Camden Town Advanced

YOUNG PEOPLE

Going global in the digital age
Introduction to advanced English skills

Lehrerband / Teacher's notes

Diesterweg

Camden Town Advanced

YOUNG PEOPLE
Going global in the digital age
Introduction to advanced English skills

Lehrerband / Teacher's notes

Erarbeitet von: Caroline Byrt, Stephanie Claussen, Pamela Hanus, Christoph Reuter, Mirja Schnoor, Sylvia Wauer

Druck A [1] / Jahr 2015
Alle Drucke der Serie A sind im Unterricht parallel verwendbar.

Redaktion und Satz: Caroline Byrt p.u.n.k.t.genau, Speyer
Herstellung: Harald Thumser, Frankfurt am Main
Umschlaggestaltung: blum DESIGN & KOMMUNIKATION GmbH, Hamburg
Layout: Jesse Konzept & Text GmbH, Hannover
Druck: pva, Druck und Medien-Dienstleistungen GmbH, Landau

ISBN: 978-3-425-**74015**-7

Inhaltsverzeichnis

Camden Town Advanced YOUNG PEOPLE: Going global in the digital age ist ein auf die Einführungsphase der Oberstufe zugeschnittenes Angebot. Es trägt der Bewertung vieler Lehrkräfte Rechnung, die Schülerinnen und Schülern (fortan: S) seien in dieser Phase noch recht unselbstständig und bräuchten dringend ein sie anleitendes Einstiegswerk.

Da **Camden Town Advanced YOUNG PEOPLE: Going global in the digital age** noch nicht direkt auf das Abitur vorbereitet, weist es eine starke Kontinuität zum Sekundarstufe-I-Bereich von **Camden Town** auf. Der *Skills*-Ansatz von **Camden Town** wird fortgeführt, wobei das Hauptaugenmerk auf der Arbeit mit unterschiedlichen Textsorten und der Vorbereitung auf die mündliche Prüfung liegt.

Den S soll geholfen werden, sich bei textanalytischen Aufgaben klar und zielgerichtet auszudrücken. Viele S verstehen die Textanalyse zwar theoretisch, aber es fehlt ihnen das Werkzeug, um ihre Ergebnisse zu versprachlichen. **Camden Town Advanced YOUNG PEOPLE: Going global in the digital age** ist in seinem Angebot an Möglichkeiten für eine *hands-on*-Analyse einzigartig.
In jedem *Theme* wird den S anhand eines ersten Textes beispielhaft und kleinschrittig gezeigt, wie Textanalyse funktioniert, bevor sie sie dann an einem zweiten Text selbstständig umsetzen.
Camden Town Advanced YOUNG PEOPLE: Going global in the digital age bietet eine praktische Einführung in die Textanalyse:

- Ausarbeitung eigener Modellanalysen durch angeleitete, kleinschrittige Vorgehensweise und Analysebeispiele zu unterschiedlichen Textsorten
- zahlreiche Formulierungshilfen (= textanalytischer *language support*)
- authentische, schülernahe Texte zur Förderung der kommunikativen Kompetenz
- eine Auswahl an oberstufenrelevanten Themen, z. B. *gap year, studying and working abroad, multiculturalism, applying for jobs, living in the digital world, sexual identity* und *globalisation*
- ein *Skills*-Anhang mit einer Zusammenfassung der wichtigsten Schritte der Textanalyse zum Nachlesen
- ein *Glossary*-Anhang, einmal textsortenspezifisch sortiert, das andere Mal alphabetisch

Der zweite Schwerpunkt von **Camden Town Advanced YOUNG PEOPLE: Going global in the digital age:** Vorbereitung auf die mündliche Prüfung, d. h. die Kompetenzen Sprechen, Mediation und Hörverstehen stehen im Mittelpunkt der D-Teile (*Themes* 1, 2, 5, 6 und 8).

Aufbau der acht *Themes:*

- Der **A-Teil** leitet das Thema ein.
- Anschließend werden im **B-Teil** die relevanten Schritte einer Schlüsselfertigkeit kleinschrittig und systematisch an Beispielen erarbeitet,
- bevor sie, im **C-Teil,** dann selbstständig von den S angewendet werden.
- Die *Themes* 1, 2, 5, 6 und 8 verfügen zudem über einen D-Teil. Hier stehen, in Vorbereitung auf die mündliche Prüfung, Sprechen, Mediation und Hörverstehen im Mittelpunkt.
  (Hier zeigt sich der Unterschied zum Vorgängerband **Camden Town Advanced YOUNG PEOPLE** (978-3-425-06653-0), wo es keine D-Teile gab. **Camden Town Advanced YOUNG PEOPLE: Going global in the digital age** intensiviert die Kompetenzen Sprechen, Mediation und Hörverstehen und bietet somit noch mehr Möglichkeiten, sich mit den geforderten Kompetenzbereichen auseinanderzusetzen.)

Camden Town Advanced YOUNG PEOPLE: Going global in the digital age ist **modular** aufgebaut, d. h. die acht *Themes* können in jeder Reihenfolge bearbeitet werden, die L, möglichst in Absprache mit den S, festlegt.

Anhang von Camden Town Advanced YOUNG PEOPLE: Going global in the digital age:

- ***Skills*-Seiten** greifen auf die Grundlagen aus den höheren Bänden der Sekundarstufe I zurück, da es zu Beginn der Oberstufe darauf ankommt, das Erlernte der Mittelstufe kursübergreifend aufzugreifen und zu festigen und danach Schritt für Schritt auszubauen.
- Das ***Glossary – Literary terms*** (nach Textsorten geordnet) und das ***Glossary – Alphabetical*** unterstützen die S mit dem nötigen lexikalischen und inhaltlichen Rüstzeug für die Textanalyse; hier können die S immer wieder nachschlagen, wenn sie unsicher sind.

Teacher's notes

Auf Unterrichtsempfehlungen wurde in den vorliegenden ***Teacher's notes*** weitestgehend verzichtet. Stattdessen konzentrieren sie sich auf Lösungsvorschläge und Erwartungshorizonte sowie Hintergrundinformationen zu Texten und Autoren.
Ausnahme: Wiederholt fordert **Camden Town Advanced YOUNG PEOPLE: Going global in the digital age** zu kooperativen Lernformen auf: *Milling around* (*Theme* 2), *Think–pair–share* (*Theme* 2 und 3), *Placemat* (*Theme* 3 und 7), *Debate* (*Theme* 5), *Freeze frame* (*Theme* 6) und *Four corners* (*Theme* 8).
Diese Methoden sind aus dem bisherigen Englischunterricht meist bekannt, werden jedoch an den entsprechenden Stellen der ***Teacher's notes*** nochmals erläutert:
Milling around: Seite 15
Think–pair–share: Seite 20
Placemat: Seite 27
Debate: Seite 46f.
Freeze frame: Seite 58
Four corners: Seite 28

Die ***Teacher's notes*** werden durch Klausurvorschläge abgerundet (Seiten 109–135), zum Teil mehrere Vorschläge pro *Theme,* die als direkt im Unterricht einsetzbare Kopiervorlagen vorliegen und erlauben, jedes *Theme* sinnvoll abzuschließen.
Auch zu den Klausurvorschlägen gibt es Lösungsvorschläge und Erwartungshorizonte: auf den Seiten 81 bis 108.

Die **DVD für Lehrer** (978-3-425-74016-4) bietet
- die Tracks des Themenhefts:
  - Track 1: Gap Yah (*Theme* 1 A3)
  - Track 2: Spending a gap year in Australia (Klausurvorschlag *Theme* 1)
  - Track 3: Filmausschnitt 1 aus *The Social Network* (*Theme* 5 B2)
  - Track 4: Filmausschnitt 2 aus *The Social Network* (*Theme* 5 B7)
  - Track 5: Filmausschnitt 3 aus *The Social Network* (*Theme* 5 C1)
  - Track 6: Filmausschnitt 4 aus *The Social Network* (Klausurvorschlag *Theme* 5)
  - Track 7: Podcast Rachel Gleason (*Theme* 6 D2)
  - Track 8: Excerpt from podcast *Same sex marriage in Michigan* (Klausurvorschlag *Theme* 6)
- die Klausurvorschläge als editierbare Vorlagen zum individuellen Bearbeiten
- sowie folgende zusätzliche Filmclips:
  - Track 9: Internet identity
  - Track 10: Social gaming
  - Track 11: Silicon Valley
  - Track 12: Twitter
  - Track 13: What is a nerd?

Getting started

A1 **Seite 6**

Lösungsvorschlag/Erwartungshorizont:

a) *part-time job; look for a job; earn some money; start an apprenticeship; go on holiday; travel; hang out with friends; party with friends; go to bed late; sleep late*

A2 **Seite 6**

Lösungsvorschlag/Erwartungshorizont:

a) 1. *young woman from London e-mailing her parents from her gap year in Russia; telling them how cold it is (temperatures of minus 30); using examples to illustrate the cold (danger of freezing to death if you move too slowly; within minutes losing all feeling in your extremities)*
   2. *seized/being held hostage for four hours by a group of revolutionary guerrillas in Nepal: gapper was in a group hoping to catch a bus when a group of six young men with guns told them they couldn't leave and would have to wait until a (Maoist) rally was over; afterwards they were allowed to walk home; tone of e-mail is very matter-of-fact*
   3. *young female gapper teaching primary school children in Kenya and accompanying them to a music competition: she is surprised that she has become so protective and proud of "her" children as teaching them and dealing with life in Africa is quite a challenge*

b) 1. *would have found it exciting / would have tried to walk faster in the cold / would have coped OK / would have felt similar to the way the gapper in the e-mail felt*
   2. *would have felt really, really scared / would have flown back home right afterwards / would have thought of friends and family back home / would have thought I'm going to die / would have sat very quietly / would have started praying / would have tried to relax / don't think I would have coped as well as the gapper in the e-mail*
   3. *would have felt just as proud of "my" children / would have enjoyed myself / would have found it exciting / would have been very touched*

c) *exciting experiences; facing new challenges; getting to know the world – and getting to know yourself at the same time; situations that are unpredictable*

A3 **Seite 7**

Es empfiehlt sich, *to chunder* vorzugeben (siehe Randspaltenhinweis im TB): Synonym für *to throw up.*

Lösungsvorschlag/Erwartungshorizont:

- *getting very drunk, enjoying party time, throwing up all over the place*
- *thinking that they have experienced living rough, thinking that they know the hard life*
- *gap year = party time*
- *like to see themselves as hip, cool and helping the world, when in fact all they do is get drunk*
- *it's chic, cool, hip to go on a gap year; it's not about helping disadvantaged people but about doing the hip thing and having something to boast about to their friends*
- *pretending to be into spiritual, cultural and political enlightenment (but ending up drunk and throwing up all over the place most of the time)*

Zusatzinformationen im Internet (Stand April 2015):
http://www.theguardian.com/technology/2010/mar/28/gap-year-spoof-youtube

A4 **Seite 7**

Lösungsvorschlag/Erwartungshorizont:

Mum: *I don't see why you have to do that.*
Daughter: *But Mum, everyone is doing it.*
Mum: *What kind of reason is that? I don't see why you can't go straight to university after leaving school.*
Daughter: *Mum, I know you're worried. But I'll be fine. We know so many people who've taken a gap year, and they're all fine. No one was killed.*
Mum: *OK, no one was killed. But you know what happened to Tim. His passport and all his money were stolen.*
Daughter: *So? That could have happened anywhere. It could happen next time you're on holiday in Turkey with Simon.*

Mum: *Yes, I know you're right. It's just that I'm worried.*
Daughter: *But Mum, you know I'll be fine. You know I don't do silly stuff, you know you can trust me not to do anything dangerous. And you know I won't be travelling on my own. I'll be with Jess and Rebecca the whole time.*
Mum: *What do their parents think of this whole idea of a gap year?*
Daughter: *Rebecca's mum spent a year teaching English in Cambodia when she was our age. That's where she met Rebecca's dad. He was on trip around the world with a friend at the time.*
Mum: *And Jess's parents?*
Daughter: *Jess's dad thinks it's a silly idea to take off a year after school. But not because he's worried about Jess but because he thinks it's a waste of time. The sooner she starts university, he says, the sooner she will start earning her own money, which seems all he's worried about.*
Mum: *Well, that's not a very nice thing to say. But they've always been a strange family.*
Daughter: *I know. But Rebecca is great.*
Mum: *I know she is. Just give me some more time to think this through. I know I'll get used to the idea of you going on a gap year and travelling to exotic countries. It won't be easy but I know I can't stop you. And to be honest, I guess I would do the same if I were you.*

Practice section

B1 **Seite 8**

Doppelbedeutung *wasted:*
– *to waste your time = to use your time carelessly, extravagantly or to no purpose*
– *wasted = drunk, under the influence of alcohol or illegal drugs*

Lösungsvorschlag/Erwartungshorizont:
an article discussing whether or not gap years are a waste of time/whether gap years are worth it / not clear from heading in which direction the article is headed / sounds like a comment rather than a report, i.e. the heading implies that the article will give an answer to the question and will include the author's opinion

B3 **Seite 10**

Lösungsvorschlag/Erwartungshorizont:
a) *2. … the party culture of young people going abroad for a gap year.*
4. … the question of whether young people use their gap year constructively.
c) *– title of article*
– author of article
– where and when the article was published

B4 **Seite 10**

Lösungsvorschlag/Erwartungshorizont:
a) → *introduction/description of party scene/setting*
→ *facts and figures regarding scene/setting*
→ *quotation by Mary Curnock Cook*
→ *facts and figures about school-leavers taking a gap year*
→ *further description of party scene*
→ *interviewing two people (one male, one female)*
→ *author's conclusion*
b) *ll. 1–15*
ll. 16–26
ll. 27–40
ll. 41–55
ll. 56–66
ll. 67–107 (ll. 67–81, ll. 82–107)
ll. 108–end
c) *ll. 1–15: Impressions of the young people's party scene in Thailand (people, music, slogans)*
ll. 16–26: Facts and figures about the young people's party scene

ll. 27–40: Mary Curnock Cook's opinion, the chief executive of the universities and colleges admissions service, that a gap year should be seen as the beginning of your career
ll. 41–55: Facts and figures about school-leavers taking a gap year
ll. 56–66: Description/Impressions of party scene continued
ll. 67–81: Interview with 19-year-old Londoner about travelling and gap years
ll. 82–107: Interview with young woman about her gap-year experiences
ll. 108–end: The author's conclusion

B5 **Seite 10**

Lösungsvorschlag/Erwartungshorizont:
The newspaper article "Gap years: Wasted youth?" by Patrick Kingsley, published in The Guardian *on September 6, 2010, deals with the party culture of young people going abroad for a gap year. To begin with, the author describes a young people's party scene in Thailand, focussing on his impressions of the people, the music and the slogans.*
This is followed by some facts and figures about the area in Thailand where the party takes place and how things have changed over the past twenty-five years.
The author goes on to quote Mary Curnock Cook, the chief executive of the universities and colleges admissions service, who says that your gap year should not be a year of carefree fun but a year of preparing and focussing on what lies ahead at university upon your return.
Mary Curnock Cook's opinion is subsequently contrasted with the situation as it currently presents itself, where British school-leavers seem more interested in having a good time during their gap year than in concentrating on what lies ahead.
Patrick Kingsley subsequently presents two young gap-year students he has spoken to in Thailand. The first one is a 19-year-old from London who tells the author that for him there is a difference between tourists and backpackers. He considers himself a backpacker, not a tourist.
This is followed by Hailey, who is not your typical gap-year student as she has already been to university. She studied first, then went travelling to Thailand. She explains that spending a gap year travelling before starting at university prepares you for your time at university, because it teaches you how to interact with others.
The author concludes by telling his readers that he never took a gap year and that he is glad he did not, as there is nothing he has seen or heard in Thailand that appeals to him.

B6 **Seite 11**

Lösung: *evaluative article*

B7 **Seite 11**

Lösungsvorschlag/Erwartungshorizont:
- ***heading and sub-heading:*** *heading is an open question / sub-heading is a question, too / → function: reader will almost automatically answer the questions for himself/herself and will then read on to see whether his/her own opinion is confirmed or not*
- ***introduction:*** *ll. 1–26 / → function: capture the reader's attention*
- ***main part:*** *ll. 27–107, made up of four individual paragraphs*
  ll. 27–40: informative and fact-based / → function: depict what a gap year should officially/ ideally achieve
  ll. 41–55: mix of facts, i.e. statistics, and opinions (l. 41: "this is a point that has yet to trickle down", ll. 54–55: "a trend towards increasingly mindless hedonism") / → function: give the reader a clue as to what the author's personal opinion might be
  ll. 56–66: additional information about scene from introduction (Full Moon Party in Thailand) / → function: emphasis and in order to contrast with ideal depicted in ll. 27–40
  ll. 67–107: narrative elements, i.e. personal statements by gap-year travellers Jez and Hailey / → function: balance the article; author provides reader with quotes and personal statements by others so reader can make up his/her own mind about the topic presented
- ***concluding paragraph:*** *ll. 108–end; refers back to the beginning (ll. 1–3) and gives the author's opinion that the idea of a gap year does not appeal to him (ll. 113–114) / → function: round off the article; help the article come full circle; article rounded off with author's personal opinion*
- ***additional parts:*** *a photo which gives the reader a clue as to where the article is headed, i.e. gap years are all about partying*

B8 **Seite 12**

Lösungsvorschlag/Erwartungshorizont:

a)

facts	*opinions*
– *most of the introduction (ll. 1–3, ll. 9–11, ll. 17–24): description including figures ("14 beachside bars", "35 wooden stalls", "buckets filled with a litre's worth of vodka and Red Bull", "frequented every month by between 10,000 and 30,000 European youngsters")* – *"Three weeks ago, the chief executive [...] declared to a Sunday newspaper that 'the golden age of the gap year is over'" (ll. 27–30) → quotations are facts (although choice of quotations may influence the reader)* – *"In a year when the number of university applications – a record 660,000 – has dwarfed the number of university places available – 450,000" (ll. 36–39)* – *"Every year around 160,000 British school-leavers take a gap year before entering university" (ll. 46–48)* – *"Londoner Jez, 19 years old, dressed in a vest, and approaching the end of his year out" (ll. 68–69)* – *"near the centre of Had Rin, the main tourist town on Koh Phangan" (ll. 72–73)* – *all the quotations in the article (they are facts in that they represent what was said but of course, they can be seen as a way of influencing the reader)*	– *"their knees bending awkwardly" (l. 6) → "awkwardly" is a judgement* – *"deeply dubious" (ll. 11–12)* – *"ranging from the lurid to the moronic" (ll. 12–13)* – *"arguably" (l. 25)* – *"this is a point that has yet to trickle down" (l. 41)* – *"the vast majority of gappers do not use their year-out in anything approaching a fashion that might – in the eyes of universities – be viewed as 'constructive'." (ll. 43–46)* – *"increasingly mindless hedonism" (l. 55)* – *"meant to be Britain's brightest" (ll. 64–65) → "meant to" implies that author has his doubts* – *"He enlightens me" (l. 70) → sarcastic* – *"It's a slightly strange answer" (ll. 70–71)* – *"a warm, welcoming guy" (l. 76)* – *"Hailey's gap-year experiences were slightly different to Jez's." (ll. 82–83) → understatement* – *"then hurriedly starts again" (l. 104)* – *"Though I never took a gap year, never took the chance to either let my hair down like this, or do something more constructive, nothing that I've heard or seen here makes me want to join them." (ll. 110–114)*

b) *Author's personal point of view is clearly stated in concluding paragraph: "Though I never took a gap year, never took the chance to either let my hair down like this, or do something more constructive, nothing that I've heard or seen here makes me want to join them." (ll. 110–114)*
– *as regards balancing of positive and negative facts: up to the reader to decide whether s/he considers the presented facts as positive or negative; getting drunk and partying all night is a fact, but some readers will see it as something positive, others will see it as something negative → author does not expect reader to agree with him, is not presenting arguments in a structured way trying to convince the reader; chances are that readers will draw a different conclusion from the facts presented in the article; there will be plenty of readers who will consider getting drunk, partying and having sex a great way to pass your time and who most likely passed their gap years doing just that*

c) *evaluative article*

B9 **Seite 12**

Lösungsvorschlag/Erwartungshorizont:

use of strong or emotive adjectives and verbs: *"deeply dubious slogans, ranging from the lurid to the moronic" (ll. 11–12); "the ultimate destination" (l. 22), "scores of topless teenagers" (l. 59)*

informal or colloquial language: *"that kind of thing" (l. 15)*

repetition: *"peeing into the Gulf of Thailand" (ll. 2–3)/"urinating into the ocean" (ll. 59–60)/ "still [...] peeing into the Gulf of Thailand" (ll. 109–110)*

exaggeration/enumeration: *"the epitome, the pinnacle" (ll. 25–26)*

parallelism: *"why they go, however, why this is the modern gap-year experience" (ll. 56–57)*

metaphor: *"a mecca for footloose gap-year tourists" (ll. 23–24), "mopeds belching out acrid fumes" (l. 75), "let my hair down" (l. 111)*

humour/irony/ridicule: *"generic drum'n'bass" (ll. 7–8); "Welcome to the Full Moon Party" (l. 16), "modern gap-year experience" (l. 26), "this is a point that has yet to trickle down" (l. 41), "the vast majority of gappers do not use their year-out in anything approaching a fashion that might* [...] *be viewed as 'constructive'." (ll. 43–46), "teenagers who are, after all, meant to be Britain's brightest" (ll. 64–65), "Attempting to understand" (l. 56), "He enlightens me" (l. 70), "It's a slightly strange answer" (ll. 70–71), "a perfect exemplar" (l. 86)*

wordplay: *"Wasted youth?" (heading) → literal meaning of "wasted youth" vs. informal meaning: "drunk kids" ("wasted" = informal for "very drunk"* or *"having taken a lot of drugs")*

B10 **Seite 13**

Lösungsvorschlag/Erwartungshorizont:

a) *The reader strongly agrees with Patrick Kingsley and his article.*
He thinks that moral values are in decline in today's society and that gap years are a complete waste of time and money.

b) *1. I am writing in response to your article "…" from …*
2. As a firm believer in …
3. I could not agree with the author more.
4. It is beyond doubt that …
5. Your article shows precisely (what) …
6. The article raises the question whether …
7. I completely agree with the author when he concludes that …
8. Let me add, from my personal experience as well as from the example of others around me, that …
9. I congratulate you on this article and hope you will keep drawing attention to …

B11 **Seite 14**

Lösungsvorschlag/Erwartungshorizont:

Sir or Madam,
I am writing to you in response to your article "Gap years: Wasted youth?" from 6 September.
I see no reason why Patrick Kingsley feels he has to criticize young people for their choices.
I myself was a gapper not too long ago and one of many to enjoy the Full Moon Party in Thailand. The way I see it, exploring life's pleasures is what being young is all about. For most young people, the gap year is like a farewell tour to their youth before turning serious, checking in your dreams and beginning with the rest of your life.
No one has to join in the fun if they do not want to. But I think everyone should have the right to spend their gap year as they please as long as they do not hurt anyone.
Jonathan Robinson
Warrington, England

Getting to the point

C1 **Seite 15**

Lösungsvorschlag/Erwartungshorizont:

– *an informative article*
– *an article concentrating first on Owen Henry's gap year experience, followed by factual pieces of advice and information on how to make the most of your gap year*

C2 **Seite 17**

Methodische Alternative: Wenn die S Transparentpapier oder Folie haben, so können sie diese/s auf den Text legen und die gesuchten Informationen unterstreichen:
– eine Farbe für *reasons for the increase in the numbers of gappers,*
– eine andere Farbe für *their experiences.*

Lösungsvorschlag/Erwartungshorizont:
reasons for the increase in the numbers of gappers: *last year at high school is becoming more and more demanding so students need a break before going on to university/college (ll. 46–48) / more and more colleges are seeing the benefits of gap years because students who have taken a gap year seem to be more focused, better motivated and more mature than other students, so colleges/universities are making it possible for students to take a year off inbetween having been accepted to college and actually starting college (ll. 50–54) / (in addition: gap-year fairs (l. 27))*

their experiences: *on the one hand, being part of a structured program is great, but on the other hand, the more independent and the bigger the challenge, the bigger the personal benefits in terms of personal growth (ll. 95–97) / having to cope with difficult situations and getting through hardships makes you a stronger and more confident person / you cannot go wrong with a gap year: no matter whether it turns out just as planned or completely different, it will always be an invaluable life experience and you will learn and benefit from it*

C3 **Seite 17**

Lösungsvorschlag/Erwartungshorizont:
the author's attitude towards gap years: *positive attitude (ll. 22–25: "But to be beneficial, it needs to involve more than rest and relaxation."); in favour of taking a gap year (before starting at college) → clear from the start: heading is unambiguous, sums up the article*

matter-of-fact and neutral language: *"Though the concept may be new" (l. 35), "a gapper who got malaria in Africa" (ll. 131–132)*

formal and academic language: *"acquaint" (l. 27), "craving" (l. 48), "less predictable" (l. 68), "adhering to" (l. 70), "minimize the likelihood of prolonged downtime" (ll. 71–72), "businesses that cater to" (l. 81), "can hinder the maturation process that tends to happen in the absence of ample support systems" (ll. 82–84)*

facts and figures: *"about 11% of the 300,000 college-bound seniors take a gap year before enrolling" (ll. 37–39); facts and figures about Owen Henry: ll. 99–115*

quoting experts and authorities: *advice box on page 35: Center for Interim Programs, Princeton, N.J. → Princeton is one of the leading US universities (Ivy League); ll. 29–30; David Hawkins, director of public policy and research at the National Association for College Admission Counseling (ll. 55–61); Holly Bull of the Center for Interim Programs (ll. 74–79); Tom Griffiths, founder of gapyear.com (ll. 89–90); "Most experts recommend" (l. 116); Karl Haigler, author of The Gap Year Advantage: Helping Your Child Benefit From Time Off Before or During College (ll. 129–131); Samer Hamadeh, co-founder of Vault.com (ll. 136–137)*

personal statements of people affected: *ll. 119–123*

C4 **Seite 17**

Lösungsvorschlag/Erwartungshorizont:
Sir or Madam,
I am writing in response to the article "'Gap year' before college gives grads valuable life experience". I totally agree with the author's view that a gap year provides you with valuable life experience even if the experience as such might be a negative one.
A friend of mine became infected with HIV during her gap year. She would never have asked to become infected with HIV but at the same time it has given her life a sense of purpose. Upon her return, she wanted to tell young people what happened to her so that maybe they could learn from her mistake and not repeat it. She says that if her experience helps keep just one young person from having unprotected sex, she will have accomplished a lot. Everything is for good, she says – she has had to learn it the hard way but it is true.
Clare Yates
Leeds, England

Listening

D1 Seite 18

Lösungsvorschlag/Erwartungshorizont:

a) *a lecture, an interview, a radio show, a poem recital, an eyewitness report, an interview in the street, a pronunciation exercise, a song, a dialogue, a show, a routine by a standup comedian, a joke, an (extract from an) audio book, podcast, the news, a debate*

b) – *texts specifically prepared for a recording: a radio show, an audio book, a song, a pronunciation exercise, a podcast, the news*
   – *texts that 'happen' to be recorded: an interview in the street, a debate, a dialogue, a show, a routine by a standup comedian, a poem recital*
   – *texts with just one speaker: an eyewitness report, a routine by a standup comedian*
   – *texts with various speakers: a debate, a dialogue*

c) – *background noise: interview in the street*
   – *slang: in a dialogue between native speakers, an interview in the street*
   – *English spoken by non-native speakers: if you're not used to Indian English, for example, it can be very difficult to understand*
   – *different varieties of English: many people find it difficult to understand a Scottish or Yorkshire accent; they would find it difficult to understand an interview with people from Scotland*
   – *poor pronunciation: quite often, native speakers can be more difficult to understand than non-native speakers because their pronunciation is not as clear and distinct*
   – *talking too fast: native speakers are often difficult to understand for learners of English*
   – *poor acoustic quality: if recorded with amateur equipment*
   – *many different speakers, especially when speaking simultaneously: this is typical of natural speech and natural conversation; however, it's a lot easier to understand different speakers speaking simultaneously if you can see them at the same time*

D2 Seite 18

Lösungsvorschlag/Erwartungshorizont:

a) – *the picture (children in (school) uniform)*
   – *the headline: it's obviously about India; about gappers in India*
   – *section "Education & family", so it will have something to do with schools and/or learning*
   – *it's on the BBC News page, so it's probably well-researched and not intentionally funny*
   – *it's probably fairly easy to understand because the acoustic quality will be good; the recording/filming will have been done by professionals*

b) – *"where he asks British students why" → interviews with British students*
   – *possible interview questions: Why did you come here? Do you like it here? Why did you choose to spend a year away from home?*
   – *reasons for the increase in the number of young people taking a gap year*

D3 Seite 19

Lösung:
1–b 2–g 3–f 4–e 5–a 6–c 7–d

D4 Seite 20

Dauer: 3:06 min

Lösungsvorschlag/Erwartungshorizont:

a) *1. true*
   2. false (The number has risen because not all school-leavers can get into university, so decide to take a year out before they try to get into university again the following year.)
   3. false (Nikki knew that she wanted to spend a year travelling first, so she didn't even apply for university after school.)
   4. true

b) 1–b *Richard Oliver believes that those students who do a gap year after school are less likely to give up their university course because they start refreshed.*
   2–a *Another advantage of students with gap-year experience is that they can take part in seminars better because they are more aware of global problems.*

3–f *There are also many gappers like Oliver Harkus who take a year out after finishing university.*
4–c *One of the reasons why people like Oliver Harkus go abroad is that they cannot find a job after university and hope to gain skills abroad and meet new people that can help them when they look for and find a job.*

c) 1–c *According to …, gap-year travellers do **not** face the danger of **natural disasters.***
2–d *gogapyear.com provides you with information you need to prepare well for a gap year.*

DVD **D5** Seite 21

Lösungsvorschlag/Erwartungshorizont:

a) *Daniela Papi is critical of graduates from wealthy countries doing volunteer work in 'poor' countries. She says that just because they come from wealthier countries, that does not make them skilled or knowledgeable about what is actually needed.*
She does not question people's good intentions but says that it takes more than just good intentions to serve and do good.
Volunteering is seen and presented in such a positive light nowadays that nobody actually questions the good that comes from it.
In just about every other situation, we expect people to have proper training before they start doing the jobs that volunteers do. But with volunteers, nobody pays attention to their qualifications. Good intentions are considered enough by most people.
According to Papi, this is dangerous because it gives young people the impression that they are in a position of superiority, simply because they are from rich, western countries.
(147 words)

b)
- *good intentions are not enough; it takes more than good intentions to do good*
- *praise for international volunteering is virtually blind; very little attention given to the question whether volunteers have the skills, speak the language, are familiar with the culture*
- *for jobs in the UK and the US, we understand that professional work takes professional skills; however, when we go abroad, we tend to forget that we have to learn before we can serve*
- *we feel as though wearing a volunteer shirt gives us the knowledge needed to save the world*
- *it is not just the volunteers who are to blame for this "illusion of grandeur"*
- *we're teaching our next generation that just because they're from the UK or the US, they are in a position of superiority towards the people they are supposed to serve*
- *we're teaching today's young people that they get to choose how to help in a foreign country without first learning more about the issues at hand*

The email by the volunteer in Sri Lanka seems to prove the points that Daniela Papi makes in her lecture. The volunteer comes across as rather superficial and as feeling superior to the local people. There might be some irony involved when she says "I'm a volunteer, here to save them" (l. 3) but it nevertheless sounds as though she truly believes that she is on a "mission to save the world" (l. 3), as though that were the reason why she is a volunteer. She comes across as very self-centered, as more interested in the image people have of her than in doing the actual work, learning the language and getting to know the people and their customs.

D6 Seite 21

Lösungsvorschlag/Erwartungshorizont:

Hi Lisa,
Thanks for your email. I'm not entirely sure how to react … you come across as pretty superficial, if I may say so. I've never heard you speak like that before.
Have you started to learn the local language in Sri Lanka yet? I think it's a shame that you expect the children to learn our language, rather that start learning their language.
Were you being serious when you wrote that you're on a "mission to save the world", there "to save" the people and orphans of Sri Lanka? Do you seriously think they need saving? I don't. You come across as feeling superior to the local people. Do you really feel that way? Just because we come from a rich country, that doesn't in any way make us superior to the people of Sri Lanka.
I'm sorry if this sounds rude, but I really don't like the sound of your email. And it doesn't really sound like you at all, to be honest. It sounds as though people have talked you into thinking you're better or more advanced, simply because you're a volunteer from a rich country. Is that what the other volunteers are like? If so, I would stay away from them if I were you.
Bye for now, Isabel

Getting started

A1 Seite 22

Milling around in d): Die S bewegen sich im Klassenraum und nehmen mit ihren MitS Kontakt auf. Es können unterschiedliche Arbeitsaufträge vergeben werden. Die Methode kann z. B. mit einer Umfrage *(survey)* oder einer Vokabelabfrage verbunden werden.
Arbeitsschritte:
1. Die S gehen umher, zunächst ohne zu sprechen.
2. Auf ein Signal von L hin finden sie sich mit der Person, vor der sie gerade stehen, zu einem Paar zusammen und tauschen sich über ihre Aufgabe aus.
3. Die S notieren ihre Ergebnisse und gehen dann weiter, bis zum nächsten *Stop!* von L.

Alternative, falls L sich weiter zurücknehmen möchte: Der Austausch wird nicht durch ein Signal getaktet, stattdessen wird im Vorfeld eine Mindestzahl von Kontakten festgelegt.

Lösungsvorschlag/Erwartungshorizont:

a) *France and England: school exchange*
Spain, Italy and Austria: holidays

b) *I have been to Spalding in England, which is twinned with Speyer.*
It was OK but I wasn't too keen on the food.
I enjoyed speaking English and, even more so, people understanding me. That was pretty cool.

c) *an internship: Germany* | *university studies: England*
a work and travel programme: Australia | *a job: Germany*

d) *I think it would be great to spend a year studying at a university in England, one reason being that I prefer British English to American English.*
Another reason is that some English universities, e.g. Oxford and Cambridge, have a very good reputation internationally, so I think it would help with a future job if I studied in Oxford or Cambridge for a year or two.
Another reason is that England is not too far from Germany so it would be easy to fly home for Christmas or for other important events. Also, friends and family could come and visit me.
I would try and spend a bit of time at pubs. I've heard so much about British pubs.
Every now and then, I would try and visit London for a weekend. It's such a cool city.

A2 Seite 22

Dauer: 3:30 min

Excel: L kann auf die korrekte Betonung von *(Microsoft) Excel* (Betonung auf der zweiten Silbe!) hinweisen (kommt zweimal im Video vor), selbst wenn die S vermutlich weiterhin bei der deutschen Erstsilbenbetonung bleiben werden; *to excel* – sich auszeichnen.

Lösungsvorschlag/Erwartungshorizont:

a) *four-week internship in investment banking (at Deutsche Bank)*

b) ***why they applied:*** *gain experience; find out what a bank is really like*
how they applied: *paper application; two rounds of interviews*
what they gained in experience: *it opened their eyes to what a bank is really like; presentation skills; business etiquette; "personal brand"; introduction to the City; different divisions in the bank; internship was very structured, got a lot out of the short time they had; how to network with people; that you need patience; being able to communicate with people at all levels; how to use Excel; attention to detail; adapt your situation and take the opportunities available; more self-confident; better people skills; learnt an incredible amount about investment banking but also about themselves*
why they would recommend it to others: *a fantastic opportunity; felt welcome right from the beginning; "learnt so much"; they were made to feel part of the team; made good friends; had exposure to all sorts of important people without being aware of it; really busy people with their own workloads giving up their time to invest in you, as a person and as a colleague*

A3 Seite 22

Lösungsvorschlag/Erwartungshorizont:

a) ***text 1:*** *insight into a foreign country; experience another language and culture; make friends for life; improve your CV; travel; improve your language; find new friends; experience (American family life) first hand*

text 2: *valued member of a team; make a real contribution; a sense of responsibility; a job that is challenging but also satisfying; a unique opportunity to get right into (the heart of a hugely successful and competitive business world); a real taste of what life is like working in (the Investment Banking world)*
text 3: *amazing; ridiculously rewarding; see my students improve day on day; explore the wonderful culture of your temporary home; an opportunity to experience another culture; challenge yourself; develop transferrable skills; make a difference*
text 4: *meet new people; learn about new cultures; explore foreign areas; grow as a person; indulge in the (Australian) experience and culture; brave and adventurous; a whole world worth exploring*

b) ***opportunities you would consider applying for and why:*** *I would consider applying for Voluntary Service Abroad. It sounds a very rewarding thing to do. I would not want to be gone from home for a full year, but teaching for three months sounds great. I also like the idea of living with a local family in a host home. I'm sure this can give you a real taste of what life is like in a particular country.*
possible negative experiences: *As much as I like the idea of living with a local family in a host home, I can imagine that it can also be quite difficult. You might be used to having your own room but now have to share a room with people you don't know very well.*
You might feel homesick while studying or working abroad.
You might find that you don't know and understand the local customs. Cultural misunderstandings can cause problems and negative experiences, especially as it can sometimes take a while before you realise what the problem is.

A4 **Seite 24**

Lösungsvorschlag/Erwartungshorizont:

a) *young people/graduates who would like to gain work experience abroad*
b) *learn new skills; show potential employers that you're no run-of-the-mill candidate; boost your employability; secure that coveted first job in your chosen industry; distinguish yourself from the crowd; show your desire to get stuck in and work alongside local people; demonstrate to potential employers that you can cope in a multicultural, multilingual working environment and produce great work in the process; succeed despite being out of your comfort zone, away from your friends and family; spending time abroad and working alongside non-English speakers will help [your language skills] improve; moving abroad and finding work experience shows motivation, independence, maturity and adaptability; travel; expand your horizons; reap the rewards in your future career*

A5 **Seite 25**

Lösungsvorschlag/Erwartungshorizont:

Good morning, everybody. I'm here to talk to you about the benefits of work experience abroad.
I would like to encourage you to spend time abroad before you start your further education.
I'm not alone in thinking that it's one of the best things you can do at this stage of your lives.
Let me explain.
Working abroad for a limited period of time after completing school will show potential employers that you're no run-of-the-mill candidate. And that is what they are looking for in applicants nowadays. – What does that mean for you?
Specialise, make sure there is something that differentiates you from other applicants, something that makes you stand out from the crowd. This something should become obvious from looking at your CV, i.e. before anyone has actually met you. Because what's the point of a great personality and good people skills that would win potential employers over in an interview if your CV is so similar to everybody else's that you won't even make it to the interview stage?
If all this sounds too focused on your future career and on your work life in general, let me tell you that there is more to working abroad than just becoming more interesting to a potential employer. You will learn a lot about yourself, too. Travelling and working abroad will expand your horizons, not only professionally but also personally. There will, without any doubt, be challenges on the way, you will be out of your comfort zone many a time, but that is what life is all about. Dealing with challenges, learning from them, that is what makes us who we are.
To wrap up, let me wish you all the very best for your future. You have a great time ahead of you. Make the most of it.
Thank you for listening.

Practice section

B1 **Seite 26**

Lösungsvorschlag/Erwartungshorizont:

a) ***No,*** *I wouldn't want to apply for the programme. There are several reasons why the job does not appeal to me.*
I wouldn't say that I speak English fluently. My English isn't bad but also not particularly good. Also, I don't have any cash handling skills, especially not with foreign currencies.
I think I would enjoy the actual job but I don't think that I meet more than a couple of their basic qualifications and requirements so I wouldn't even apply.
Yes, *I like the sound of the job description and would like to apply for the programme.*
I would love to be able to work in California for a year. That must be so cool.
I'm not too keen on travelling so would prefer to work abroad rather than travel. I believe that you get to know a country much better by working there rather than by travelling.
I can imagine that the job can be quite stressful because you are dealing with different people all the time. Quite often, tourists can be quite big-headed because they feel they can be as rude and impolite to you as they like because they are giving you their money and will probably never see you again.
I have no problem handling confidential information, as I'm sure my friends can testify.

b) ***skills I have at my disposal:*** *at least 18 years of age; available to work Sunday through Saturday, including days and nights; strong problem solving and decision-making skills; ability to manage conflict resolution; able to handle confidential information; fluent in German*
skills I am lacking: *speak English fluently; experience in customer service and guest relations; strong computer proficiency; cash handling skills; fluent in French, Japanese, Portuguese or Spanish*

B2 **Seite 27**

Lösungsvorschlag/Erwartungshorizont:

a) ***skills he has:*** *fluent in English and German; available to work Sunday through Saturday, including days and nights; strong computer proficiency; cash handling skills; experience in customer service; most likely: able to handle confidential information*
skills he has not got: *experience in guest relations; fluent in French, Japanese, Portuguese or Spanish; at least 18 years of age?; possibly: strong problem solving and decision-making skills; ability to manage conflict resolution*

b) *I think Daniel has a good chance of being accepted for the programme, unless he is not yet 18.*
I believe that if he is not 18 yet, none of his other qualifications will help him. I'm sure it's a legal requirement than anybody working at the Sunshine Village Resort must be 18 years and over. However, all his other qualifications sound very convincing.
Daniel is fluent in English and German, has a high level of computer competence and is experienced in the handling of cash and credit card transactions and in dealing with customers.
I think Mr Rodriguez will be very impressed with Daniel's application.
I'm sure that the fact that Daniel's letter reads well and is without mistakes or typos will help Daniel's application, too. It shows that he is serious about wanting the job. It proves what he says at the beginning of the fourth paragraph: that he is a conscientious person.

B3 **Seite 28**

Lösungsvorschlag/Erwartungshorizont:

Daniel is used to working under pressure.
He is interested in team sports, which shows that he is used to dealing with people. He probably has good people skills.
He might not be fluent in French but he has a GCSE in French, so he knows a bit of French ("good conversational French"), which will help him with guests from France and other French-speaking countries.
Daniel took part in "a peer mediation program" in year 9, which will be perfect for the Sunshine Village Resort, as they say in their job description that they are looking for someone with "strong problem solving [...] skills" and the "ability to manage conflict resolution".
I don't think there will be many applicants more suited to the programme than Daniel.

B4 **Seite 28**

Milling around: → Seite 15 hier in den *Teacher's notes.*

Lösungsvorschlag/Erwartungshorizont:

b) *internship with an advertising agency*

c) *creativity, enthusiasm; reliability; being prepared to put in a lot of hard work; a passion for advertising; full of ideas; interested in art; fluent in English; excellent command of the English language; impeccable grammar and spelling skills; strong problem-solving and decision-making skills; able to handle confidential information; be flexible about ideas and about working hours; high level of computer competence; enjoy working in a team; good people skills: networking is very important in the advertising industry; resilience; don't be put off easily; determination and persistence*

d) *Nina Eid*
Blumenstraße 21, 67346 Speyer, Germany
Phone: +49 (0)6232 678876   Email: nina@dieeidfamily.de
EDUCATION
2009–present Mathilde-Knerr-Schule Speyer
2005–2009 Woogbachschule Speyer
WORK EXPERIENCE
since 2015 Assistant editor of school magazine.
Work in a team of six people, often under pressure. Design and layout of advertisements by local shops. Write and edit articles. Help with typesetting and layouting pages.
INTERESTS
Sport: *Have been doing ballet for eight years.*
Drama group: *Joined a local drama group for young people in 2013. Regular performances.*
SKILLS
Computing: *Proficient in MS Word. Basic knowledge of Adobe InDesign.*
Tutoring: *Became a tutor last year for pupils starting at our school. Help them get to know their school.*
Languages: *Fluent English (C1-2) and good conversational Spanish (B2).*
Referee details available on request

B5 **Seite 29**

Lösungsvorschlag/Erwartungshorizont:
It's a summer internship in banking, for school-leavers before they start university in the autumn.

B6 **Seite 29**

Lösungsvorschlag/Erwartungshorizont:
The advert in B5 sounds, as it says in the advert, more "rigorous" than the advert in B1.
My feeling is that the theme park advertising in B1 is looking for far more people than the bank in B5. In order to be able to fill all the positions available (and keep their theme parks going throughout the busy summer months), they cannot be very strict or too particular when looking for suitable applicants. I'm sure it's a lot easier being accepted for the job in B1 than the internship in B5.
The advert in B1 reads more like a fun job, the advert in B5 more like a proper, serious job.
Working in a theme park does not need to have anything to do with what you want to do later. It's more like a fun job for young people.
The internship in B5 is aimed at young people who have already spent time thinking about their career, people who have decided that they would like a career in banking. It's not aimed at school-leavers who want to earn a bit of money while at the same time having a good time.
The job that is offered in B1 is a twelve-month programme. The internship in B5 only lasts for a few weeks, a couple of months at the most.
There is no detailed mention of money in the internship ad in B5, it just says "paid internship programmes". The advert in B1 says that successful applicants "will earn an hourly rate of $10.75 per hour". From the sound of it, I don't think that the people accepted for the internship in banking will be earning a lot. They're in it for the experience, not the money.

B7 **Seite 29**

Lösungsvorschlag/Erwartungshorizont:

Blumenstraße 21
67346 Speyer
Germany
Tel.: +49 (0)6232 678876
Email: nina@dieeidfamily.de

Bank of America Merrill Lynch

Dear Sir or Madam,
I am writing to apply for your Internship Programme – Summer 2015, as advertised on your website.
I am in my last year of school in Germany and hope to gain some experience working in banking before starting a university course in economics and international studies in October.
It would be a fantastic opportunity to work in one of your investment or corporate bank divisions.
Having grown up in Germany, I speak German fluently. My father, however, comes from England, and since I speak English with him and visit my relatives in Bristol regularly, I can also claim to be fluent in English.
I have always enjoyed learning. I believe that both my CV and my most recent school report, both of which are enclosed, are a testament to this.
My teachers describe me as driven, reliable and prepared to take the initiative whenever needed.
I have on numerous occasions led the school team in local and national debate competitions, which I believe proves both my teamwork skills and my leadership qualities. If necessary, I would be happy to provide a reference from both my maths teacher and the teacher who runs the debate club.
I became interested in the financial market about three years ago. I find it highly fascinating to follow international developments and predict how the market might change and adapt in the near and further future.
I believe I could fit easily into your programme and successfully accomplish any of the tasks you choose to set me.
I would like to add that I have opted for maths as one of my main subjects for my final two and half years at school.
I would like to apply for an internship in Chester. An aunt of mine lives in Chester, so I would be able to stay with her during the internship.
Thank you for taking the time to consider my application. I would feel privileged if I were given the opportunity of a pre-university internship with your company.
I look forward to hearing from you.
Yours sincerely,
Nina Eid

Getting to the point

C1 Seite 30

Think–pair–share: Studien belegen, dass wir bessere und ausführlichere Antworten geben, wenn wir nach einer Frage zunächst Zeit zum Überlegen haben. Hierauf fußt die Methode *Think–pair–share,* die die Vorteile der Wartezeit und des kooperativen Lernens kombiniert. Die Methode kann jederzeit ohne Vorbereitung eingesetzt werden.

Think–pair–share besteht aus drei Phasen:

1. ***Think*-Phase:** Die S denken jede/r still für sich über eine Frage/einen Arbeitsauftrag nach. Abhängig von der Aufgabenstellung machen sie sich ggf. Notizen.
(L: *Spend a few minutes brainstorming ideas/thinking about the question/problem on your own and write/note down your ideas on a piece of paper/organize your thoughts on paper.*)
2. ***Pair*-Phase:** In Partnerarbeit tauschen sich die S über ihre Ergebnisse der *think*-Phase aus. Wichtig ist dabei das aktive Zuhören.
(L: *Pair up with a partner to compare and discuss the ideas you have collected./Agree on some ideas and collect them in a list.*)
3. ***Share*-Phase:** Die Paare stellen ihre Ergebnisse im Plenum vor. (L: *Summarize and share your comments in class.*) oder finden sich in Vierergruppen zusammen, um ihre Ergebnisse auszutauschen und zu diskutieren. (L: *Team up with another pair to summarize and share your comments.*)

Lösungsvorschlag/Erwartungshorizont:
a) *teacher, dentist, architect, engineer, lawyer, accountant, physiotherapist, translator*
b) ***healthcare & social sector:*** *doctor, dentist, nurse, physiotherapist, social worker*
business & management: *accountant, tax consultant, financial controller*
science & engineering: *chemist, lab assistant, engineer*
education: *teacher, educational editor*
law: *lawyer, solicitor, judge*
crafts: *carpenter, (fashion/furniture/…) designer, web designer*

c)

benefits	***challenges***
to have your own office	*to fufill the company's expectations (e.g. higher sales, new customers)*
to travel abroad/to foreign countries a lot	*to work for a boss/with colleagues/people you don't like*
to have a company car	*to worry about losing your job*
to be able to take important decisions that affect many people	*to worry that you are not good enough for your job*
to be in a position of authority	*to be dependent on other people's good will*
to earn good money	*to have to work fixed hours*
to prove that you are capable of dealing with various challenges	*to be afraid of making mistakes that cost the company a lot of money*

C2 Seite 30

Lösungsvorschlag/Erwartungshorizont:
a) + b)
photo 1: *a solicitor/lawyer; being a solicitor must be exciting and challenging; you know that it might be down to you and your ability to convince people whether your client walks free or not; but I think I would find it very difficult to defend someone in court who has done something really bad*
photo 2: *a doctor; I think I like the job of a doctor; it must be nice to be able to help people feel better; at the same time, it must be difficult to accept that there are some things you can't change or make better for your patients; I think you carry a lot of responsibility as a doctor*
photo 3: *a teacher; I've always wanted to become a teacher; I like the idea of helping others learn and understand; education is a basic human right and I would love to help people, especially children, discover and understand the world around them*

photo 4: *a pilot; I would probably be useless as a pilot but I think it's a nice job if you don't mind being responsible for the safety of a plane full of people; I don't think you have to be very good at maths, though; I think computer skills are far more important: you need to be able to read and understand the plane's instruments*
photo 5: *an engineer; I don't like maths and I don't really know what engineers do all day long, so I would say that it is a job I dislike*
photo 6: *an architect; it must be great to design your own home or help friends or customers build their dream home; however, I think you must be good at maths in order to be a good architect, so it probably wouldn't be the right job for me*
photo 7: *a scientist; science has never been my strong point, so I'm sure I wouldn't be happy working in a lab all day*
photo 8: *a stock trader; I wouldn't want to work as a stock trader; a stock exchange is much too busy and hectic for my liking; you have to take important decisions very quickly, I would hate that*

C3 **Seite 32**

Lösungsvorschlag/Erwartungshorizont:
a) – ***top left:*** *working overtime from home late at night; having to answer two phones at the same time; being overworked; close to burnout /* ***possible reasons:*** *too much work but not enough employees; not very good at time management; unfair boss/management; responsible position /* ***possible consequences:*** *burnout; difficulties sleeping; depression; angry at family*
– ***top right:*** *working from home; being self-employed with a young baby; bringing your child in to work /* ***possible reasons:*** *can't afford to take maternity leave; childminder is ill /* ***possible consequences:*** *caught between the roles of an employee and a parent; unable to put in your normal working hours; unable to concentrate on your work properly*
– ***bottom left:*** *the woman has been made redundant; packing her things on her last day of work /* ***possible reasons:*** *company is downsizing and is laying off people; company has gone into administration /* ***possible consequences:*** *depression; feelings of unworthiness; unemployed*
– ***bottom right:*** *bullying; people talking behind your back; sexual harassment /* ***possible reasons:*** *you got the job/position they wanted; woman efficient and competent, thereby drawing attention to the men's incompetence; misogyny /* ***possible consequences:*** *high blood pressure; depression or anxiety; feeling like an outsider*

C4 **Seite 32**

Think–pair–share: → Siehe oben, Seite 20 hier in den *Teacher's notes.*

Dauer des Videos in b): 4:57 min

Lösungsvorschlag/Erwartungshorizont:
a) – *where in your home do you want the interview to take place? pay attention to the background (tidy; not too personal, but at the same time not too clinical; make the background work to your advantage)*
– *make sure you have all your phones (landline as well as mobile) switched off*
– *make sure everyone in your family knows you're about to have a job interview on Skype, i.e. they should not walk into the room or call out to you while you're on Skype*
– *pay as much attention to the video interview as if you were going for a 'normal' job interview: be ready on time, think about what you're going to wear*
– *don't be fooled: you might be in your home, but it's still a job interview*
– *doublecheck your equipment (computer, microphone)*
– *carry out a few video calls on Skype with friends to make sure you know how to work the programme, where and at which distance from the screen to sit, the best angle at which to hold your head; experiment with the volume of your voice*
b) – *suitable background (create some amount of depth; create some warmth, e.g. plants, wood, bookshelves; if possible, avoid a plain white wall)*
– *lighting (ideally natural light from outside; fluorescent lighting is not very flattering)*
– *no bright background, as it will distract from your face and make your face dark*
– *a dark/black top is fine, ideally a dark/black jacket*
– *don't do any "cute" stuff, like trying to "shake" your Skype partner's hand*
– *perfectly OK to acknowledge the unnaturalness of the situation*
– *simulate eye contact, which is very important when you are dealing with someone in person, so try to look directly into the webcam; what might help: stick photo of a friend, anyone you*

feel comfortable with, next to or on top of the webcam (punch a hole in first!)
– do a warm-up with a friend on Skype shortly before your actual interview to check how you look in the small frame
– turn your email off so you're not interrupted by the sound of an incoming email during the interview
– framing/angle: turn your body slightly to the left, then turn your head to face the screen, i.e. avoid sitting flush to the camera (= facing the screen with your whole body) (→ too much like a police mugshot)
– in short: put yourself in the light, sit up, dress up

c) *– make sure there are no inappropriate posters in the background*
– no sipping on a beer
– check the lighting and the surroundings (no inappropriate posters in the background)
– check alignment of camera and screen: make sure you're making eye contact with the interviewer
– think about what to wear: dress as you would for any job interview
– do a mock interview (with a friend or someone who is used to interviewing people)
– make sure you're not caught out by technical issues (make practice calls to friends to make sure you know the ins and outs of Skype)
– bear in mind that an interview through Skype gives you less time to make a positive impression
– pay attention to your non-verbal communication: make eye contact, smile and check your posture (sit up straight, shoulders back and down, chest open); speak clearly; make sure you match your tone and your message (tone makes more lasting impression than message)
– if you have to interview in a public place, make sure you let the interviewer know

C5 Seite 34

Lösungsvorschlag/Erwartungshorizont:

Aspect of the interview	***What you shouldn't do***	***What you should do***
Clothes and make-up	*– wear large jewellery, loud colours or too much make-up*	*– dress appropriately (man: suit (e.g. navy blue or charcoal grey, white shirt, nice tie); (woman: skirt suit or pant suit)*
Handshake	*– give a limp or a bone-crushing handshake – forget to make eye contact and smile*	*– give a firm, but not a bone-crushing handshake – make eye contact and smile*
How to answer some key questions	*– tell the interviewer your life story*	*– give a concise summary of your career, abilities and goals*
Other dos and don'ts	*– mention possible personality or character flaws – feel obliged to volunteer information about your age or marital status (it's illegal for interviewers to ask you certain personal questions) – wear too much perfume or cologne – leave your mobile on during the interview – answer your mobile phone (in case you forgot to turn it off)*	*– when asked about your weaknesses, avoid mentioning personality or character flaws – instead: focus on weaknesses that might be improved upon over time – stand up and greet your interviewer – bring a copy of your résumé – ask for interviewer's business card – turn off your mobile phone – should your mobile go off (because you forgot to turn it off), apologize immediately and turn it off without checking who's calling or answering it*

C6 Seite 34

Lösungsvorschlag/Erwartungshorizont:

c) ***Q1: What is your greatest weakness?***
– tricky question
– don't mention anything that is vital for the position you are applying for
– narrow your weakness down, i.e. make it very specific, limited to specific situations → this implies that it is manageable and can be worked and improved on

Q2: What is your greatest strength?
– focus on personal qualities, skills and experience directly related to the job
Q3: How would you describe yourself?
– strike a balance between being truthful and saying something that will benefit the company/ position you are applying for
Q4: How do you handle stress and pressure?
– make sure you come across as someone who can handle stress
– specify how you deal with stress/working under pressure
– give a detailed reply, rather than a general one
Q5: What are your hobbies?
– pay attention to/think carefully about what hobbies you want to mention/talk about
– leave out any hobbies that might be considered superficial (partying, clubbing, chilling, …)
– concentrate on hobbies that show qualities that might be of interest to a potential employer
– a mix of different kinds of hobbies is best so you come across as diverse and interested in different areas
Q6: What motivates you?
– there is no right or wrong answer here
– just make sure you don't come across as too fun-oriented
Q7: Describe a difficult work situation and how you overcame it.
– give a specific example
– don't complain about other people and their mistakes
– concentrate on what you did to overcome the situation, not on what/who caused the situation
Q8: What do people most often criticize about you?
– tricky question
– show that you take criticism on board but at the same time don't admit to being criticised for a behaviour that might cause a problem if the company decided to take you on

C7 **Seite 37**

Lösungsvorschlag/Erwartungshorizont:

a) *interview B: more personal than interview A, without being informal; formal and personal can go together; more lively; Francesca steers the interview in her direction; not afraid to lead the conversation; they seem to be talking at eye level, whereas in interview A there is a sense of hierarchy, with the interviewer being the superior*
Interview B runs a lot more smoothly. There is a nice flow to the interview. Interview A, however, feels more like 'stop and go'.
Interview B feels like a conversation, rather than a mere question and answer session.
The questions in interview B are indirect (I hope … / It would be great if you could …), whereas in interview A they are direct and don't allow for much room.
James in interview A doesn't elaborate on his answers; doesn't take the questions as a starting point to bring his ideas/personality across; doesn't show initiative; dull, rehearsed replies

b)

interviewer	***interviewee***
– I'm glad you were able to come and see us here in person. *– I hope you've had no problem finding your way here.* *– Please tell me a little bit more about what …* *– I hope (coming to see us here in person) didn't mean too much hassle for you.* *– You sent in a very interesting application, so …* *– Although I've got your application in front of me, it would be great if you could …* *– You're right that …* *– Coming back to …* *– We can definitely arrange a tour of the company and you may be able to talk to the members of staff.* *– In order to make the most of your time, however, I'd like to know …* *– That was exactly what I was hoping for.*	*– No, not at all. Actually, it was even more … for me to …* *– Thank you for inviting me.* *– As I already pointed out in my application, …* *– There are basically two reasons why … First of all, … Secondly, …* *– It would be a great opportunity to …* *– I know that you are a firm that …* *– I don't know if it is possible, but …* *– I would really like to get to know …* *– That sounds fantastic, even better than what I was hoping for.* *– As I have already written in my CV, …* *– I hope I could be of help in that respect.* *– Maybe there are other skills that might be useful to you.*

C8 Seite 38

Lösungsvorschlag/Erwartungshorizont:

b) *(Delta Summer Sports Camp)*

Interviewer: *Thank you for agreeing to do the interview on Skype. It makes things a lot easier for us.*

Interviewee: *No problem at all. I used Skype a lot during my high school year in the US. I would use it at least once a week to speak to friends and family back home in Germany.*

Interviewer: *Yes, I can tell from your application that you like travelling and spending extended periods abroad. So I believe that was why you decided to apply for a position with us, am I right?*

Interviewee: *Yes and no. Of course, I find it appealing to live and work abroad but that is not all. The main reason is that I'd be able to work with children. As I pointed out in my application, I have experience working with children, in particular children aged 7 to 11. I started out as an assistant coach at our local hockey club, coaching our kids' teams, both boys and girls, but eventually went on to become head coach for the girls' team. I think you will see that I have a fair amount of experience working with children.*

Interviewer: *Thank you. How about some of the other essential requirements we stated in our advert? Although I have your application in front of me, it would be great if you could point out additional reasons why you think you would be the right person for the job.*

Interviewee: *Yes, gladly. I took a first-aid course about five years ago, then a refresher course about six months ago. I've never been in an emergency where I've had to put my knowledge into practice but I'm confident that I would know what to do.*

Also, I took my driving test about eighteen months ago. I don't have my own car but often use my mum's car, so I get a fair bit of practice.

Other than that, I must admit I find it difficult to tell you about my personality, simply because I think it is probably easier for you to tell my attitude and nature, simply by talking to me.

Interviewer: *OK, fair enough. I was wondering whether there is anywhere in particular that you would want to work? Or would you be open as to whether you'd be based in the UK or somewhere else?*

Interviewee: *I have studied your website and am very impressed. I think I would prefer an activity camp in the UK. But at the same time, I know it all depends on your vacancies. So whereas I have a preference for the UK, I would be happy to go wherever I'm needed.*

Interviewer: *That's what I was hoping to hear. We try to accommodate people's preferences but, as you can imagine, it makes things easier if people are flexible. We sometimes even have changes at the last minute.*

Interviewee: *That's no problem at all.*

(Sussex Serengeti Safari Park)

Interviewer: *Thanks for applying. And thank you for agreeing to do the interview on Skype. Not everyone is happy with that.*

Interviewee: *Well, it's my first interview on Skype, so yes, I'm a bit nervous. I'm sorry.*

Interviewer: *Not to worry. We've all been there. Well, let's start. You sent in a very interesting application. I would now like to find out a little bit more about you in person. If you don't mind, would you just briefly explain what made you apply for a job with us?*

Interviewee: *Sure. There are basically two – or two and half – reasons why I've applied for the position. First of all, I enjoy a nice challenge. I can imagine that working shifts in a safari park can be quite demanding as I'm sure it's extremely busy at times. However, I actually quite enjoy working under pressure, not necessarily continuously, but from time to time. Secondly, I much prefer flexible working hours. I'm not really a 9 to 5 person. And finally, although it's only half a reason, the fact that it's a safari park really appeals to me. I'm aware that I probably won't get to see much of the animals but still, it's nice to know that they are there. I find them fascinating.*

Interviewer: *Don't worry, you'll get to see plenty of wild animals. So I take it you wouldn't mind working weekends and bank holidays?*

Interviewee: *No, not at all. I'd much rather have time off during the week.*

Interviewer: *That's good to know. However, as you know, this interview is only a first step. As a next step, you would be required to attend an Assessment Centre in London.*

Interviewee: *Yes, I'm aware of that. I would love to get the chance to prove myself there. Do you have any idea when you would let me know whether I have progressed to the next stage?*

Interviewer: *You should hear from us no later than the end of next week. We're planning the Assessment centre for the end of March.*

Interviewee: *Thank you very much. That sounds fine.*

Mediation

D1 Seite 42

Lösungsvorschlag/Erwartungshorizont:

a) **A** *1. former classmate from the US; thinking of studying in Germany; wants to know more about "duales Studium"*
2. email
3. definition/explanation; advantages and disadvantages
B *1. young people from all over Europe; at a conference about youth unemployment in Europe; introducing the situation in Germany*
2. descriptive/informative article
3. presenting the situation in Germany to young people from other European countries
C *1. colleagues/employees in Irish partner company; explain to them what kind of internship you're doing*
2. short article for the company intranet
3. what the internship is about; why internships abroad are becoming more popular

b) **A** *personal view; colloquial expressions; possibly incomplete sentences and slang; you're emailing a friend/former classmate, so you don't have to be too particular about the wording*
B *objective and matter-of-fact style; technical terms; you've never met the people you're addressing; most of the people you're addressing will be the same age as you; you're representing Germany at the conference, so you will feel obliged to do a good and accurate job*
C *heading; objective and matter-of-fact style; you've never met the people you're addressing; most of them will be older than you; you're acting as a representative of all the people doing an internship after you; you're an employee so you want to come across as professional*

D2 Seite 43

Lösungsvorschlag/Erwartungshorizont:

a) *Text 2 fits task A best.*
reasons for my choice:
- *balanced, informative, straight-forward, easy to read and understand; up to Kyle to decide whether he likes the idea of "duales Studium" or not*
- *text 1: too personal, too negative, too opinionated*
- *text 3: too formal for email between friends/classmates; will need reading twice*

good in the other versions:
- *text 3 offers a lot of valuable information; (good if you think or know that Kyle is very posh)*
- *can't see anything good or useful in text 1*

D3 Seite 45

Lösungsvorschlag/Erwartungshorizont:

1. die Hörsaalbank drücken: *attend university, study, go to university*
2. Abitur: *German school-leaving certificate that qualifies you to study at a university*
3. im Doppelpack bekommen: *receive two things at the same time*
4. seinen Preis haben: *come at a price*
5. fix und fertig sein: *very tired, worn out*

D4 Seite 45

Lösungsvorschlag/Erwartungshorizont:

a)
- *becoming more and more popular*
- *three-year programme: you divide your time between studying at university and working for a company*
- *hard work because of the switch back and forth between company and university, which might involve having to pay rents in two different places*
- *the company pays your university fees and pays you a salary*
- *very practice-oriented: you get a chance to put into practice what you've learnt at university*
- *good chances of being offered a permanent position after you graduate*
- *available for many but not all subjects: mostly economics; also engineering; gradually becoming more readily available for health and social care*
- *ideal for people who want to start and move on with their career as quickly as possible*

- *not so ideal for people who prefer in-depth studies and/or who would like to enjoy the benefits of student life*
- *with most companies, you have to commit to staying with them for two to five years after having graduated*
- *should you decide to drop out of the course mid-way, you might have to pay back the university fees*

b) *Hi Kyle,*
Good to hear from you. It's been a while.
Great to hear you're thinking of coming to Germany to study. You asked me about Duales Studium. *Here's what I've found out:*
It is an increasingly popular form of a three-year degree course at university. However, as the word 'dual' suggests, you don't only spend time at a university, but somewhere else as well, meaning a company which has selected you in an application process and pays for your studies, but expects you to work for them when you are not attending lectures. This can make it quite stressful, but you are paid a salary as well and usually stand a good chance of being offered a job after you graduate. That's why more and more school-leavers do it.
Furthermore, those who choose this kind of a course like the combination of theory and its direct practical application at the company.
However, there are a couple of things to consider.
Duales Studium *is not available for all subjects. It's currently mostly economics but also engineering. It also seems to be becoming more and more available for health and social care, too.*
You have to commit to working for the company for two to five years after having graduated.
Should you decide to drop out of the course mid-way, some companies will ask you to pay back the university fees.
If you decide to do a duales Studium, *you will most likely not be able to enjoy the usual benefits of student life, simply because you won't have the time. Also, a* duales Studium *is considered not to be as detailed or thorough as a traditional university course.*
Although the company will pay you a salary, things might still get tight money-wise, especially if you have to pay two rents, one while you're at university and one while you're working at the company.
Duales Studium *is particularly suitable for people who are more interested in their career than in a university course as such.*
I hope this helps.
Bye for now,
Hannes

Getting started

A1 Seite 48

Lösungsvorschlag/Erwartungshorizont:
different aspects of identity: *religion, family, nationality, language, customs and traditions, sport, sports team, music, party, friends, hobbies/interests, shopping, clothes, work/job, tribe, gender*

*picture **1**: Praying together / United in faith*
*picture **2**: Family get-together / Happy family / Blood is thicker than water*
*picture **3**: United we stand / Home country / Fatherland / Home is where the heart is*
*picture **4**: Stand strong as a team / We're in this together*
*picture **5**: Fatherland and mother tongue / Home is where the heart is / Back to the roots*
*picture **6**: The sound of music / Fans united*
*picture **7**: Being with friends / Beach party / Dancing on the beach*
*picture **8**: Shop till you drop / I shop, therefore I am*
*picture **9**: Rush hour / 9 to 5 / Busy business / Rat race*
*picture **10**: Goth / Goth tribe / Black is beautiful*

A2 Seite 48

Placemat in Vierergruppen: Jede Gruppe findet eine gemeinsame Position zum Thema.

a) ***Placemat*-Phase 1** (Einzelarbeit)
  – Jede Vierergruppe legt eine *Placemat*-Vorlage an, gefaltet oder gezeichnet. Jedem/r der vier S wird eines der äußeren Felder zugewiesen.
  – (Falls gefaltet: Die S nehmen ein großes Blatt (DIN-A3-Format oder größer, z. B. Rückseite von Plakaten), falten es zweimal diagonal und wieder auseinander. In der Mitte wird ein Rechteck ausgespart. L-Anweisung: *Fold a large sheet of paper twice, from corner to corner. Draw a rectangle in the middle.*)
  – Jede/r S denkt allein über die Ausgangsfrage *What three aspects of identity are most important for you?* nach, schreibt seine/ihre *three most important aspects of identity* plus kurze Begründung in sein/ihr Feld (und unterschreibt die Notizen ggf.).
  – Tipp: Jede/r S verwendet eine andere Farbe.

b) ***Placemat*-Phase 2** (Lesen/Kommentieren der Beiträge)
  – Das Blatt wird so lange gedreht, bis jede/r in der Gruppe die Beiträge der anderen gelesen und schriftlich kommentiert hat.
  – Tipp: Wichtig ist, dass in den *Placemat*-Phasen 1 und 2 nicht gesprochen wird.

c) ***Placemat*-Phase 3** (Diskussion/Einigung)
  – Die Gruppe diskutiert die Beiträge, einigt sich auf *the top three aspects of identity* und schreibt diese in das ausgesparte Rechteck in der Mitte des Bogens.
  Language support zur Entscheidungsfindung:

  We need to decide between … and …
  We have to agree on the top three aspects.
  So we all agree that X should go in the centre, right?
  Let's take a vote on this.

  – (Mögliche ***Placemat*-Phase 4** (Präsentation): Ein/e Gruppensprecher/in (z. B. nach *Placemat*-Phase 3 spontan von L bestimmt) stellt die Diskussionsergebnisse begründet im Plenum vor. Die anderen Gruppen bzw. Gruppensprecher/innen nehmen jeweils Stellung.)

Lösungsvorschlag/Erwartungshorizont:
a) ***place/country of birth:*** *identity is about roots and where you originate from*
language: *will always define who you are; language and thoughts are related*
customs and traditions: *unwritten rules that hold a society together; it's only when you've lived somewhere completely new and different that you realize how many customs and traditions, i.e. unwritten rules, there are*

A3 Seite 49

Lösungsvorschlag/Erwartungshorizont:
a) *1. your identity is determined by how you see the world; in other words, your identity changes as you go through life; your take on life is bound to change by your experiences as you grow*

older; according to this quotation, identity is determined/influenced by the outside world

2. *it's impossible to separate your identity from your family background; you need to know who your parents are in order to know who you are; which would imply that it is very difficult/virtually impossible to know who you are, i.e. to have an identity, if you were adopted and don't know anything about your biological parents*
3. *I work, therefore I am; the work you do tells you who you are; emphasis on your work rather than your family or your free time; which would imply that you lose your identity if and when you lose your job*
4. *if you know yourself, if you know who you are, you're bound to be successful; knowing what you want from life means knowing your identity and being successful; identity is like your inner self, your calling in life; ignoring/sacrificing your calling means ignoring who you are*
5. *identity as a synonym for 'life experience'; you live and learn; you acquire an identity by going through life; the older you are, the stronger or more pronounced your identity; which would imply that young people can't have an identity/a pronounced identity because they don't have as much experience as an older person / (similar to quotation number 1)*
6. *having a sense of identity requires other people; you need to interact with other people in order to develop your sense of identity; which would imply that anyone living in isolation, for whatever reason, can't have an identity/would inevitably struggle to develop a sense of identity*
7. *the name given to us by our parents determines who we are, determines our sense of identity; which is why you should never change your name because it would impact on your sense of identity; in other words, your sense of identity is given to you by your parents, i.e. it is predetermined; implies that your identity is a constant that can't and won't undergo any changes during the course of your life*

A4 **Seite 49**

Alternative (Kooperative Lernform): ***Four corners***

- Vier der Zitate werden in den vier Ecken oder an den vier Wänden des Raumes aufgehängt. Die S gehen im Hinblick auf die Frage *Which statement do you agree with most?* umher und entscheiden sich jede/r für sich für eines der Zitate als Antwort. Sie gehen in die Ecke und bleiben bei dem gewählten Zitat stehen.
  Dort begründen die S ihre Wahl zunächst in Paaren, dann erfolgt ein Austausch mit all den MitS in der Ecke, die sich für dasselbe Zitat entschieden haben.
  Ein/e als *presenter* bestimmte/r S trägt die Diskussionsergebnisse der Gruppe im Plenum vor. (Eine mögliche Bestimmungsmethode ist die aus dem Kooperativen Lernen bekannte Methode des „demokratischen Zeigefingers"/*democratic finger:* Alle Gruppenmitglieder heben den Zeigefinger einer Hand und zeigen dann auf ein Signal hin gleichzeitig auf ein Mitglied ihrer Gruppe. Der/Diejenige, auf den/die die meisten Zeigefinger weisen, übernimmt die Präsentation.)
- Zweiter Durchgang mit *Which statement do you agree with least?*
- Alternative, um ein Meinungsbild abzurufen: Die S können ihre Zustimmung/Ablehnung zu jeweils einem *statement* deutlich machen, indem sie sich folgenden vier Plakaten zuordnen, die in den vier Ecken des Raumes hängen: *I strongly agree / I agree / I disagree / I strongly disagree.*
  L liest jeweils ein *statement* vor und die S ordnen sich den Ecken zu.

Lösungsvorschlag/Erwartungshorizont:

- ***statements I most agree with:*** *statement number 2 by Mary Pipher (the father of a friend of mine was adopted from Vietnam as a baby and he doesn't know anything about his biological parents; he says that although he loves his adopted parents and that although he now has a biological family of his own, he still feels lost and lacks a clear sense of identity because he does not know his roots; I think you need to know your past in order to know yourself, your present and your future)*
- ***statements I least agree with:*** *statement number 3 by Kay Stepkin (I'm not saying that work isn't important but it's a poor show if your identity depends on work alone; your identity should not depend on things that are beyond your control, can easily change or be taken away from you; the more independent your identity, the stronger it is; there's more to life than work, so there should be more to your identity than work)*

Practice section

B1 Seite 50

Think–pair–share: → Seite 20 hier in den *Teacher's notes.*

Lösungsvorschlag/Erwartungshorizont:
strict upbringing; parents arranging a marriage for him; Manjit wanting to go out with an English or non-traditional girl; talking back to his parents; being into "Western" habits and interests; having non-Asian friends

B2 Seite 50

Hintergrundinformationen:
- *Bali Rai (*1971) is an English author; was born and grew up in Leicester;* (Un)arranged Marriage *was his first novel for young adults*
  What he says about (Un)arranged Marriage: *"The novel is partly autobiographical with the rest based on the true life experiences of friends and family."*
- Bali Rai **im Internet** (Stand April 2015): http://www.balirai.co.uk

Lösungsvorschlag/Erwartungshorizont:
a) ***Manjit:*** *angry and scared, more angry than scared; I feel sorry for him because he seems very alone; he feels very different from the other members of his family; I think it takes a lot to stay true to yourself and to your interests and values if everyone around you is different and tells you or makes you feel that you don't belong*
his situation: *Manjit's family is more traditional than he is; he seems like the outsider/black sheep of the family (ll. 30–32); his father beats him, is very strict; Manjit's two older brothers, Ranjit and Harry, are different from Manjit, i.e. they take after their father; Manjit and Harry have to share a room; Harry harasses and verbally abuses Manjit (ll. 59–63); no-one in the family shares and/or appreciates Manjit's interest in education and literature; the males dominate the household: Manjit does not mention his mother (or his sister-in-law) much*
b) – *quotation **4:** possibly too early to say but it seems as though Manjit will not "sacrifice" his identity; at the moment he still seems to manage to do what he really wants to do; which, if you believe quotation 4 to be accurate, will mean that Manjit will be successful in life*
– *quotation **5:** Manjit seems to be very aware of what goes on around him; he can see and analyse his family and their interactions very clearly; the way he deals with being the black sheep of the family informs his identity; his experience informs his identity*
– *none of the quotations really fit: we can't really tell from the extract what it is that informs Manjit's identity; it seems as though his identity is a result of being different, of not belonging*

B3 Seite 52

Lösungsvorschlag/Erwartungshorizont:
a) *very reliable, always there when I need her; very funny; green eyes; doesn't talk forever about the same thing; nice balance of talking and listening; talks with her hands; modest; shy in a nice kind of way; her favourite colour is green*
b) *personality/character; voice; gestures; looks/outer appearance (height, build, hair, eyes); clothes*

B4 Seite 52

Lösungsvorschlag/Erwartungshorizont:

aspect and definition/ explanation	***example***
1. Outer appearance/ Looks/Physical features	
	4. *"I had answered back calling him a 'bastard'" (ll. 19–20)* *"Not that I was that bothered by it." (ll. 26–27)* *"I was more influenced by the whole Western culture thing than my brothers had been" (ll. 35–36)* *"getting hit all the time made me feel an outsider and the feeling just got stronger as I grew older." (ll. 38–40)* *"I hated having no privacy, no time to myself that wasn't intruded on" (ll. 64–65)*

5. Habits	
	8. *"Not that I was that bothered by it. […] I just saw it as one of the daily hazards of growing up" (ll. 26–29)* *"getting hit all the time made me feel an outsider and the feeling just got stronger as I grew older." (ll. 38–40)* *"Sharing a room with Harry was like my worst nightmare." (ll. 50–51)* *"I hated having no privacy, no time to myself" (l. 64)* *"I couldn't even do my homework in peace because no-one in my family saw it as being important." (ll. 81–83)*
	10. *"And my dad, well," (l. 1)* *"I had seen him hit my brothers though," (l. 10)* *"With me though it was like open season" (l. 15)* *"He'd hit me" (l. 16)* *"he'd clipped me round the head" (l. 18)* *"I had answered back calling him a 'bastard'" (ll. 19–20)* *"I got beaten" (l. 20)* *"He hit me all the time" (ll. 23–24)* *"since I was a kid" (l. 28)* *"the whole Western culture thing" (ll. 35–36)* *"getting hit all the time" (l. 38)* *"He was so bloody thick" (ll. 66–67)*
11. Social background / Family background	
	14. *"He'd hit me for asking him too many questions or for daring to say something back to him." (ll. 16–17)* *"He hit me all the time, sometimes I reckon just because I was in his range" (ll. 23–25)* *"Not that I was that bothered by it." (ll. 26–27)* *"I did wonder though why he singled me out. Sometimes I thought it was because I was the youngest and other times I really thought that he hated me for some reason" (ll. 30–33)* *"Maybe he could see that I was more influenced by the whole Western culture thing than my brothers had been." (ll. 34–36)* *"He definitely didn't like the fact that my best friend wasn't Asian." (ll. 36–38)* *"[Ranjit and his wife] were the ones who had nicked my room from me" (ll. 48–49)* *"Sharing a room with Harry was like my worst nightmare." (ll. 50–51)* *"At night I used to pretend that he wasn't there by pulling the duvet over myself like a tent and reading by torchlight. Even then he'd throw things at me or call me a poof." (ll. 56–59)* *"I hated having no privacy, no time to myself that wasn't intruded on by a brother who still found fart jokes incredibly funny. He was so bloody thick." (ll. 64–67)* *"I hated him. And he'd turn up like a bad smell every time I wanted some peace" (ll. 68–69)* *"Ranjit and his wife had started doing the same, […] giggling at each other like kids" (ll. 71–73)* *"My mum was always in the kitchen, cooking, or watching the Asian channels on Sky in the living room" (ll. 74–76)* *"And Dad? Well, he was a law unto himself, walking around the house like a drunken zombie, belching all the time." (ll. 76–78)* *"To escape, I'd tried locking myself in the bathroom once but only succeeded in getting a smack in the mouth from him for my trouble." (ll. 78–81)* *"I couldn't even do my homework in peace because no-one in my family saw it as being important. They thought that school was a waste of time, like quite a lot of working-class Punjabi families. All they were interested in was trying to earn money" (ll. 81–86)* *"It was a wonder that I ever got the high grades that I did – not that anyone in my family cared." (ll. 89–91)*

	16. *"And my dad, well, he ran the family with fear." (ll. 1–2)* *"He hit me all the time" (ll. 23–24)* *"made me feel an outsider and the feeling just got stronger as I grew older." (ll. 39–40)* *"I hated having no privacy, no time to myself that wasn't intruded on" (ll. 64–65)* *"It was a wonder that I ever got the high grades that I did – not that anyone in my family cared." (ll. 89–91)*

B5 **Seite 53**

Lösungsvorschlag/Erwartungshorizont:

a) – *family (brothers, i.e. not an only child)*
– *culture (his family's culture is not "Western"; his family is critical of the "Western culture')*
– *relations to others (outsider in the family)*

b) *Manjit = outsider in his family; he seems to be the only member of the family interested in education; for the rest of his family earning money is more important; he is and feels very different from everyone else in his family*

B6 **Seite 54**

Lösungsvorschlag/Erwartungshorizont:

category	***direct/explicit***	***indirect/implicit***	***interpretation***
looks		*"[W]hat are you, a gorah (white) …]?" (ll. 61–62)*	*Manjit is not white; he is a member of a visible minority; Asian-looking: dark complexion and dark hair*
personality/ character traits	*"an outsider and the feeling just got stronger as I grew older." (ll. 38–40)*		*Manjit is the black sheep of the family, feels different from the others, as though he does not belong.*
	"Not that I was that bothered by it." (ll. 26–27)		*Manjit does not seem to mind being beaten by his father. It is probably fair to say that he does not mind being an outsider in his family, either.*
	"I hated having no privacy, no time to myself that wasn't intruded on" (ll. 64–65)		*Manjit likes having time to himself. He is a bit of a loner, partly because it is forced upon him (outsider), partly because he prefers it that way, it is just the way he is. Manjit isn't a family man; he appreciates having time and space to himself; independent*
		"I had answered back calling him a 'bastard'" (ll. 19–20)	*Manjit does not seem scared of his father although his father beats him a lot. → strong character*
		"With her [= Manjit's mum] and my sister-in-law he just shouted a lot which scared them enough anyway." (ll. 8–10)	*Other members of the family (Manjit's mum and his sister-in-law) are scared of Manjit's father. This again shows that Manjit is different. He reacts differently from the other members of his family.*
		"I did wonder though why he singled me out." (ll. 30–31)	*Manjit reflects on his own and other people's behaviour. → thoughtful*
		"my best friend wasn't Asian" (ll. 37–38)	*Manjit is different and not afraid to do things his way.*

category	*direct/explicit*	*indirect/implicit*	*interpretation*
personality/ character traits *(continued)*		*"Even then he'd throw things at me or call me a poof." (ll. 58–59)*	*Manjit comes across as centred and strong. His brother continually tries to provoke him but Manjit doesn't react to the taunting.*
		"but that was their problem" (ll. 47–48)	*Manjit seems quite defensive; distances himself from his family.*
habits	*"At night I used to pretend that he wasn't there by pulling the duvet over myself [...] and reading by torchlight" (ll. 56–58)*	*"What you wanna read for, man? Bloody Dickens" (ll. 60–61)*	*Manjit refuses to let the outside world interfere with/his family affect his inner world and his values. He protects himself against the outside; manages to stay true to himself and do the things that are important to him, e.g. reading. Likes reading: 19th century English/Victorian literature in particular (Charles Dickens: 1812–1870)*
mood	*"made me feel an outsider and the feeling just got stronger as I grew older." (ll. 38–40)*		*Manjit feels like an outsider.*
	"Sharing a room with Harry was like my worst nightmare." (ll. 50–51) *"I hated having no privacy, no time to myself" (l. 64)* *"I couldn't even do my homework in peace because no-one in my family saw it as being important." (ll. 81–83)*		*Manjit is happy to spend time all by himself. His happiness does not depend on sharing time with others. In fact, he quite often prefers being alone to spending time with others. He seems self-sufficient.*
		"Not that I was that bothered by it. [...] I just saw it as one of the daily hazards of growing up" (ll. 26–29)	*Manjit's inner state is not particularly affected by what goes on around him. → inner strength* *Manjit is the black sheep of the family but he is used to it and has accepted it; in fact, he in turn has distanced himself from his family; the feeling of distance/alienation seems to be mutual*
language/ idiolect		*"And my dad, well," (l. 1)* *"pissed" (l. 3)* *"I had seen him hit my brothers though," (l. 10) / "With me though" (l. 15)* *"He'd hit me" (l. 16)* *"calling him a 'bastard'" (ll. 19–20)* *"I got beaten" (l. 20)* *"He got angry all the time" (l. 4) / "He hit me all the time" (ll. 23–24)* *"since I was a kid" (l. 28)* *"the whole Western culture thing" (ll. 35–36)* *"bloody thick" (l. 67)*	*– colloquialisms* *– spoken, informal language* *– exaggerations ("all the time"), typical of colloquial English, especially among younger people* *– short forms, not just in direct speech but throughout the text* *– the odd swear word ("bastard", "bloody")* *– Manjit uses a lot of informal language and slang: he can be quite rude and impolite*

category	*direct/explicit*	*indirect/implicit*	*interpretation*
social background / family background	*"I was the youngest" (ll. 31–32)* *"We lived on Evington Drive, in an area that was popular with Punjabi families. […] three bedrooms […] I had to move […] in with Harry when Ranjit got married and his wife moved in with us." (ll. 41–46)* *"[My family] thought that school was a waste of time, like quite a lot of working-class Punjabi families" (ll. 83–85)*	*"he'd […] call me a poof." (l. 59)*	*– youngest son of three; working-class Asian family* *– Manjit has two (older) brothers: Ranjit (married) and Harry* *– three-bedroom house for six people: parents, Ranjit and his wife, Manjit and Harry* *– Manjit is the only one in his family with an interest in education and literature* *– Manjit's family are portrayed as hostile to British culture and the educational system; identity of male members of the family is very much based on macho hostility/underlying siege mentality towards the rest of the society/culture they live in; Manjit is seen by them as traitor/collaborator with the enemy* *– Evington Drive in Leicester; family does not mix with non-Asians much; keep to themselves; ghettoization/autonomous co-existence of minority communities*
relations to others		*"They thought that school was a waste of time, like quite a lot of working-class Punjabi families. All they were interested in was trying to earn money" (ll. 83–86)*	*He refers to his family and all "working-class Punjabi families" as "they", rather than "we". This emphasises the fact that Manjit is and feels different. He does not seem to have anything in common with his family/his cultural background.*
	"I couldn't even do my homework in peace because no-one in my family saw it as being important." (ll. 81–83) / "a wonder that I ever got the high grades that I did – not that anyone in my family cared." (ll. 89–91)		*Manjit feels like an outsider, and his family see it that way, too.* *The feeling that Manjit does not belong, that he is the odd one out, seems to be mutual.*
	"And Dad? Well, he was […] like a drunken zombie, belching all the time." (ll. 76–78) / "He hit me all the time, sometimes I reckon just because I was in his range" (ll. 23–25) / "Maybe he could see that I was more influenced by the whole Western culture thing than my brothers had been." (ll. 34–36) / "He definitely didn't like the fact that my best friend wasn't Asian." (ll. 36–38)	*"Ranjit and his wife […], […] giggling at each other like kids" (ll. 71–73)*	*Manjit is very critical of his father and his brothers.* *He does not get on with his father or his brothers. Things seem to be particularly difficult between Manjit and his father and Manjit and Harry.* *Manjit and his brother Harry do not get on at all.* *Manjit does not seem to take Ranjit, his other brother, seriously.*

category	*direct/explicit*	*indirect/implicit*	*interpretation*
relations to others *(continued)*	*"Sharing a room with Harry was like my worst nightmare. He was fat and hairy, and had a horrible habit" (ll. 50–52) / "Even then he'd throw things at me or call me a poof." (ll. 58–59) / "I hated him [Harry]." (l. 68)*	*"He was so bloody thick" (ll. 66–67)*	*Manjit is very critical of people who are not as intelligent and well-educated as he is; it makes you wonder whether he might not be just be as intolerant as his father and his brothers: they are prejudiced against non-Asian people, Manjit seems prejudiced against working-class people* *Manjit is very critical of his traditional Asian/Punjabi background; he feels more at home in Western/British culture*
function for the story		*"made me feel an outsider and the feeling just got stronger as I grew older." (ll. 39–40)* *"It was a wonder that I ever got the high grades that I did – not that anyone in my family cared." (ll. 89–91)*	*Manjit is the protagonist and first-person narrator.* *You can guess from the extract that Manjit is/will be at the centre of the story/plot unfolding.* *It will most likely be Manjit against the rest of his family/against his culture.*

B7 **Seite 54**

Lösungsvorschlag/Erwartungshorizont:
- *Manjit is both the protagonist and the first-person narrator of the story*
- *the story/novel is set in Leicester, England; Manjit is the youngest of three sons in a traditional Punjabi family; one of his brothers, Ranjit, is married; his other brother is called Harry*
- *Manjit not only feels like the outsider in his family, he is treated as the odd one out by everybody in the family: his father and his brother Harry are particularly aggressive towards him*
- *one of the reasons why Manjit is so different from the other people in his family is that he is interested in books and in education, whereas his family "thought that school was a waste of time, like quite a lot of working-class Punjabi families" (ll. 83–85); this implies that Manjit is an outsider on more levels than one: not just in his family, but also in his culture*
- *however, Manjit seems perfectly capable of standing up to his father and his brother; if we believe what he says in the extract, he is not "that bothered" (l. 27) by his position in the family and by the aggression and abuse he has to endure at the hands of both his father and Harry*
- *as far as Manjit's brother Ranjit is concerned, Manjit does not seem to take him very seriously; instead, he compares him and his wife to children when he describes them as "giggling at each other like kids" (l. 73)*
- *Manjit strikes me as strong-willed; it takes a lot of inner strength to cope with being the black sheep in the family and being beaten by your father on a regular basis*
- *at the same time, Manjit comes across as headstrong and stubborn in places; he seems no less critical or stubborn than his brother Harry, or his father, for that matter; all of them seem to be good at hurling insults and abuse at each other (cf. ll. 19–20, ll. 58–63)*
- *Manjit seems to have developed coping mechanisms for how to cope with his position in the family; he refuses to let the outside world interfere with/his family affect his inner world and his values. He protects himself against the outside; he manages to stay true to himself and do the things that are important to him, e.g. reading.*
- *Manjit is very critical of his traditional Asian/Punjabi background; he feels more at home in Western/British culture*
- *The fact that Manjit enjoys reading 19th century English/Victorian literature (cf. ll. 60–61) highlights the fact that he is "more influenced by the whole Western culture thing" (ll. 35–36) than both his brothers.*
- *What strikes me as interesting is the fact that Manjit hardly ever mentions his mother (or sister-in-law) in the extract. On the one hand, he wants to portray himself as different from this culture, on the other hand he seems just as ignorant of women as the other male members of the family.*

B8 **Seite 55**

Lösungsvorschlag/Erwartungshorizont:

b) *first person narration*

c) ***text B:** not as direct as text A (which is the original); it is easier to identify with a first-person narrator than with a third-person narrator; in this case, it is a* **third-person limited narrator,** *which is the most distanced of all possible narrative perspectives; as a consequence, you feel a distance between yourself as a reader and the protagonist; this distance is created by the narrator*
***text C: omniscient narrator;** as a reader you get an insight into how the different characters feel; this helps you feel close or closer to not just one character but all characters; in text C we get an idea of how Manjit's mother feels about her son being beaten by her husband; we also find out how Manjit's father feels about Manjit; the omniscient narrator provides the reader with more answers and information than a first-person narrator could; with the original text, the reader is left to guess why Manjit gets beaten by his dad; text C provides some answers; also, there is a bit of foreshadowing in the final line: "One day he would either turn against his father or simply walk out." As a reader, you can guess that either of the two things will happen in the novel.*

B9 **Seite 56**

Lösungsvorschlag/Erwartungshorizont:

(dialogue between Ranjit and a Punjabi friend)
***Ranjit:** I need your help, Amrit. Manjit's dishonouring the family.*
***Amrit:** What do you mean?*
***Ranjit:** He behaves not like a Punjabi but like a gorah. This must stop.*
***Amrit:** What are you saying?*
***Ranjit:** Not sure. But it's upsetting our father. Manjit's disobeying him all the time.*
***Amrit:** Why don't you give him a good beating?*
***Ranjit:** That's what our father has tried. But it's not enough. You can see it in Manjit's eyes. He hates all of us. He shows no respect. Respect, man. That's what Manjit needs to learn.*
***Amrit:** Would you like one of my cousins to talk some sense into him?*
***Ranjit:** I was hoping you'd suggest that, Amrit. Our family would be eternally grateful. Thank you.*

(last three paragraphs: third-person limited narrator focusing on Manjit)
Manjit hated having to share a room with his brother Harry. He had had to move out of his own room and in with Harry when Ranjit got married and his wife Jas moved in with them.
Harry would often hurl insults at Manjit when all Manjit wanted to do was have a bit of peace and quiet and read. "What you wanna read for, man? Bloody Dickens – what are you, a gorah or something? Read about bloody man's stuff, innit."
Manjit hated having no privacy, no time to himself that wasn't intruded on by a brother who still found fart jokes funny. Manjit did not think much of Harry, he sometimes felt like he was talking to a gorilla. In so many words, Manjit hated Harry. Harry would turn up like a bad smell every time Manjit wanted some peace, no matter where Manjit was – the garden, the garage, wherever. To make matters worse, recently Ranjit and Jas had started doing the same, always around and giggling at each other like kids.
Manjit's mum was always in the kitchen, cooking, or watching the Asian channels on Sky in the living room. And Manjit's dad? Well, he was a law unto himself, walking around the house like a drunken zombie, belching all the time. To escape, Manjit had once tried locking himself in the bathroom but only succeeded in getting a smack in the mouth from his father. Manjit often felt like a stranger in his own family. Not that he was that bothered by it. He was used to it by now. He truly did not mind – if only they ignored and left him alone more.
Manjit couldn't even do his homework in peace because no-one in his family saw it as being important. They thought that school was a waste of time, like quite a lot of working-class Punjabi families. All they were interested in was trying to earn money and you couldn't do that at school or college. Ranjit and Harry had both got jobs in factories as soon as they left school. It was a wonder that Manjit ever got the high grades that he did. However, his family seemed entirely indifferent to Manjit's efforts and it was a shame that they cared so little about the achievements of the youngest member of the family.

Getting to the point

C1 **Seite 58**

Think–pair–share: → Seite 20 hier in den *Teacher's notes.*

Lösungsvorschlag/Erwartungshorizont:
- *white/western people suspicious of/worried about members of visible minorities*
- *societies/people becoming wary and suspicious of Muslims*
- *people becoming increasingly worried about large crowds of people*
- *people becoming distrustful of other people and cultures → decrease in tolerance*
- *people spying on each other, prepared to spy on each other; governments spying on people's phone calls and e-mail communications*
- *people prepared to compromise on freedom in return for an increase in safety, if only a perceived increase*
- *increase in security checks at airports and other places where many people come together*

C2 **Seite 58**

Lösungsvorschlag/Erwartungshorizont:
- *Khalid is with his friends Holgy and Tony*
- *close to where they are a group of other boys start harassing a woman in order to distract her and steal her mobile phone*
- *Khalid steps in, tells the boys to leave the woman alone and gives the mobile phone back to the woman, apologizing for the boys' behaviour → the woman reacts in a strange way, as though she doesn't want Khalid's help*
- *when Khalid returns to Holgy and Tony, they make fun of him; to them it is obvious that the woman was scared of Khalid because of his Asian/Arabic/"Bin Laden" looks*
- *Khalid is very upset that he might be mistaken for a terrorist; he is aware that it has to do with the political situation in the world, that people are starting to see a terrorist in anyone resembling Bin Laden, i.e. anyone with Asian/Arabic looks; he becomes acutely aware that the political situation in the world is having an impact on his very own life and situation in England; that he is becoming an outsider in his own country, in the country he grew up in*

C3 **Seite 59**

Lösungsvorschlag/Erwartungshorizont:
- *narrative perspective in "Guantanamo Boy": third-person limited narrator focusing on Khalid (narrator provides insight into Khalid's thoughts and feelings: ll. 22–32, 43–44, 62–64, 71–75)*
- *narrative perspective in "(Un-)arranged marriage": first-person narrator*

C4 **Seite 59**

Lösungsvorschlag/Erwartungshorizont:
direct characterization:
- *"likes a beer now and then" (l. 24) → average teenager*
- *"stolen a couple of things […] for a bet" (ll. 25–26) → didn't steal of his own accord but because of a bet; didn't steal because he has seriously criminal tendencies but because he considers it part of growing up and because he wants to fit in; at the same time, it proves that he pretends to be "more confident and stronger" (ll. 27–28) than he actually is: because if he were really confident and strong, fitting in wouldn't be that important, i.e. he wouldn't feel the need to steal for a bet*
- *"pretending to be wilder, more confident, and stronger than he really is to prove he can hold his own with some of the older kids" (ll. 27–30) → wants to fit in with the others*
- *"resentment at the steroid heads' stupid behaviour rises in him like never before" (ll. 30–32); "angrily" (l. 34) → strong sense of what is right and wrong; but also points to strong emotions (aggression)*

→ *interestingly enough, Khalid does not seem strong enough to say no to a bet that involves stealing but he is strong enough to tell off a group of boys trying to steal a woman's mobile phone; Khalid is a lot stronger than he thinks; his actions prove him to be strong and courageous*
- *"'These are dangerous times for Muslims,' his dad said the other day. And he was right" (ll. 64–66) → Khalid realizes that his life is changing; realizes that he's being judged not by the things he does but by the way he looks and by the religious beliefs he has/judged not by his actions but by his looks and his religion*

indirect characterization:

- *"They're at it again" (l. 22) → it's not the first time Khalid is witnessing a situation like that; suggests that he has been angry at groups of boys trying to steal things before*
- *"screams at the top of his voice" (l. 23), "push the kids aside" (ll. 34–35), "knocks the mobile out of the [...] hand" (ll. 35–36), "grabs" (l. 37) → shows that Khalid is angry; it also suggests aggression; when the woman watches him behave like that, all she probably sees is the aggression which she is afraid he will direct at her next*
- *"the steroid heads' stupid behaviour" (ll. 30–31) → distances himself from the other boys' rude behaviour*
- *"'Push off, you jerk!' [...] 'Do it again and I'll thump you.'" (ll. 49–50) → Khalid feels strongly about this; however, it also shows strong emotions and potential aggression*
- *"'They're a bunch of losers.'" (l. 40) → he is different from the boys who tried stealing the woman's mobile phone; wants to distance himself from them; wants to make it clear that he has nothing to do with them, that he is far from attacking her*
- *"Hands tucked deep in his pockets" (l. 67) → inner withdrawal; tries to make himself invisible; sad; truly upset that his helping the woman could be mistaken for a possible attack*
- *"suddenly unable to remember why he's here. Unable to remember anything" (ll. 71–72) → lost in thoughts; in shock; clearly upset by what has happened; obvious that he doesn't take things lightly but is sensitive*
- *"'If you had a beard, you'd be a dead ringer for Bin Laden" (ll. 59–60) → tells us about Khalid's looks: brown skin, dark hair*

→ Khalid is very different from the way he is perceived by the woman; in fact, he is very thoughtful and sensitive (→ round character) and has a very keen sense of what is right and wrong; which is why he is very upset, both by the woman's reaction and by his friends' laughing and joking, but also when he realizes that this is something he will most likely have to get used to

C5 **Seite 59**

Lösungsvorschlag/Erwartungshorizont:

I think Khalid's behaviour might develop in three possible ways:

- *he might withdraw from his friends and become passive: this would be in line with his initial reaction after the incident; he confronts neither the woman nor Holgy and Tony; in fact, he remains quiet apart from a short "Yeah?" (l. 62); not only does he not confront anybody, he doesn't even begin to explain or justify himself; instead, he stands with his hands "tucked deep in his pockets" (l. 67)*
- *OR he might become active in a positive way, i.e. by speaking out against prejudice: again, there is possible evidence in the text that things will go this way; Khalid has a very strong sense of what is right and wrong and is prepared to stand up and speak out when he feels somebody is treated unfairly; he didn't hesitate when he saw the woman being harassed, so there is reason to think/hope that he wouldn't hesitate to stand up and speak out for himself and all the other Muslims living in England and feeling at home in England*
- *OR he might become active in a negative way, i.e. by taking it out on other people or possibly even joining a terrorist youth camp: on the one hand, I don't see Khalid giving up his life in England and joining a terrorist youth camp in say, Pakistan, but on the other hand, the text makes it clear that Khalid's emotions are quite strong and he is prepared to use physical violence in order to do what he thinks is right; his actions when he confronts the group of boys are described in a rather aggressive way ("screams [...] runs over to push [...] aside [...] knocks [...] grabs"; ll. 23–37); also, he seems prepared to use violence if he sees the boys harassing anybody again ("I'll thump you."; l. 50); but there is no telling whether he might not just say that in order to impress the boys, as he is previously described as "pretending to be wilder [...] than he really is" (ll. 27–28)*

I would like to think that Khalid responding in a negative, openly hostile way is the least likely option of the three options I have described. From what we learn about Khalid's father in lines 64–65 of the extract, there is nothing to indicate any history of extremism in Khalid's family that might encourage Khalid to turn aggressive in an organized fashion.

I would like to think that Khalid will go for the second option I have pointed out, i.e. speaking out against prejudice and becoming active in order to change the world for the better. It will make him a stronger person, it will prove that a bad experience can be turned into something good.

Khalid opting for withdrawal and passivity would be a shame and a sign of defeat.

C6 Seite 59

Lösungsvorschlag/Erwartungshorizont:
(from Khalid's point of view)
'By the way,' Holgy says, laughing, 'Mikael's parents are bunking off somewhere on Saturday so he's having a party.'
As I'm about to get the details, as I've never been to Mikael's before, a commotion starts up outside the fish-and-chip shop a few doors down. A woman in a grey tracksuit and trainers, about thirty years old, is arguing with the steroid heads from school.
A fat kid swigs from a bottle of beer. What an idiot! He starts jumping up and down as if bouncing on a trampoline, while the others surround her, grabbing her chips and flinging them in the air. 'There goes another one – wooeee!'
Taunting her with a blizzard of daft hand movements, they pump her space with their shoulders so one of them can dip his hand in her tracksuit pocket to steal her mobile.
They're at it again. 'Hey!', I find myself screaming at the top of my voice. I often find myself pretending to be wilder, more confident and stronger than I really am. You have to show you're tough, you have to prove you can hold your own with some of the older kids. If you don't, they turn on you. But today resentment at the steroid heads' stupid behaviour rises in me like never before.
I run over to push them aside. I can hear Holgy and Tony laugh their heads off behind me. 'Give it here!' I knock the mobile out of the little fair-haired one's hand, then grab the bag of chips from the tubby one, who now has them.
'I'm sorry,' as I hand the phone back to the woman. 'They're a bunch of losers.'
She thanks me briefly with a nod but refuses the remaining chips with a sour expression. Something's off, something's not quite right. She makes me feel as though she doesn't want my help, then strides off proudly, swishing her ponytail as if she was never in any danger in the first place.
'Whaddya do that for?' One of the kids frowns. 'We were only having a bit of fun.'
'Push off, you jerk! Do that again and I'll thump you.'
When I turn back to Holgy and Tony, they are still killing themselves laughing.
'What are you like? Fess up, Kal. Didn't you see – ha-ha-ha – how pale she went – ha-ha – when you screamed at them?' Holgy says.
'I mean, you're pretty tall, Kal. She was more scared of you than – ha-ha – of that lot.'
'If you had a beard, you'd be a dead ringer for Bin Laden, mate,' Tony adds, and both of them crack up again.
'Yeah?' Suddenly it dawns on me that the woman maybe thought I was a terrorist or something. 'These are dangerous times for Muslims,' Dad said the other day. And he was right. I know he was. Some time later, I find myself standing under the green canvas of the shop, hands tucked deep in my pockets, staring at the display of grapefruits, cabbages, tomatoes, peppers, ginger and garlic, suddenly unable to remember why I'm here. Unable to remember anything but the look of contempt on the woman's face and Tony's words. I know they were supposed to be a joke, but even so … It's the first time world events and the so-called 'War on Terror' have really come home to me.

Getting started

A1 **Seite 60**

Lösungsvorschlag/Erwartungshorizont:

a) *I spend about three hours on the Internet every day.*
- *chat with friends*
- *watch TV*
- *buy books and DVDs from Amazon*
- *look up information (on Wikipedia)*
- *check my e-mails*
- *check my Facebook/Instagram page*
- *write a blog entry*
- *read my favourite blogs*
- *play online games*
- *watch videos/tutorials on YouTube*

A2 **Seite 60**

Lösungsvorschlag/Erwartungshorizont:

"our nights in together" implies a romantic evening with just two people; however, here it is an evening spent in front of two separate computers; in addition, the cartoon makes fun of "friends"; shift in meaning of "friends"; a friend used to be a person you know really well; in the real world there's a limit to the number of friends you can have; you can't have 756 friends; you can have 756 online friends but that's far from the traditional/original meaning of the word "friends"

A3 **Seite 60**

Lösungsvorschlag/Erwartungshorizont:

possible reasons: *meet new people who share your interests / find romance / lonely and/or unhappy / want to escape the life you lead / want to pretend to be someone else / take on a new/different identity / many people find it easier to talk about problems when they don't have to look you in the eye / being able to say nasty things without having to deal with the consequences of having abused/hurt someone / anonymity / talk with and stay connected to friends and family who live far away / people are not judged based on how they look / flirting / cybersex/online sex*
possible problems: *misunderstandings/arguments because you don't have people's voices, facial expressions and gestures to guide you / many people lose all their inhibitions online and believe they can act any way they like → a lot of abuse and insults / criminals looking for easy targets / cyberbullying/cyberstalking / some people are more likely to speak honestly when they are online, which is why conversations may quickly become intimate*

A4 **Seite 60**

Hintergrundinformationen:

- *Mary Hooper (* 1944) is a British author of teen fiction; her novel* Amy *was published in 2002*
  Im Internet (Stand April 2015): www.maryhooper.co.uk
  E-Mail-Adresse: contact@maryhooper.co.uk
- *Val McDermid (* 1955) is a Scottish crime writer;* Fever of the Bone *was published in 2009*
  Im Internet (Stand April 2015): www.valmcdermid.com
  E-Mail-Adresse: info@valmcdermid.com

Lösungsvorschlag/Erwartungshorizont:

a) ***Amy:*** *creepy; she meets Zed and he moves very quickly, i.e. asks her personal questions (about her looks, her body, her bra size) and invites her to come and stay the night at his place; Amy doesn't ask Zed any personal questions but answers all his questions about her; she tries to talk about Zed's work but he keeps returning to private/personal/intimate matters; she does not refuse to answer his questions; she comes across as a bit naive ("You mean meet up 4 real?")*
Jeni: *scary and threatening; Jeni starts chatting with someone who calls himself or herself ZZ; ZZ tells Jeni that s/he knows her secret; s/he says no more but it sounds as though s/he will try and blackmail Jeni into doing something; Jeni says that she does not know what ZZ is on about*

b)
- *people who are unhappy/bored in their relationships*
- *looking for new friends after you have fallen out with your old/best friends*
- *look for/find someone for a one-night stand / blackmail*

Practice section

B1 Seite 62

Lösungsvorschlag/Erwartungshorizont: *Colin uses the Internet to check his e-mails but ends up doing things he had not planned to do, i.e. buy a really old car and get married to an underage girl.*

B2 Seite 62

Lösungsvorschlag/Erwartungshorizont:

a)

terms: visual elements	*description*	*effect*
dominant colours	*red*	*symbolizes danger*
caricature: focal point in this cartoon	*a character of unspecific age with thick glasses, an unathletic figure and old-fashioned clothes sitting at his computer; facial expression is difficult to describe as you cannot see his eyes*	*suggests that he is a nerd, i.e. a boring person who is socially isolated; his goggle-type glasses and his hanging cheeks imply frustration and ignorance*
text font	*childish clumsy writing*	*indicates lack of maturity or intelligence*

terms: text elements	*description*	*effect*
headline	*the title of the cartoon*	*specifies the message of the cartoon*
caption	*explains what happened to the character while he was checking his e-mails*	*illustrates the pitfalls of indiscriminate Internet use*

b) ***visual elements:*** *The cartoon "The Dangers of the Internet" shows a character of unspecific age sitting at his computer, with thick glasses, an unathletic figure and old-fashioned clothes. His facial expression is difficult to describe as you cannot see his eyes.*
The way the character is depicted suggests that he is a nerd, i.e. a boring person that is socially isolated; his goggle-type glasses and his hanging cheeks imply frustration and ignorance.
The above is emphasised by the childish clumsy writing that is used for the caption. This indicates a lack of maturity or intelligence on the part of the character.
The dominant colour of the cartoon is red, which symbolizes danger.
what makes the cartoon humorous: *many of us know the feeling of having klicked on something, then wondering how it is we got there; people's tendency to do things online that they would never do or achieve in real life, either because they'd be too scared or because they'd think it through first; the thought of the character in the cartoon being attractive to a 17-year-old girl*
the cartoonist's message: *The problem with the Internet is that you tend to get sidetracked, i.e. you end up doing things you hadn't wanted to do or certainly hadn't planned to do.*

B3 Seite 63

Lösungsvorschlag/Erwartungshorizont:

a) ***cartoon 1:*** *fact that people don't always tell the truth online; that people put false information in their online profile in order to attract particular people*
cartoon 2: *people are so used to doing their shopping online that they are no longer aware of the dos and don'ts in the real world / we have become so dependent on the Internet that we no longer know how to act in the real world/that we lose all inhibitions when the computer fails us*
cartoon 3: *online communication (e.g. Facebook) has come to replace face-to-face communication; generation Facebook often seems ignorant of other ways of communicating*
cartoon 4: *the parent generation knows very little about the online world; the parent generation is out of touch with what goes on in their children's lives; parents often freak out for no reason at all; they freak out because they lack the necessary experience/information*

b) ***cartoon 1***
visual elements: *dominant colours red and orange for the cat → symbolizes danger / black and white for the mouse → inferiority; the cat dominates the mouse / grin on the cat's face → feeling of superiority / eyes and mouth of mouse wide open → angry, indignant, annoyed / cat looks plump, on the heavy side → suggests that the cat likes its food and is anything but a vegetarian*

***text elements:** caption/punch line presented as direct speech, as though spoken by the mouse*
***what makes the cartoon humorous:** that it's animals rather than people/animals are personified; that the cat is more clever than the mouse; cartoon will remind many readers of Tom & Jerry cartoons: Tom the cat usually loses out to Jerry the mouse; here the situation is reversed: the plump cat which would never have caught the mouse if they'd had a race/chase has won/ has used its brains/criminal energy/online anonymity to beat the mouse*
***the cartoonist's message:** Beware of the risks of online anonymity! Don't trust anyone online!; Don't believe what anyone says online about who they are!; there are too many people on Facebook et al pretending to be someone else in order to attract others / Don't meet up with anyone whom you've met online without some form of safety net, e.g. taking someone along.*

cartoon 2
***visual elements:** couple/husband and wife in their underwear; he is unshaven with a cup of tea in his hand, she with her curlers in → suggests that they consider the supermarket their living room; they feel at home; no inhibitions; oblivious to other woman's disapproval / woman on the right: thick glasses staring at other woman's underwear; hair in a bun; plump figure → her stare implies disapproval; her hairstyle, her figure, her outfit and the fact that she has partly turned away from the husband and wife imply old-fashionedness, disapproval and possibly bigotry / no-name products on shelves, empty trolleys → makes the reader concentrate on the people*
***text elements:** punch line presented as direct speech by woman in underwear / swear word "bloody" → underlines their lack of inhibitions / they blame the computer for their outfit → they have become totally dependent on the computer/Internet; have forgotten how to act, speak and dress appropriately in the real, outside world*
***what makes the cartoon humorous:** that the couple are in the supermarket in their underwear obviously unaware of the other woman's stares/unaware of the inappropriateness of their attire*
***the cartoonist's message:** the computer/Internet makes you lose all your inhibitions; we have become so used to using the computer that we have forgotten how to behave properly in the real world outside our homes, away from our computers*

cartoon 3
***visual elements:** cartoon is black and white / mother and daughter in living room; mother sat in armchair, daughter standing in front of her; expression on mother's face: upper lip protruding over lower lip → suggests that she is perplexed/baffled by her daughter's assumption/ignorance*
***text elements:** punch line presented as direct speech by the daughter*
***what makes the cartoon humorous:** that the daughter seems ignorant of normal human interaction; that young people take everything to do with Facebook as "normal"; they can't imagine a time/life before or without Facebook*
***the cartoonist's message:** Children/The younger generation will always think their parents old-fashioned. They are so sure of themselves that they forget that their parents have lives, too. / Internet interaction has come to replace human interaction.*

cartoon 4
***visual elements:** father and son in living room; father sat in armchair reading his newspaper, son standing in front of him; expression on son's face: huge eyes, upper lip protruding over lower lip → suggests that he is perplexed and baffled by his father's ignorance, is lost for words*
***text elements:** punch line presented as direct speech by the man on the left (= father)*
***what makes the cartoon humorous:** that the father pretends to know what is good for his son; some things never change: children growing away from their parents but parents still pretending that they're on top of things*
***the cartoonist's message:** parents don't know what goes in their children's lives but still try and tell them what to do; they try and hold on to their position of authority in the family*

B4 **Seite 64**

Lösungsvorschlag/Erwartungshorizont: *The authors' attitude towards the Internet is very critical. / The headline suggests that the authors think the Internet is to blame for a student's suicide. / The authors' attitude is clearly stated in lines 1–5, the article's introduction.*

B5 **Seite 66**

Hintergrundinformationen: *The article was published in* The Washington Post *in October 2010.* The Washington Post *is a leading daily US newspaper. (Others are* The New York Times *and* The Wall Street Journal.*)* Im Internet (Stand April 2015): www.washingtonpost.com

Lösungsvorschlag/Erwartungshorizont:

a) ***choice of language/words that trigger(s) associations:***
– "shocking" (l. 1), "alarming" (l. 2), "tormenting" (l. 2), "cruel" (l. 4), "vengeful" (l. 4), "shocked and disturbed" (l. 20), "teasing, harassing or intimidating" (l. 32), "cruelly" (l. 38), "nasty" (l. 44), "damaging" (l. 48) → imply danger and violence
– "yet again" (l. 2) → implies impatience
– "can even distinguish" (l. 3) → implies condescending attitude towards young people
quotations to give weight to the arguments: *statement of a New Jersey lawyer (ll. 6–9, ll. 56–58), Rutgers student Lauren Felton (ll. 21–27), Gregory Jantz, founder of A Place of Hope, a Seattle mental health care center (ll. 52–56)*
facts and figures to back up the arguments: *"at least 12 cases in the U.S. since 2003 in which children and young adults between 11 and 18 killed themselves after falling victim to some form of 'cyber-bullying'" (ll. 28–31)*
appealing to emotions and awakening human interest:
– "jumped to his death" (l. 11), "a shy, gifted 18-year-old violinist" (ll. 19–20), "hanged herself" (ll. 35–36), "cruelly dumping her" (l. 38), "Ravi's lawyer and a lawyer believed to be representing Wei did not return calls." (ll. 65–67), "where Clementi grew up and attended high school" (ll. 69–70), "Childhood friend" (l. 71), "who played in a summer music academy with him" (ll. 71–72), "destined for greatness" (l. 73), "'I've never heard anyone make a violin sing the way he did'" (ll. 73–75)
– repeated references to sex: "whose sex life was broadcast" (l. 1), "sexual encounters" (ll. 14–15), "in bed with" (ll. 21–22), "wouldn't have been outed" (ll. 24–25), "having sex" (l. 63), "a second encounter" (l. 64), "homophobic" (l. 79), "gay friends" (l. 79) → sex sells

b) *the authors are clearly/heavily biased: their bias is evident right from the start, i.e. headline plus introductory five lines (a less biased alternative would have been to keep the introduction neutral/matter-of-fact and only move on to bias towards the end of the article, after having presented their arguments/evidence) / article heavily reliant on words that imply danger and violence / many phrases that appeal to reader's emotions and awaken human interest: "jumped to his death" (l. 11) sounds a lot more sensational than 'committed suicide'; there should be no need to specify how Clementi committed suicide in order to make your point that cyber-bullying causes young people to kill themselves / ll. 65–67: there might be all sorts of reasons why the two lawyers didn't return the authors' calls; the way it is put implies wrongdoing/guilty feelings/ ignorance on the part of the lawyers / "destined for greatness" (l. 73): pathos, over the top, exaggeration, tearjerker / sex sells (repeated reference to sex)*

B6 **Seite 66**

Lösungsvorschlag/Erwartungshorizont:

Both the article and the four cartoons illustrate possible Internet dangers.
cartoon 1: *deliberate use of false identity on Internet to deceive/mislead others or to create sense of anonymity (which is a prerequisite, i.e. necessary, for bullying) / the article and the cartoon both deal with the fact that information that is put online can put people's lives at risk; that you should not believe what other people say about you or about themselves on the Internet; the mouse in the cartoon believed what the cat said about itself on its Facebook profile; as a consequence, the cat will kill the mouse; 13-year-old Megan Meier in the article (ll. 34–38) believed the cruel messages she had received on MySpace, took them to heart and killed herself as a consequence; fits line 2: "the Internet's alarming potential as a means of tormenting others", and lines 55–56: "the often-false sense of anonymity that the Internet provides"*

cartoon 2: *dependence on Internet for basic transactions; lack of awareness of division between private and public, cf. people going shopping in underwear, blurring of sense of privacy / fits lines "raises questions whether young people in the age of Twitter and Facebook can even distinguish public from private" (ll. 3–4) and "a world that has blurred the line between public and private" (ll. 50–51); the couple in the cartoon don't seem to be able to distinguish between what's socially acceptable in private and what's socially acceptable in public; the couple have lost all inhibitions as to how to act properly, respectfully and decently outside their home; the deaths/suicides of the young people mentioned in the article were triggered/caused by other people's lack of respect for their privacy*

cartoons 3 and 4: *over-dependence on Internet for basic human communication and interaction; lack of sense of privacy (Facebook and blogs are public forms of communication)*

Getting to the point

C1 **Seite 67**

Hintergrundinformationen:

- *The article was published in* The New York Times *in February 2008.* The New York Times *is a leading daily newspaper in the USA. (Two others are* The Washington Post *and* The Wall Street Journal.*)*
  David Pogue is The New York Times*'s technology columnist.*
- **Im Internet** (Stand April 2015):
  – *The New York Times:* www.nytimes.com
  – David Pogues *Technology blog:* pogue.blogs.nytimes.com
  Diesem Blog ist auch der vorliegende Artikel entnommen.
  Den ungekürzten Blog-Beitrag finden Sie unter:
  pogue.blogs.nytimes.com/2008/02/28/assessing-the-dangers-of-the-internet-for-children
  – David Pogues E-Mail-Adresse: pogue@nytimes.com
  – Die in dem Artikel empfohlene Sendung – *"excellent hour long PBS 'Frontline' documentary" (ll. 34–35)* – finden Sie unter:
  www.pbs.org/wgbh/pages/frontline/kidsonline/view/main.html
  (PBS (= Public Broadcasting Service) is a non-commercial, non-profit public broadcasting television service in the US.)

Lösungsvorschlag/Erwartungshorizont:

– *The article "How dangerous is the Internet for children?" by David Pogue is about just that: about the question of how dangerous the Internet is for children.*
– *The author claims that the Internet is far less dangerous for children than many people think.*
– *The author reviews and recommends a TV documentary that examines the situation of children online, including possible dangers and risks. The TV documentary confirms the author's view that the Internet does not pose as big a threat for children as many people think.*
– *According to both the article and the TV documentary the threat of criminals/paedophiles looking for easy targets online is exaggerated.* (Hinweis: *pedophile (line 9 of article) is the American spelling, paedophile is the British spelling.*)
– *In addition, children and teenagers are a lot less naive about the possible risks and dangers of the Internet than many adults and experts think.*
– *However, cyberbullying is a realistic threat.*
– *The article concludes by stating that though not everybody might approve of everything that happens online, there is no denying that the Internet is hugely influential in teenagers'/young people's lives.*

C2 **Seite 67**

Lösungsvorschlag/Erwartungshorizont:

visual elements: *cartoon is in black and white / a character with bulging eyes (one eye more bulging than the other), very few teeth, full of wrinkles; looks as though he is trembling → suggests that he is very old / bulging eyes, open mouth, unshaven → gives the character a leering quality and implies unpleasant and lascivious thoughts and intentions / large text font → indicates bad eyesight, which in turn underlines that the character is very old / old computer with massive screen, old keyboard and floppy disk drive → again, helps to underline the character's age*

text elements: *caption/punch line presented as writing on computer screen; has been entered into the computer by the old man*

what makes the cartoon humorous: *the huge contrast between the old man's age and the image of himself that he is presenting in the chat room (he is neither 21 nor tall nor dark-haired nor good-looking; the only accurate piece of information is that he is male)*

the cartoonist's message: *Don't believe what people say about themselves on the Internet! / people rarely tell the truth online; people put false information online in order to attract people who wouldn't be interested in them if they told the truth about themselves*

C3 **Seite 67**

Lösungsvorschlag/Erwartungshorizont:
the author's point of view: *the Internet is far less dangerous for children and teenagers than many people think*

point of view is presented openly and directly: *"Sure, there are dangers. But they're hugely over-hyped" (ll. 7–8), "I realize that not everybody shares my nonchalance" (ll. 28–29), "cyber-bullying is a far more realistic threat" (ll. 90–91), "You'll learn that some fears are overplayed, others are underplayed, and above all, that the Internet plays a huge part in adolescence now." (ll. 99–102)*

most of the time the tone is matter-of-fact: *the article starts off with an open question, i.e. no bias: "How dangerous is the Internet for children?" / "I realize that not everybody shares my nonchalance" (ll. 28–29), "The show carefully examines each danger of the Net." (ll. 47–48), "cyber-bullying is a far more realistic threat" (ll. 90–91), "In any case, watch the show." (l. 99)*

no aggression towards people who think differently: *"I realize that not everybody shares my nonchalance" (ll. 28–29), "if you live in terror of what the Internet will do to your children, I encourage you to watch" (ll. 32–34) → makes the article all the more convincing; you are far more likely to win someone over if you present your arguments in a non-aggressive, matter-of-fact, non-sensational way*

tone is humorous in parts (in a good-natured way, without being ironic or sarcastic): *"she literally dove for the computer, crashing over a chair, yanking out the power cord" (ll. 22–24)*

informal language (characteristic of blog entries): *short forms (ll. 29, 35, 44, 46), "You know what?" (l. 25), "Turns out I had it relatively easy" (l. 39), "the sexual-predator thing is way, way overblown" (ll. 48–49), "That one blew my mind" (l. 60), "hammers repeatedly on this point" (l. 62), "never, ever" (l. 63), "idiot" (l. 73), "an online sicko" (ll. 74–75)*

the author refrains from sensationalism (which puts the article in strong contrast to the article on page 65): *"Internet horror stories" (ll. 17–18), "scattered anecdotes about terrible things that happen online" (ll. 30–31) → makes his point without going into gory details which would awaken human interest without strengthening his argument*

quotations to give weight to the arguments: *quoting from and recommending the PBS "Frontline" documentary; quoting documentary producer Rachel Dretzin (ll. 54–60, 65–71), a teenager from the TV documentary (ll. 75–77), David Finkelhor, author of a report by the Crimes Against Children Research Center (ll. 84–87)*

facts and figures to back up the arguments: *"teenagers, 90 percent of whom are online every single day" (ll. 41–42) → supports author's claim in last paragraph of article: "the Internet plays a huge part in adolescence now" (ll. 101–102) / "As my own children approach middle school" (l. 88) → clever move to mention that he has children of his own; helps to make him a credible expert on the topic of children and teenagers*

C4 **Seite 67**

Lösungsvorschlag/Erwartungshorizont:
- *both the article and the cartoon are biased: the cartoon suggests that the Internet is all about people deliberately putting false information online in order to deceive/mislead others, i.e. young people in particular; whereas the article takes the opposite stance: that the Internet is nowhere near as dangerous for teenagers and young people as some of us think*
- *cartoon is biased in that it emphasizes the Internet's potential dangers and risks; the way in which the man in the cartoon is depicted fits lines 9–10 of the article ("pedophiles luring children out of their homes"); fearmongering; parents living in terror of what the Internet will do to their children will find their fears confirmed in the cartoon; they might fail to see the humour and exaggeration that are typical of a cartoon*
- *article is biased in that the author claims that the risks/dangers are exaggerated and that the Internet is far less dangerous for children/teenagers than many people think and than is often assumed; he recommends people to watch a TV documentary that has arrived at the same conclusion*

Getting started

A1 **Seite 70**

Lösungsvorschlag/Erwartungshorizont:

a) *chatting during breaks at school, meeting up in the afternoon/evening/at the weekend, doing sports together, hanging out together at the park; texting, emailing, instant messaging, online chat, chatting on social media (e.g. Facebook, Twitter)*

A2 **Seite 70**

Lösungsvorschlag/Erwartungshorizont:

a) *The line graph* ***"The March to a Billion"*** *shows how Facebook's membership numbers have developed since Facebook's early days, in 2004./shows the increase in Facebook users between 2004, when Facebook started, and 2014.*
The horizontal axis shows the years from 2004 to 2014.
The vertical axis shows the number of Facebook members in millions.
For the first three years after Facebook was launched in 2004, the membership figures remained constant, at about one million users.
In 2007, there is a considerable increase, after Facebook started admitting anyone of 13 years and older towards the end of 2006.
There is a fairly slow increase in the number of users between 2007 and 2008.
There is a rapid increase in the number of users between about July 2008 and early 2009. It is during that time that the like button was introduced.
Membership figures doubled between 2008 and 2009 (from 100 to 200 million users) and between 2009 and the beginning of 2010 (from 200 to 400 million users).
The most recent figure in the graph is from approximately July 2014, when there were about 1.4 billion Facebook users.
Facebook reached the threshold figure of one billion users in the second half of 2012.

The pie chart ***"Facebook friend count"*** *provides information on the number of Facebook friends that people have.*
The majority of people, that is 39% of the people questioned, have between one and one hundred so-called "Facebook friends".
A mere 15% of all Facebook users claim to have more than 500 Facebook friends.

The bar chart ***"How men and women compare"*** *provides information on how men and women use Facebook.*
For women, seeing photos or videos is the most popular Facebook activity. 54% of the women questioned use Facebook to see photos or videos. This compares with just 39% for men.
For men sharing with many people at once seems to be the most important Facebook feature. 42% of men use Facebook to share with many people at once. However, even more women use Facebook to share with many people at once: exactly 50% of women use Facebook to do that.
Men and women seem to agree that getting feedback on content you posted is not very important. Only 17% of men and 16% of women cited getting feedback as important.
Some of the figures are identical for both men and women. For 39% of both men and women receiving updates or comments is an important Facebook feature. 31% use Facebook to keep up with news and events.

b) *The statistics for the numbers of Facebook users reveal that allowing anyone of 13 years and over to join the social networking site in 2006 was a clever move as there was a marked increase in the number of users after that.*
Facebook really started taking off in 2007.
The pie chart about Facebook friends proves that Facebook friends are different from real-life friends. No-one in real life would claim to have more than 500 friends.
It seems likely that the figures for Facebook users worldwide will continue to rise./It seems unlikely that the figures for Facebook users will start to fall.
The world population is approximately 7 billion. The fact that Facebook had about 1.4 billion users in 2014 translates as meaning that about 1 in 5 people worldwide were on Facebook/had an account with Facebook at the time.
Facebook is all about sharing information and keeping in touch with many people at the same time. Social interactions that used to involve meeting up, e.g. in order to show a friend photos from your last holiday, now happen online in a matter of seconds.

With Facebook, people are able to share and spread personal information a lot more quickly and more easily than they used to.
With the introduction of Facebook, personal information has become a lot more open and less confidential and private than it used to be.
As sharing information on Facebook is so easy and not at all time-consuming, staying in touch with people has become a lot easier.

c) *1.* (Stand April 2015)
***Facebook:** 1.4 billion active users (open to anyone 13 and up)*
***WhatsApp:** 700 million active users (instant messaging app for smartphones; was bought by Facebook in 2014)*
***LinkedIn:** 347 million active users (business and professional networking; age: 18 and up)*
***Instagram:** 300 million active users (photo-based networking; anyone 13 years or older; Facebook bought Instagram in 2012)*
***Google+:** 300 million active users (open to anyone 13 years or older)*
***Twitter:** 288 million active users (microblogging; open to anyone 13 years or older)*

Social networking sites started out as online communities geared to particular groups of people (e.g. school, university, workplace). Their intention was to help people find people they had lost contact with and/or wanted to stay in touch with.
Eventually, most social networking sites became more general in their approach. You no longer have to be a member of a particular social group in order to sign up. You just have to be of a certain age, usually 13 or older.
Social networking sites are constantly adding new features.
Organizations and companies have started using social networking sites as an advertising tool and communication tool by creating profiles for a particular product and/or service.
Some social networking sites remain popular over a reasonable length of time. The world of social networking sites is fast-moving. New sites are launched, take off, which in turns means that others start losing users. Once the 'cool kids' realise that their favourite site has attracted 'normal', mainstream users, they tend to move on to the next site. As an example: Facebook is still very popular and successful as a whole, but is becoming less and less cool among teens. Whereas in 2013, 94% of all 13- to 17-year-olds in the US were on Facebook (compared with 95% in 2012), by the end of 2014 this figure had slipped to 88%.

2. Mark Zuckerberg: born in 1984; dotcom entrepreneur; geek/nerd; very bright; became a student at Harvard University (never finished his course, but dropped out in order to concentrate on Facebook); co-created and co-founded Facebook with fellow students at Harvard in 2004; Facebook's chief executive and president; has been through a number of court cases in which he has been accused of stealing the ideas for Facebook from fellow students at Harvard University; among the 100 wealthiest people in the world; also considered among the 100 most influential people in the world; in 2010, he signed up for "Giving Pledge" (an initiative set up by Microsoft co-founder Bill Gates and billionaire investor Warren Buffett), morally but not legally committing himself to donating the majority of his wealth to charity; got married in 2012; apart from that, not much is known about his personal life: he prefers to guard his privacy; is said to be shy and socially awkward (as is often said of geeks/computer nerds)

d) ***Yes,** I think Mark Zuckerberg deserves the title: Facebook is the world's busiest website / as TIME magazine put it, Facebook is the "connective tissue for nearly a tenth of the planet" / anyone who can take a company from its beginnings to such popular prominence in less than seven years deserves the title "Person of the Year" / the title is not about good or bad but about being influential, about having influenced the news and having become a household name*
***No,** I don't think Mark Zuckerberg deserves the title: the title should be awarded to people who have changed our world for the better, who have made the world a better place / Facebook is a household name today but in today's Internet-dominated world fame fades fast and chances are that hardly anyone will remember Facebook ten years from now*

A3 **Seite 71**

Verschiedene Möglichkeiten der Durchführung der ***debate*** in Teilaufgabe c):
– *A class discussion*
– *A formal debate*
– *American debate*
– *Fishbowl discussion*
– Pro-Kontra-Analyse

A formal debate
Nach *Make notes on the arguments* in Teilaufgabe a) und *Add more arguments of your own* in b):
- ***Form two groups of three:*** *the* ***proposition*** *to argue in favour of the motion 'Making and keeping friends is impossible without Facebook.', the* ***opposition*** *to argue against it.*
- ***Choose a chairperson*** *to act as a 'referee'. He/She opens the debate and keeps track of the time (e.g. a one-minute time limit for each speaker).*
- ***Start of debate through chairperson:*** *Ladies and gentlemen, today's motion is 'Making and keeping friends is impossible without Facebook.' Team A is going to argue in favour of the motion, team B against. May the best team win! We'll start with a first person in favour of the motion.*
- ***1st speaker team A*** *argues for the motion.*
- ***Chairperson:*** *Thank you. Now X will speak against the motion.*
- ***1st speaker team B*** *argues against the motion.*
- ***Chairperson:*** *Thank you. Let's have a second person for the motion.*
- ***2nd speaker team A*** *argues for the motion.*
- ***Chairperson:*** *Thank you. Let's have a second person against the motion.*
- ***2nd speaker team B*** *argues against the motion.*
- ***Chairperson:*** *Thank you. Now a third person will argue for the motion.*
- ***3rd speaker team A*** *sums up the team's arguments.*
- ***Chairperson:*** *Thank you. Let's have a third person against the motion.*
- ***3rd speaker team B*** *sums up the team's arguments.*
- ***Questions from the floor*** *(Chairperson: The debate is now open to the floor./Now for some questions from the audience.)*
- ***Conclusion of debate through chairperson:*** *I would now like to ask the audience to vote on the motion: would those in favour of the motion please raise your hands? … Those against the motion? … The motion is accepted/lost.*
- Weitere Redemittel für die moderierende *chairperson: I must ask you to keep within the agreed time limit.*
- **Landeskundlicher Hinweis:** In USA und Großbritannien haben *debating societies* eine lange Tradition. Inzwischen gibt es Bemühungen, diese Tradition auch in Deutschland zu etablieren. Im Internet: www.schoolsdebate.org

American debate
Bei der amerikanischen Debatte sind alle Lerner einbezogen.
- Die Klasse wird in zwei gleich große Gruppen, Gegner und Befürworter der *motion,* und eine Beobachtergruppe *(= reporters/commentators),* bestehend aus zwei bis vier S, geteilt.
- Die beiden Großgruppen stellen oder setzen sich einander gegenüber und tragen abwechselnd ihre Argumente vor (*time limit* vereinbaren: max. 30 Sekunden), dabei Bezug aufeinander nehmend (L: *The argument that has come before has to be repeated …*) und die Gegenargumente entkräftend (L: *… before reacting with an appropriate counter-argument.).*
- Die Beobachtergruppe notiert die Argumente mit, fasst sie im Anschluss zusammen und gibt den beiden Gruppen Rückmeldung über Sachbezug, Überzeugungskraft, Glaubwürdigkeit, rhetorisches Geschick usw.

Fishbowl discussion/**Aquarium**
Kooperative Arbeitsform, die eine dynamische Alternative zu Diskussionen in großen Gruppen bietet. Vier bis sechs S tauschen ihre Argumente aus. Sie sitzen im Kreis (= Aquarium); die MitS platzieren sich in einem Außenkreis um sie herum und beobachten.
- *First, prepare your arguments as you would for a normal discussion.*
- *Then form two circles with your chairs – an inner circle with 4–6 chairs and an outer circle.*
- *Decide on 4–6 students to start the discussion in the inner circle (= fishbowl). Each of them prepares a statement that refers to the topic of the discussion/debate.*
- *Then the students in the inner circle present their statements and start the discussion.*
- *The students in the outer circle listen to the discussion. Whenever one of them wants to join the discussion, s/he touches one of the students in the inner circle, then takes his/her place.*
- *When the discussion is over, the students in the outer circle supply feedback to those in the inner circle.*

Closed fishbowl: Die S im Innenkreis diskutieren einige Minuten. Dann werden sie von MitS abgelöst. Dies setzt sich so lange fort, bis möglichst viele die Gelegenheit hatten, ihre Argumente vorzubringen.
Open fishbowl: Ein oder zwei leere Stühle werden zusätzlich in den Innenkreis gestellt, sodass sich jederzeit jemand aus dem Außenkreis dazusetzen kann, der/die etwas beitragen möchte.

Pro-Kontra-Analyse
Die Lerngruppe wird in zwei gleich große Gruppen geteilt, Gegner und Befürworter der Ausgangsthese.
Die beiden Gruppen tragen abwechselnd ihre Argumente vor (*time limit* vereinbaren), nehmen dabei möglichst immer Bezug aufeinander.
Nach fünf bis sieben Minuten wechseln die Gruppen ihren Standpunkt und tauschen erneut Pro- und Kontra-Argumente aus.
Anschließend sollte die Methode reflektiert werden. Mögliche Frage: *What did you find easier: arguing for or against your own opinion?*

Lösungsvorschlag/Erwartungshorizont:
a) *arguments* ***in favour*** *of the extensive use of Facebook (text A):*
- *more and more people are on Facebook: the more people join, the more powerful Facebook will be (l. 1)*
- *serves many purposes, not just chatting and sharing photos (ll. 2–5)*
- *Facebook is "more than just a website" (l. 7)*

arguments ***against*** *the extensive use of Facebook (text B):*
- *lack of privacy (l. 6)*
- *Facebook may use/abuse the information you post for its own purposes (ll. 7–9)*
- *you never know who might end up reading your posts and seeing the photos you have put online (ll. 9–12) → potentially embarrassing*

b) ***arguments in favour*** *of the extensive use of Facebook:*
- *great for finding long-lost friends*
- *great for making new friends*
- *great for finding people who have the same interests as you*
- *helps staying in touch with people*
- *staying in touch with people you want to stay in touch with but don't really want to spend time hanging out with in person*
- *great advertising tool*
- *saves a lot of time because you can reach many people at the same time*
- *it's fun!*
- *can help start a revolution and overturn governments (→ Arab Spring 2011: the revolutions in Tunisia and Egypt are sometimes referred to as 'Facebook revolutions' or 'Twitter revolutions')*
- *devolution of power: redistribution of power from governments and big institutions down/back to individuals and small institutions and companies; Facebook is a lot more flexible and can react a lot faster to facts/incidents/natural disasters than any government or major company*

arguments against *the extensive use of Facebook:*
- *information you put on Facebook can come back to haunt you (it might seem fine when you post it but turn embarrassing at a later date)*
- *a waste of time*
- *devalues the term "friend"*
- *Facebook will never replace face-to-face encounters*
- *risk of becoming addicted to checking your Facebook page and what your 'friends' are up to*
- *identity theft*
- *cyber-bullying/cyber-stalking*
- *by concentrating on Facebook 'friends', you will eventually start neglecting your real friends*
- *Facebook is just a phase: it will pass as so many others have in the past*

Practice section

B1 **Seite 72**

Lösungsvorschlag/Erwartungshorizont:
- *close-up of computer screen with Facebook page open*
- *someone (= no-one in particular, i.e. viewer does not get to see who it is) carrying out typical Facebook actions, e.g. adding photos, approving friendships, updating his/her status, 'liking'*
- *camera showing some typical Facebook features, e.g. wall posts, relationship status*
- *after that: flashback to how things started back in 2004*

B2 **Seite 72** DVD

Lösungsvorschlag/Erwartungshorizont:

a)
- *young man/Mark Zuckerberg wearing pool sliders, no socks → expectation: what kind of guy is that? it's fall/autumn, i.e. unusual not to be wearing any socks (everybody else seems to be bundled up) → strange, weird guy*
- *wearing a Gap hoodie (Gap: all-American iconic fashion brand) and a rucksack slung over his right shoulder → student (is later confirmed by setting: Harvard University, fall 2003)*
- *starts walking at normal pace → walking fast → breaking into a jog; a clear sense of direction, in a hurry to get somewhere*
- *lost in his thoughts → expectations: Where is he going? What is he up to?*
- *in contrast to his surroundings: lonely figure hurrying along, no socks, moving faster than everybody he passes; his brisk, hurried walk/jog makes him stand out; no interaction whatsoever with people around him; no eye contact with anyone; keeps to himself → socially awkward/autistic/oblivious to his surroundings → nerd/geek*
- *interestingly enough, none of the people he passes seem to be paying any attention to him (as though it were quite normal for someone wearing pool sliders and no socks in the middle of autumn to hurry past you) → expectations: makes the audience wonder about the setting, whether a situation like that isn't that unusual in this particular setting*
- *he has been dumped by his girlfriend Erica so you're wondering whether he is on his way to a friend to talk to him/her about it*
- *you would expect him to go and see a friend to tell him/her what has happened; instead, he goes straight to this computer (two computers!), then fetches a bottle of beer from the fridge, signs on to his blog and writes nasty, personal comments about Erica and her family, i.e. he 'confides' in his blog → a blog is public so not the best place to share confidential/personal information; suggests that computers are central to the character, his life and his dealing with problems; seems unaware of the potential damage he's causing by posting nasty comments*
- ***topic:** founding of Facebook/computer/social media/social networking; character who is socially inept and oblivious to his surroundings and to the feelings of others*
  ***setting:** Harvard University, fall 2003; 8:13pm (when he sits down at his computer to write his blog entry; so he probably left the pub "Thirsty Scholar Pub" at about 8pm) and 9:48pm*
  ***main character:** Mark Zuckerberg; computer nerd*

b)
- *computer nerd/geek; oblivious to surroundings; different from your average person/student; loner; no need for human company; happy with himself, a bottle of beer and his computers*
- *central character does not seek out human company after having been dumped by his girlfriend but the company of his computer/blog → socially inept; importance of computer/blogging/social media; no respect for other people's privacy; ignorant of other people's feelings*

B3 **Seite 72** DVD

Lösungsvorschlag/Erwartungshorizont:
- *piano music; very slow, melancholic; accentuated → helps to underline the atmosphere of a lonely, strange, weird character; a loner*
- *violins → make the atmosphere more dramatic; create a feeling of suspense*
- *not much lighting; dark; soft dark shades; cosy fall colours → makes you think of cosy nights in; instead Mark is on his own, out in the dark, wet, damp and cold*
- *mysterious lighting → creates a feeling of suspense: Who is he? What kind of guy is he? What is he up to? Where is he going?*
- *brownish lighting → transports an atmosphere of tradition; in line with prestigious Ivy League tradition (wood, library)*

B4 **Seite 73**

Lösungsvorschlag/Erwartungshorizont:

a) *film still **1**: full shot / long angle shot*
*film still **2**: over-the-shoulder shot*
*film still **3**: high angle shot*
*film still **4**: low angle shot*
*film still **5**: medium shot / eye-level shot*
*film still **6**: close-up*
*film still **7**: eye-level shot/straight-on angle*
*film still **8**: medium shot / medium long shot / establishing shot*

b) *film still **1**: isolation and superiority; Mark lives in a world of his own*
*film still **2**: confrontational; opponents*
*film still **3**: distance between Mark and the people sitting; feeling of superiority (Mark feels superior towards the other people in the room)*
*film still **4**: distance; feeling of inferiority towards whatever it is Mark is looking at (photos of club alumni, i.e. former members of the exclusive final club he is visiting / he is in awe of previous members of the final club)*
*film still **5**: closeness; equals; they share the same goal/focus*
*film still **6**: Mark on his own*
*film still **7**: loneliness/isolation (empty chair in the background; separated from people outside)*
*film still **8**: equal partners; partners at eye level; Mark's body language is defensive, he uses his arms to shield himself/keep his distance from Erica*

DVD **B5** **Seite 75**

a)–c) Lösungsvorschlag/Erwartungshorizont:

scene	*action/picture content*	*filmic devices*	*function/effect/meaning*
1 *Thirsty Scholar Pub*	*Mark is seen leaving the pub, walking by himself, head down low, past the pub window that shows that the pub is packed*	*long shot, establishing shot*	*university town; humiliation (has been dumped by his girlfriend); seems embarrassed; isolated from the crowds*
2 *Out on the street*	*Mark running, seems to be obsessing about sth.*	*long shot → panning shot → tilting shot → tracking shot*	*Mark is a loner; oblivious to his surroundings; comes across as obsessed with sth.*
3 *On the campus*	*Mark still running*	*tilting shot → long shot → medium long shot*	*Mark is a loner; comes across as slightly autistic*
4 *Kirkland House*	*Mark running up stairs to door of "his" house/dorm*	*tilting up to name*	*high expectations, haven*
5 *"Home"*	*wakes up his computers; goes to fridge for a beer; opens the bottle of beer; types his blog entry*	*close-up/point-of-view shot of open fridge and beer / close-up of Mark sitting at his computer*	*Mark needs some intoxication to get over his hurt feelings / feelings of frustration and pent-up humiliation*

B6 **Seite 75**

Lösungsvorschlag/Erwartungshorizont:

– *Mark's running along the street and across campus continues for about two minutes → atmosphere of anticipation; helps to expose Mark as obsessive, oblivious to his surroundings, a nerd*
– *close-up of Mark sitting at his computer → shows the character's feelings of frustration and pent-up humiliation after being dumped by his girlfriend*
– *point-of-view shots of beer in the fridge and of computer → reveal Mark's focus: these are the two things that will keep him company and help him get over his disappointment*
– *no-one around Mark seems to be taking any notice of him → confirms the impression of a geek/nerd who does not interact with his surroundings much*
– *typically American details (Gap hoodie, car horns, police/ambulance horn, campus) → suggest prestigious US university setting (helped/confirmed by insert "Harvard University, fall 2003")*

B7 Seite 76 DVD

Lösungsvorschlag/Erwartungshorizont:
- *Mark spends the evening hacking into Harvard's databases; setting up a website; with his friends sitting around; drinking beer (he admits being "intoxicated", i.e. drunk); having fun, enjoying the intellectual challenge of hacking; the site finally goes online at approximately 3am*
- *female students arrive at Phoenix club house by bus; all dolled up; scene is sexually charged; alcohol and drugs; techno music; having fun at "the Phoenix first party of the fall semester"; pseudo-lesbian snogging as party entertainment; strip poker; party atmosphere*

B8 Seite 76

Lösung: A–3; B–2; C–1; D–4

B9 Seite 77 DVD

Lösungsvorschlag/Erwartungshorizont:
a) *cross-cutting/parallel action*
b) *present two sides of the same plot development; creates a feeling of suspense as you start to suspect that the evening will turn unpleasant/embarrassing for some/most of the girls at the party*

B10 Seite 77

Lösungsvorschlag/Erwartungshorizont:
b) *in Mark's dorm:*

aspect	*function/effect*
characters and character constellation: *– Mark: "I need you."; referring to algorithm but Eduardo thinks Mark needs him emotionally (because Erica has broken up with him)* *– Eduardo has his doubts about Facemash website*	*→ Eduardo supplies the emotional intelligence that Mark is lacking: worried about his friend's emotional well-being and voicing moral doubts about the Facemash website*
actions: *– "Let the hacking begin!"* *– hacks into one university house after the other* *– Mark talks very fast*	*→ fun, challenge; unaware of potential damage* *→ shows how very bright Mark is; quick thinker* *→ audience not expected to understand everything*
objects: *– dart* *– beer*	*→ focus, mission accomplished* *→ intoxicated; addicted to the thrill of hacking*
visual effects and acoustic effects: *– voice-over (= Mark commenting on what he is doing; posting his comments on his blog)* *– techno music from party at the Phoenix club* *– quiet music when Eduardo enters the scene*	*→ Mark is very fast, very brainy, very clever (= too clever and fast for the average audience)* *→ expectations are raised: what's going on at party?* *→ change in pace: Eduardo is different, calm*

at the party at the Phoenix club:

aspect	*function/effect*
characters and character constellation: *– sexually charged: female students all dolled up; male and female students eyeing each other*	*→ guys are using girls as a turn-on; girls are using guys as an entry to a prestigious club*
actions: *– doors opening* *– pseudo-lesbian snogging; strip poker*	*→ entry/access to exclusive club* *→ sexually charged atmosphere: physical*
objects: *– pills*	*→ girls lose their inhibitions*
visual effects and acoustic effects: *– dark, gloomy lighting* *– techno music* *– Mark's typing on keyboard*	*→ allows/makes girls do things they might otherwise be ashamed of the next morning* *→ drowning out all other sounds; numbing effect* *→ expectations are raised: what's going on at dorm?*

e) – *girls are all dolled up, as though the party were a beauty contest; girls seem ready, prepared and happy to be judged and rated on the basis of their looks*
- *Mark: "Let the hacking begin!" / girls arriving at party: Let the party begin!*
- *two girls on screen being rated / two girls snogging at party → both situations serve as a turn-on for boys; girls are being used / potentially demeaning for the girls, although they don't seem to mind it at the party (because they are allowed to play an active part in it?), but mind being rated on the website*
- *both scenes leading to climax: the Facemash website going online → party: foreplay; the party gets raunchier as the evening/night progresses, as the website nears completion*
- *women/girls are judged by their looks: both on the website and at the party → on closer inspection the scene at the dorm and at the party aren't all that different; beauty contest, men judging people/women by their looks*
- *Mark and friends get a kick out of hacking and setting up Facemash website → people at party get a kick out of partying (drugs, alcohol, flirting/sex)*
- *Mark and friends get high on beer and hacking → people at party get high on drugs and sex*
- *Mark hacks his way into the university's databases → being invited to the party at the Phoenix club provides access to one of the most prestigious university clubs in the world*
- *"one picture at a time" (Mark) → one-to-one conversation at party*

B11 **Seite 78**

Lösungsvorschlag/Erwartungshorizont:
Sir or Madam,
I am writing to you in response to the article "Hot or Not? Website Briefly Judges Looks" from 4 November.
I am appalled to think that a fellow student of ours would hack into our university's databases to help himself to ID photos in order to create a website that allows users to vote for the "hotter" of two students. But at the same time, I am even more appalled that this website, during the course of just a few days, received 450 visitors and more than 22,000 votes.
It is one thing to enable other people to be vicious and nasty. But it is up to every one of us to decide whether to become accomplice to such a hideous act. In my opinion, criticism has been focusing too much on Mark Zuckerberg, who created the site, rather than on all the people who secretly, or not so secretly, accessed the site to judge other people by their looks. I think it is a fair bet to assume that many of them saw nothing wrong with what they were doing, that they were in fact enjoying themselves immensely.
For Mark Zuckerberg, the challenge was the computer science behind the website, not the website as such. For everyone else, the challenge was to withstand the urge to judge their peers by their looks, rather than by their merits. Mark rose to the challenge. Everyone else did not.
Michael Narayan, Quincy House

B12 **Seite 78**

Lösungsvorschlag/Erwartungshorizont:
Girl: *Zuckerberg? Are you Mark Zuckerberg?*
Mark Zuckerberg: *Yeah.*
Girl: *Are you the one who created this website Facemash?*
Mark Zuckerberg: *Guess so.*
Girl: *You're pathetic. Erica Albright is right. You're not just a nerd, you're an asshole.*
Mark Zuckerberg: *Hey, listen, I'm sorry. I didn't mean to insult anyone. I just thought it would be cool. I just wanted to see how difficult it would be to hack into House online facebooks and compile ID photos onto a website, that was all. I never expected such widespread publicity.*
Girl: *How can anyone be so naive? Don't you have a life?*
Mark Zuckerberg: *Well, I've shut down the site. So there's nothing to get upset about anymore.*
Girl: *Nothing to get upset about anymore?! Don't you see the damage you've done? Shutting down the site won't make the shame and humiliation go away. And the looks some of us get in the corridors.*
Mark Zuckerberg: *Hey, I've said I'm sorry. What else?*
Girl: *You say you're sorry. But I don't really think you are. I don't think you feel sorry at all. I think you don't feel anything at all. You're a freak.*
Mark Zuckerberg: *Hey, listen. That's enough.*
Girl: *Yes, you're right. That's more than enough. Get out of my sight, you moron.*

Getting to the point

C1 Seite 79 DVD

Vokabelhilfen/Landeskundliche Informationen:

- 21.10 min: *Tyler Winklevoss: "We row crew."*
  - *to row crew: to be a member of a crew on a rowing boat (US usage; referring in particular to US college/university rowing teams)*
  - *refers back to the opening scene at the* Thirsty Scholar Pub, *where Mark's ambition to make it into the exclusive circles of Harvard becomes obvious. Mark and Erica discuss "guys that row crew": athletic types, i.e. quite unlike Mark, who work out at the gym; Mark understands Erica to mean that she's into athletic guys more than into guys like him; Mark seems self-conscious of the fact that he's not the athletic type*
- 21.20 min: *Tyler Winklevoss: "So you've ever been inside the Porcellian?"*
  the Porcellian club: one of the most exclusive final clubs at Harvard

Lösungsvorschlag/Erwartungshorizont:

The Winklevoss twins, Cameron and Tyler, approach Mark outside one of the lecture halls at Harvard (they have obviously been waiting for him) because they want to talk to him about an idea of theirs. It's only when Tyler Winklevoss mentions that they're on the Harvard rowing team that Mark's eyes light up and he says "Yeah, I've got a minute."

Cameron and Tyler Winklevoss take Mark to the bike room at their club, the Porcellian club (as a non-member he's not allowed further than the bike room). Mark is visibly impressed by being inside the club: he studies the wall with photos of club alumni, i.e. former members of the Porcellian club.

The Winklevoss twins and a friend of theirs, Divya Narendra, want Mark to build the site and write the code for a social networking site they have in mind, the special feature being that it would be exclusive to Harvard students.

Cameron and Tyler Winklevoss are surprised when Mark readily agrees to work with them, without asking any specific questions about the website and without inquiring about the financial conditions. The viewer knows more about Mark than the Winklevoss brothers do, so it's obvious for the viewer that it's the term "exclusivity" that is the main attraction for Mark.

C2 Seite 79

Lösungsvorschlag/Erwartungshorizont:

scene	*action/picture content*	*filmic devices*	*function/effect/meaning*
1 *corridor in university building*	*Tyler and Cameron Winklevoss approach Mark*	– *high angle shot: the camera looks down at Mark* – *low angle shot: the camera looks up at the Winklevoss twins* – *point-of-view shot* – *reverse angle shot: perspective changes from Mark to twins*	– *Winklevoss twins are superior to Mark as regards their social standing and as regards their physicality* – *difference in size between Mark and the taller and broader twins is emphasized*
2 *bike room at the Porcellian club*	*Tyler and Cameron Winklevoss and Divya Narendra make their business proposition*	– *high angle shot: the camera looks down at Winklevoss twins and Narendra* – *low angle shot: the camera looks up at Mark* – *reverse angle shot: perspective changes from Mark to twins and Narendra* – *over-the-shoulder shot* – *medium shots* – *three to one: twins and Narendra sitting at one side of the room, Mark standing at the other (i.e. at opposite ends)*	– *roles are now reversed: Mark is in a strong position, twins want sth. from him, i.e. his brains/his expertise* – *Winklevoss twins and Narendra are looking up at Mark* – *Mark looks up at photos of club alumni → that is where his ambitions lie: becoming a member of an exclusive club* – *shows the social divide between Mark and the other three (emphasized by their difference in clothing)*

C3 Seite 79

Lösungsvorschlag/Erwartungshorizont:

description of Zuckerberg in the film

- *nerd/geek*
- *socially awkward, socially inept, not very good at keeping eye contact, easily embarrassed*
- *an outsider*
- *driven by his ambition to make it into the exclusive circles of Harvard*
- *oblivious to other people's feelings*
- *lacking emotional intelligence*
- *talks fast, thinks fast*

description of Zuckerberg in the extract from TIME

- *"a warm presence" (l. 6)*
- *"a quick smile and doesn't shy away from eye contact" (ll. 6–7)*
- *"thinks fast and talks fast" (l. 7)*
- *"exudes not anger or social anxiety, but a weird calm" (l. 8)*

version I would agree with

- *Zuckerberg as described in the extract from TIME*
- *TIME magazine has an obligation to stay true to the facts*
- *a news magazine has a much stronger obligation to stay true to the facts than a film*
- *a film is a literary genre and provides a fictionalized take on Mark Zuckerberg and the creation of Facebook*
- *it's a film, not a documentary*
- *there's nothing in the article in* The Harvard Crimson *(page 78) that supports the description of Zuckerberg as portrayed in the film; instead the Zuckerberg quotes in the article (ll. 37–39) portray Mark as someone who is prepared to take the issue of people's privacy into consideration*
- *Aaron Sorkin, the film's scriptwriter, has said: "I don't want my fidelity to be to the truth; I want it to be to storytelling."*

Speaking

D1 Seite 80

Lösungsvorschlag/Erwartungshorizont:

a) ***When teenagers are online*** *(statistics)* ⚀

1. *a bar chart; it tells us when teenagers are online; the horizontal axis shows the different times of day; the vertical line shows the per cent*
2. *It proves that social networks are very popular as all the teenagers surveyed spend more than an hour a day online; three quarters of teenagers are online within an hour of waking up in the morning; more than half the teenagers questioned go online while at church*

What users dislike *(statistics)* ⚁

1. *a bar chart; it tells you what users dislike about social networking sites; the vertical axis shows the things that people dislike; the horizontal line shows the per cent*
2. *Facebook and other social networks are very popular but that does not mean that users like everything about them; just over a third of people are critical about people sharing too much info about themselves and about others posting things about you without asking permission; so, although social networks like Facebook are all about sharing, most people seem to agree that there is such a thing as oversharing; about a quarter of the people feel temptation or pressure to share too much info about themselves*

I'm happy to finally meet you in person *(cartoon)* ⚂

1. *a man and a woman meeting for a romantic dinner; meeting for the first time; they must have met online (most likely through an online dating site or in a chat room); rather than talk to each other face to face, they communicate online although they are sitting together at the same table; instead of looking into each other's eyes romantically, they are staring at their screens in front of them*
2. *online communication has taken over and there is a risk of online communication taking over even in situations where you are with the person you are 'talking' to; the cartoon makes fun of people 'hiding' behind their screens, rather than talking to and looking at each other; the two people in the cartoon seem to feel that they are actually 'meeting' each other when, in fact, they are simply typing away on their mobile devices*

Anything you say may be used against you *(cartoon)* ⚃

1. *cartoon in black and white; man and woman sitting at a table; woman is talking; man looks baffled; woman warns him that anything he might say might be used against him on social media.*
2. *the cartoon criticises that very little information is treated as confidential nowadays; you will quite often find information online that was originally shared in private and not intended to be shared in public, i.e. on social media; you might find yourself at the centre of a 'shitstorm' because something you said in private is put online by someone without your knowledge; you can never be sure what information about you might show up online at a later date*

11 Reasons to Quit Facebook in 2014 *(article)* ⚄

1. *according to the extract from the article, Facebook is on its way out; it is no longer as popular with young people as it used to be; young people have moved on from Facebook to Twitter and Instagram because it offers other, better features than Facebook*
2. *I agree; I was really into Facebook a couple of years ago; but since I've had my smartphone, I'm all into WhatsApp; it's so much quicker and more fun; Instagram is also great as a picture can say so much more than words*

Teenagers Tell Researchers It's a Cruel, Cruel Online World *(article)* ⚅

1. *according to the extract from the article, the Internet is not as dangerous for young people as some people want to make us believe; according to a survey, bullying in real life is more common than cyberbullying; fewer teenagers than you might expect seem to be affected by online abuse, most young people just ignore online abuse when they see it; young people are more likely to turn to people their own age for help than to their parents*
2. *I agree; my parents see online abuse as a much bigger problem than I do; what they consider abuse would be what I consider banter or teasing among friends; I've never suffered really bad online abuse; it might be my friends leaving teasing comments about a photo I put up but most of the time they're right: I sometimes post a terrible, unflattering photo of myself and my best friend because we think it's fun and we don't take ourselves too seriously*

D2 **Seite 82**

Lösungsvorschlag/Erwartungshorizont:

a)

Agreeing	*Disagreeing*	*Partly agreeing*	*Clarifying*	*Expressing your view*	*Interrupting*
I couldn't have said it better.	*In spite of what you have just said, I still think …*	*You may have a point there, but I still have some doubts about …*	*What I'm trying to say is …*	*Personally, I feel that …*	*Let me interrupt you for a second.*
You can say that again.	*I see your point, but …*	*I know, but it isn't as simple as that.*	*What I mean is …*	*From my point of view …*	*Hang on a second.*
I couldn't agree more.	*That is definitely not the case.*		*Look, it's like this: …*	*To my mind …*	
Exactly!	*That is just not right.*		*That's not what I meant. I was just pointing out that …*	*The way I see it …*	
	That's news to me. Where did you get that from?				
	That might be the case, but …				

b)

Agreeing	*Disagreeing*	*Partly agreeing*	*Clarifying*	*Expressing your view*	*Interrupting*
You're absolutely right.	*I'm afraid I don't agree.*	*I see your point, but …*	*Are you saying that …?*	*I strongly believe that …*	*I'm sorry to interrupt but …*
Yes, that's a good point.	*Absolutely not!*		*You don't really mean that, do you?*	*I'm convinced that …*	*My apologies for barging in but …*
I absolutely agree.			*Let me add that …*	*In my opinion, …*	

D3 **Seite 83**

Lösungsvorschlag/Erwartungshorizont:

a) **A1:** ***the problem:*** *critical of Facebook as it helps and encourages people to project an image of themselves to the world; Facebook makes people wonder how they are going to announce certain moments or events from their lives, i.e. they post about them rather than experience them /* ***evidence and arguments:*** *author admits that she spends time thinking and worrying about her online image; her online identity/image has become a lot more important to her than is wise or healthy; you leave online traces of your life years after you have moved on to a new phase of your life, which can become embarrassing; photos and posts can come back to haunt you; the author has become aware of the discrepancy between her real life and her virtual life*

A2: ***the problem:*** *Facebook has changed the way we interact with other people; so many positive examples of Facebook transforming people's lives /* ***evidence and arguments:*** *Facebook opened up a whole new world to users; it helps you stay connected with family and friends even though you might live hundreds of miles apart; Facebook makes it easier to reconnect with old/former friends or colleagues; Facebook helps you be remembered as you leave traces*

B1: ***the problem:*** *Facebook has lost a lot of its appeal, particularly for teenagers; the way people use Facebook has changed over the years /* ***evidence and arguments:*** *there are now fewer daily Facebook users, i.e. active users who check and update their Facebook page every day; people have started reducing the personal information they share on Facebook; instead, they have moved on to other social media sites, e.g. WhatsApp; the 'cool kids' have moved elsewhere → Facebook is in no immediate danger of becoming insignificant as there are still plenty of active users, even if teenagers are drifting away but still, it might be the beginning of Facebook's end*

B2: ***the problem:*** *social media and going online are nowhere as dangerous for young people as some people try to make us believe; they have not changed our world as much as some people might think /* ***evidence and arguments:*** *some people will always worry about new inventions, be it the telephone back in the day or social media/new technologies today; people worry too much about potential dangers; the environment for young people growing up has changed but their goals, e.g. socializing and finding their place in the world, have stayed the same*

Getting started

A1 **Seite 88**

Lösungsvorschlag/Erwartungshorizont:
a) *embarrassed, confused, sad, angry, touched, upset*
b) *your sexual orientation does not make you any less human/doesn't devalue you as a person; many people are discriminated against because of their sexual orientation; there is a lot more to being a human being than your sexual orientation*
c) *they seem embarrassed and isolated; they don't want to openly talk about their sexual orientation; they are afraid they will be discriminated against if they talk about their sexual orientation; or maybe they have been bullied because of their sexual orientation and feel stigmatized; sexuality is a taboo; most people feel embarrassed to talk about sexuality/their sexual orientation*

A2 **Seite 88**

Hintergrundinformationen: *Mark Ravenhill (* 1966) is an English playwright.*

Lösungsvorschlag/Erwartungshorizont:
d) ***most appropriate version:*** *frightened (Amy and Tom don't seem to know each other very well; Tom is unsure of his sexual orientation; he feels a need to talk in order to understand and come to terms with it)*

A3 **Seite 89**

Lösungsvorschlag/Erwartungshorizont:
a) ***Amy***
l. 4: *Is he making fun of me?*
l. 6: *He really means it.*
l. 10: *Didn't he want me to do that?*
l. 13: *He's weird. They usually all want that. This is strange.*
l. 16: *This is very strange.*
l. 18: *I don't believe this.*
l. 20: *I really don't believe this.*
l. 22: *This guy is weird.*
l. 24: *Gosh, he's really frightened.*
l. 34: *Is he trying to tell me he's gay?*
l. 36: *Maybe he's bi.*
ll. 38–39: *He's really, really frightened. I must call Jess and tell her. But what's the big deal?*
l. 41: *Don't be stupid. Just decide whether you're gay or bisexual.*
l. 43: *Maybe I should just have sex with him and show him.*
ll. 45–47: *What's the big deal? I wouldn't mind having sex with him. I think it would be good.*

Tom
ll. 2–3: *She seems really nice. I feel relaxed and safe around her.*
l. 5: *She doesn't believe me. She thinks I'm making fun of her.*
l. 7: *She's really nice.*
l. 9: *Why did she do that?*
ll. 11–12: *Why did she do that?*
ll. 14–15: *I need to explain so she understands.*
l. 17: *I don't know how to say this.*
l. 19: *So what?*
l. 21: *It just doesn't feel right.*
l. 23: *I'm frightened. I don't want to talk about it. I don't know how to say it.*
ll. 25–33: *I have to talk to someone about this. This dream is driving me crazy.*
l. 35: *I don't know. I really don't know.*
l. 37: *Oh no! Why did I tell her? Oh no, what if she tells everyone about me?*
l. 40: *Decide what?*
l. 42: *I don't think it's as easy as that.*
l. 44: *I don't think I'm ready for that yet. I need to be sure first.*
l. 48: *She doesn't understand.*

c) *helps to understand Tom's insecurities and fears; it seems to be weighing heavily on his mind that he is unsure about his sexual orientation / Amy seems more experienced than Tom*

A4 **Seite 89**

Lösungsvorschlag/Erwartungshorizont:

a) ***setting:*** *party, e.g. at youth club (definitely not at school); early evening*
props: *old, shabby sofa, soft drinks*
lighting effects: *hazy, soft, shady; no glaring lights*
scenery/stage design: *black, empty stage, just sofa and the two people*
costumes: *jeans and T-shirts; average teenage outfits (as in photos in A 1)*
sound effects: *soft background chatting and soft background music*

Practice section

B1 **Seite 90**

Think–pair–share: → Seite 20 hier in den *Teacher's notes.*

Lösungsvorschlag/Erwartungshorizont:

a) ***at school:*** *rarely; in more general terms (biology class: HIV and AIDS); not relating to me personally; possibly relating to celebrities (chatting with friends about celebrities who are known to be gay, e.g. Ellen Page, Neil Patrick Harris, Tom Daley, Jim Parsons, Zachary Quinto, Tom Ford, Ellen DeGeneres, Ian McKellen, George Michael, Freddie Mercury, Elton John, Hape Kerkeling, Bruce Darnell) or to characters in works of fiction (subjects: German and English); don't really feel comfortable talking to teachers about sexuality or sexual identity; most teachers don't seem to feel comfortable, either*
in private outside school: *relating to me personally and to friends and family; talking to friends about contraception, sexual experience and sexual orientation*

b) *many people are embarrassed when it comes to talking about sexuality; people tend to feel more comfortable talking about sexuality when they can be sure that no-one is eavesdropping on them, i.e. not at school / there is a lot of teasing/bullying/discrimination going on when it comes to sexuality, which is why most people prefer to talk about sexuality in private only*

B2 **Seite 90**

Hintergrundinformationen: *Moira Buffini (* 1965) is an English playwright.*

***Freeze frame*/Standbildbauen:** Mit der Methode des Standbildbauens können Texte oder Textstellen gedeutet und Beziehungen von Figuren zueinander erarbeitet werden.
Zu einer Textstelle, in der die Beziehungen der Figuren zueinander deutlich werden und die zu unterschiedlichen Deutungen herausfordert, bauen die S in Gruppen ein Standbild, ein eingefrorenes Szenenbild *(freeze frame),* das die Gefühle und Beziehungen der Figuren zueinander widerspiegelt. Es sollte eine inhaltliche Erarbeitung vorausgehen.

b)
- 10–15 Minuten Vorbereitung, d.h. Textdeutung und Standbildbau, in Gruppen von sieben S: Jedem/r S sollte aus seiner/ihrer Perspektive klar werden, in welcher Beziehung die Figuren zueinander stehen und welches ihre äußerlich wahrnehmbaren Charakteristika sind.
- **Konkretisierende Impulse:**
  - *Imagine the situation your character is in. / Tune into your character (character traits, current situation): How does your character feel? What is his/her state of mind? Imagine the way s/he stands/sits/... Think of her/his facial expression/body language. Is s/he puzzled/irritated/angry/happy/...? Is s/he about to smile/laugh/cry/scream/...?*
  - *In your groups, talk about how to present the characters and their relationships by arranging the characters in your corner of the room. Make sure you use facial expressions, body language and gestures to show the characters' relationships.*
  - *Now find your final position and don't move.*

c)
- Nacheinander positionieren sich die Gruppen im Raum.
  - Das Standbild wird jeweils 30–60 Sekunden lang gehalten und von den MitS gedeutet und besprochen.
  - Bevor die nächste Gruppe dran ist, äußern die darstellenden S ihre Intentionen.
- Erweiterung: Das Verfahren wird sprachaktiver, wenn die Zuschauer die Rollendarsteller/innen zusätzlich interviewen (auf der Grundlage des Ausgangstextes).

- Erweiterung *Thought tracking:* Die Standbildfiguren sagen, was sie in ihrer Rolle gerade denken und empfinden oder wie sie ihre Beziehung zu den anderen Figuren sehen. Dazu werden sie von L oder einer/m MitS an der Schulter berührt.

Lösungsvorschlag/Erwartungshorizont:

b) ***relationships between the characters***

Frank (male): *"sensitive" (l. 1), "nervous" (l. 1); different from Briggs, Point, Debit and Moon (cf. ll. 3–7); new in class (cf. ll. 26–27); ironic (cf. ll. 88–89); heartbreakingly honest, not trying to protect himself (cf. ll. 105, 107, 120–132); emotionally scarred from his experience at home (cf. ll. 120–132, 158–160, 162–173); grows more confident as the hot seat continues (cf. ll. 141–150); Ella and Frank are the only two characters showing respect and compassion*

Briggs (male): *bored (cf. l. 5); sarcastic, nasty, cruel (cf. ll. 48, 79, 92)*

Moon (male): *bored (cf. l. 5); only one to voice moral concerns (cf. ll. 57, 59–60, 63, 65) but joins in nevertheless → seems more interested in talking back at Mint than in the principle of protecting Frank from pain/"psychological torture" (l. 57)*

Debit (female): *bored (cf. l. 5); a fast thinker (cf. l . 21); sarcastic (cf. l. 35); disrespectful towards Mint (cf. ll. 18, 21, 35); slightly more respectful towards Frank (cf. ll. 144–161, 176)*

Point (female): *bored (cf. l. 5); disrespectful towards teacher (cf. ll. 23–24) and towards classmates (cf. ll. 90, 106)*

Ella (female): *bored (cf. l. 5); new in class (cf. ll. 26–27); doesn't join in, keeps to herself, asks Frank just one question (cf. l. 174), which makes her come across as considerate and caring*

Mint (drama teacher; male): *"full of fervour and frustration" (ll. 2–3); sarcastic (cf. ll. 17, 19, 22, 31); cynical (cf. ll. 9–11, 13–15); makes fun of his students in a rude/contemptuous/cynical way; experimental teaching methods (cf. ll. 51–56); "an instinctive teacher" (ll. 52–53); oblivious to other people's feelings (cf. ll. 58, 114–115); ignores Moon's cautioning and criticism (cf. ll. 58, 61–62, 64); doesn't address Moon's criticism openly, only indirectly (cf. l. 67); oblivious to Frank's pain (disguised as defensiveness); vetoes questions relating to sexuality (cf. ll. 92–93, 135–136)*

→ Frank and Ella are both isolated from the others/by themselves; but still stand closer to each other than to any of the others (unspoken bond between the two new ones); Briggs, Moon, Debit and Point stand fairly close together, but not really close (= a gang or group made up of unrelated individuals who are strong and lose all respect for others when in a group); Mint by himself, but not isolated; overlooking the group; equal distance from everyone

atmosphere: *menacing, threatening, "full of dread" (l. 73); makes breathing difficult*

B3 **Seite 92**

Lösungsvorschlag/Erwartungshorizont:

A play needs to be performed, needs to be brought to life, needs to be put on stage, before an audience, only then is it complete; it is not enough for a play to be written and read; not just a relationship between author and reader (as, for example, with novels, short stories and poems) but a relationship between author, director, actors and audience

B4 **Seite 93**

Lösungsvorschlag/Erwartungshorizont:

a) – ***Moon:*** *"You could leave him permanently scarred" (ll. 59–60); "You're infringing his human rights" (l. 63); "These are torture chamber conditions" (l. 65); "Do you feel that in doing this, Mint is infringing your human rights?" (ll. 74–75)*
→ voices moral concerns; critical of Mint's decision; but remains quiet once Frank hasn't replied to his question about how he feels about being put on the hot seat
– ***the other students, i.e. Briggs, Point, Debit and Moon,*** *seem indifferent, bored (cf. l. 5) and "detached" (l. 6); they don't join Mint when he claps (l. 187); Ella does but not clear whether she claps to applaud Frank or because she feels she has to do as her new teacher does*

b) – ***Mint being disrespectful:*** *"You actually passed an exam?" (l. 17); "So there's a brain somewhere under all that hair spray" (ll. 19–20); "Well, let's see how long you last" (l. 22)*
– ***language contributing towards creating atmosphere:*** *"To scald your arse" (l. 48) → threatening / "Um" (ll. 68, 76), ll. 87–89, 112–113, 134, 177 → dread (cf. l. 72) and uneasiness*

B5 **Seite 94**

Lösungsvorschlag/Erwartungshorizont:
I can state quite clearly that I would not enjoy having Mint as my teacher; I do not consider irony, sarcasm and disrespect human values worth cultivating, and I certainly would not accept them as anybody's way of teaching; Mint seems to be quite full of himself (cf. ll. 51–56) and oblivious to the potential damage he is doing to Frank and the other students

B6 **Seite 94**

Lösungsvorschlag/Erwartungshorizont:
Mint: *Moon – you're next*

– Moon goes to a seat apart from the group. –

Mint: *Right people, have your questions for Moon ready*

– Moon is bored. Mint claps. –

Briggs: *Scared?*
Moon: *No*
Debit: *Sure?*
Moon: *Yeah*
Briggs: *Why are you so worried about psychological torture?*
Moon: *Wait until you get to sit here*
Point: *I thought you weren't worried*
Moon: *I'm not*
Briggs: *What are your deepest fears?*
Moon: *People like you*
Mint: *Moon, say yes*
Moon: *No*
Briggs: *What's your deepest fear?*
Moon: *My dog dying*
Point: *Why?*
Moon: *He's my best friend*
Briggs: *This is just as bad as Frank. Have you got no other friends?*
Moon: *A dog is a man's best friend*
Briggs: *You consider yourself a man?*
Ella: *This is not fair*
Mint: *Question not allowed*
Debit: *Why?*
Moon: *Because Mint says so*
Point: *This sucks*
Moon: *Yes, it does*
Ella: *Where do you live?*
Moon: *Just down the road from school*
Debit: *Why do you ask? Do you fancy him?*
Mint: *Debit! It's Moon's turn on the hot seat, not Ella's*
Point: *Do you live with your mum?*
Moon: *My grandmother*
Briggs: *Bet your mum couldn't bear you*
Moon: *She bore me alright*
Debit: *Where's your mum?*
Moon: *Dead*
Point: *And your dad?*
Moon: *Don't know. Don't care*
Debit: *Sure?*
Moon: *Yeah*
Debit: *How did your mum die?*
Moon: *Cancer. She died within three months of being diagnosed*
Mint: *One last question: what made you choose Drama, Moon?*
Moon: *So I can pretend to be someone else. It makes the pain easier to bear*
Mint: *OK. Well done, Moon. Debit – your turn*

Getting to the point

C1 Seite 95

Lösungsvorschlag/Erwartungshorizont:
conversation between Tom and his teacher de Clerk; Tom is hoping to find out whether de Clerk is gay/wants confirmation for his assumption/suspicion that de Clerk is gay but de Clerk refuses to reveal any information about his personal life
(Tom tries to seduce de Clerk by starting to massage him; he then tells de Clerk about his recurring dream of being kissed and not knowing whether he is being kissed by a man or by a woman; de Clerk does not want to listen and tells Tom to leave; the extract ends with Tom saying he wants to talk to someone gay; de Clerk tells Tom that he should not worry about being gay)
Tom's interest: *he wants to find out whether he is gay and whether de Clerk is gay / he wants de Clerk to help him find out whether he is gay / he wants to talk to someone gay about what it is like to be gay*
de Clerk's interest: *he wants to protect his privacy; he does not want to reveal any information about his personal life; he does not want anybody at school to know that he is gay*

C2 Seite 95

Lösungsvorschlag/Erwartungshorizont:
indirect questions, *i.e. Tom keeps nagging without explicitly asking questions: "Might have been important." (l. 6); "I was just wondering." (l. 25); "It makes you wonder. We all wonder." (l. 30); "You've got good clothes, sir. For a teacher." (l. 93) → an attempt to wear de Clerk down, make him open up and talk and admit that he is gay*

hesitation: *"If you want to go home – go home to your … partner." (ll. 46–47); "With your … partner." (l. 73); "Sir … I keep on having this dream […]" (l. 96) → creates an atmosphere of hesitation; shows that Tom is treading carefully; is thinking about how to make de Clerk lower his guard and admit to his homosexuality, either openly or by mistake*

ellipsis: *"Sir – I'm really sorry, but I've –" (l. 76); "If you want me to get you another one, sir –" (ll. 85–86); "Don't." (l. 98) → creates an atmosphere of hesitation; Tom does not want to offend de Clerk, he just wants him to open up and talk to him; de Clerk wants to say as little as possible*

sexual innuendos: *"I can do a massage, sir. I know how to do a massage." (ll. 49–50); "Sssssssh-hhh. Our secret." (l. 57); "You're quite developed, sir." (l. 70) → again, Tom is hoping that this will make de Clerk admit that he is gay, which in turn would give Tom the chance to finally talk to someone who is gay*

short answers by de Clerk: *"Well, that's up to them." (l. 29); "I can't." (l. 48); "You talk to someone." (l. 115) → he wants to give as little about his personal life away as possible; wants to keep up his guard; afraid that if he starts talking in longer sentences, he might say more than he wants to, might say things he will later regret*

de Clerk being defensive and trying to stop Tom from going any further: *"I'm not talking any more." (l. 24); "Well, don't." (l. 26); "No." (l. 51); "Listen. Physical contact is –" (l. 54); "Back to your work now. That was wrong." (ll. 74–75); "No no." (l. 87); "Tom – get on with your work." (l. 90); "Tom." (l. 94); "Don't." (l. 98); "This isn't Biology. I'm Citizenship." (l. 101); "I don't want to know about that." (l. 104); "Please. Don't do this." (l. 107); "You don't talk to me." (l. 117); "Alright. Go away. Go home." (l. 122); "Shut up, please shut up." (l. 132) → he wants to give as little away about his personal life as possible; it takes a lot of willpower on de Clerk's part to stick to his role as teacher vs. student and to not slip into his other, private role as a gay man*

swearing by de Clerk: *"Well fuck 'em, fuck 'em, fuck 'em." (l. 15); "Oh, fuck." (l. 81); "Shit. Shit. Shit." (l. 83) → reveals his private self, he lets down his guard*

sarcasm/irony: *"Nothing else matters. Nothing else matters but your coursework and the inspectors and that we don't become a failing school, okay? There is nothing else in the whole wide world that matters apart from that." (ll. 7–12); "maybe I don't have a personal life" (ll. 33–34); "Maybe I'm not a person at all. Maybe I'm just lesson plans and marking." (ll. 36–37) → indication that he is bottling up emotions, such as anger and unhappiness at having to pretend to be someone he is not; unhappy about the double life he is leading, not admitting/feeling comfortable to admit to his homosexuality at work*

de Clerk letting down his guard: *"Mmm." (ll. 62 and 69); "Sometimes." (l. 72); "Well – it's fine. It's normal. It's just fine." (ll. 135–136); "Well – you should do." (l. 142) → de Clerk's inner conflict; he is stressed out by having to keep up pretences; he would like to help Tom but he feels he can't without jeopardizing his own position at the school*

C3 **Seite 95**

Lösungsvorschlag/Erwartungshorizont:

- *de Clerk tries to reassure Tom that it is fine, normal and okay to be gay; however, his own reaction in the extract seems to prove the opposite; if it is so okay to be gay, why does de Clerk not openly admit to Tom that he himself is gay but instead dodges all of Tom's indirect and not so indirect questions? Tom explicitly says that he wants to "talk to someone gay" (l. 130) but does not know anyone who is gay. This would have been de Clerk's chance to finally open up and show himself as living proof that it is okay to be gay. Young people who are thinking of coming out need role models but instead de Clerk lets Tom down.*
- *I agree with the advice that de Clerk gives to Tom but I think there are still very many people out there who do not think it is okay for people to be gay, especially openly gay; I think you should only give that piece of advice if you are prepared to support the person you are giving the advice to through his or her coming out*
- *de Clerk chickens out when he mentions the school policy of "we celebrate difference" (ll. 138–139) to prove to Tom that it is okay to be homosexual; he takes the official line rather than open up to Tom and give him some advice from his own personal experience*

C4 **Seite 95**

Lösungsvorschlag/Erwartungshorizont:

(Tom waits for de Clerk after school.)
Tom: *Sir, do you have a minute?*
De Clerk: *I'm on my way home, Tom. Can't this wait until tomorrow?*
Tom: *I really need your help, sir. … I need to talk to someone.*
(Pause.)
De Clerk: *Alright then.*
Tom: *I really need to talk to someone gay and know what it was like for them.*
De Clerk: *What do you mean, what it was like for them?*
Tom: *What it was like for you when you came out.*
(Pause.)
De Clerk: *Tom, please. There must be someone else you can talk to. This is very difficult for me.*
Tom: *I don't know anyone who is gay. Please, sir.*
De Clerk: *Uhhh. Alright. – Yes, I'm gay.*
Tom: *When did you decide to come out?*
De Clerk: *Well, have I come out? The way I've been dodging your questions makes me wonder whether I have come out at all. My family and friends all know. But no-one at school knows.*
Tom: *But didn't you say it's fine, it's normal, it's okay to be gay.*
De Clerk: *Yes, it's okay to be gay. And as I've told you before, you should feel okay about it. You know the school policy: we celebrate difference.*
Tom: *But why don't you feel okay about it?*
De Clerk: *I'm afraid to lose my job. I've only been here six months. There are still many people out there who do not think it is okay for us to be gay. They will never tell you to your face, though. They will just give some other reason if they don't hire me again next year. And I couldn't prove them otherwise. But it's different for you, Tom. You have nothing to lose.*
Tom: *I'm being bullied.*
De Clerk: *I'm sorry, Tom. Have you reported the bullies to your form tutor?*
Tom: *He hates me.*
De Clerk: *You must report the bullies. You mustn't let them do this to you.*
(De Clerk touches Tom's arm.)
Tom: *Thanks.*
De Clerk: *Listen, if there's anything I can help you with, let me know. I'm sorry I've not been much help until now. But just try to understand my position, too, Tom.*
Tom: *It's okay. I'm just glad I can talk to you now. Can we talk again?*
De Clerk: *Yes, I promise. Just come and see me whenever, Tom. And listen, you must report the bullies. Promise me that you will. Do people in your class know?*

Tom: *Yes, most of them were great.*
De Clerk: *It will get easier, I promise you it will. Don't stop talking about how you feel. You'll be fine. And come and see me whenever. There are limits as to what I can do but I'll do what I can.*
Tom: *Thanks a lot, sir.*
De Clerk: *Thank you, Tom! I'm sorry I ignored your cry for help earlier.*
Tom: *That's okay. Thanks. Bye.*
De Clerk: *Bye, Tom.*

Listening

D1 **Seite 98**

Lösungsvorschlag/Erwartungshorizont:

a) *I think that more often than not the church dodges the question of homosexuality. They know that the vast majority of people nowadays don't care whether someone is gay or not. Homosexuality isn't a big issue for most people. However, the church can't bring itself to fully endorse homosexuality as traditionally it was considered immoral, so most of the time they say very little about it, hoping not to offend anybody either way.*

b) ***arguments for*** *possible rules: if there are rules, you don't have to start arguing every time someone utters homophobic slants, instead you can just refer them to the school rules; for a lot of people, it takes rules to make them change their behaviour; school rules won't change people's opinions over night but they will make people shut up; over time, this new behaviour will change their behaviour and opinions, too*
arguments against *possible rules: rules don't change anything about people's opinions and prejudice; it is people's opinions that need changing and that can only be achieved by talking about and discussing homosexuality with people as often as possible; many people tend to rebel against rules so if a school introduces anti-discriminatory rules, I'm sure there will be some students who will act against the rules on purpose and out of principle*

c) *My guess would be that Rachel realised that she was lesbian and decided to come out, not only to her family but also to friends at her church. I'm sure that people at her church started discriminating against her, focussing on her sexual orientation rather than on her as a person, the same person they've known for years. I wouldn't be surprised if some people tried talking her out of being lesbian as though it was merely a lifestyle choice, rather than an orientation. In the context of religion, you will usually find at least one person to tell gays and lesbians to "pray the gay away".*

D2 **Seite 99** DVD

Lösungsvorschlag/Erwartungshorizont:

a) – *a very small church, 60–70 people on any given Sunday*
– *the church was Pentecostal* [*a movement within Christianity that places emphasis on a direct personal experience of God;* = Pfingstbewegung]
– *Rachel learned there that being gay was the worst thing you could be*
– *her mother made her change the TV channel if there was anything about gay people on TV*
– *by the time Rachel was in high school, she was going to church four or five times a week*
– *church was different from most other churches, in that people would fall down and cry and roll around and march around the sanctuary → made them believe that they had a deeper connection with God than anybody else*
– *Rachel loved the energy and rituals; it made her feel good, it was empowering*
– *there were ushers ready to catch you if you fainted during the rituals*
– *always felt as though she was not good enough, as though she had "sin" in her*
– *Rachel does not know how consciously aware she was that she was gay*
– *she was always hiding something, not necessarily knowing what it was*

b) **3** *She starts to read gay literature.*
7 *Her mother finds her books; Rachel agrees to have counselling "to pray the gay away".*
9 *The pastors ban her from certain church duties until she is "healed".*
4 *Rachel feels humiliated.*
2 *Rachel has to make a decision: stay and pray and never get married or run away.*
1 *At college she writes her coming-out paper "My closet has a window".*

8 *She decides to come out and not go to church anymore.*
5 *Her friends turn away from her.*
10 *She can't forgive the pastors at her former church.*
6 *She is at peace with herself but still has nightmares about church.*

D3 **Seite 99**

Lösungsvorschlag/Erwartungshorizont:
a) + b)
– ***her church and high school friends:*** *unforgiving, surprised, shocked, appalled / they didn't care about Rachel as a person, as a human being with feelings; their beliefs and their ideology were more important to them than Rachel; once Rachel didn't fit the picture they had of her, they dropped her*
– ***her mother:*** *disappointed, strict / her mother didn't want to deal with Rachel's homosexuality; she wanted her daughter to undergo counselling "to pray the gay away".*
– ***her pastors:*** *cruel, unforgiving / The pastors banned Rachel from certain church duties and were hoping that Rachel would eventually be "healed" from homosexuality; none of them seemed to try and talk to Rachel to find out how she was coping; they dropped her with immediate effect*
– ***her professor:*** *understanding, encouraging, help, Rachel's lifeline / Rachel's professor made her realise that she was ready to come out; the professor seemed to treat it as no big deal, which made everything easier for Rachel*

D4 **Seite 99**

Lösungsvorschlag/Erwartungshorizont:
– ***what I think of Rachel's story:*** *a very sad story; I feel really sorry for Rachel; I can't imagine what it must feel like to be hiding something so important from your family and friends; I'm sure Rachel's story is typical of so many others; I think coming out has become easier for young people today but I still don't think it's easy; there are still many so-called jokes about gay people around*
– ***what I think of people's reactions to her coming out:*** *incredible to think that ideology might be more important to people than a human being's feelings; Rachel was in need of people understanding her; the worst thing you can do when people reach out and open up about who they are is turn away from them; our sexuality says nothing about our character, about our goodness of heart; I find that people who are caught up in some kind of ideology/religion are particularly intolerant when it comes to accepting people who are different from them; to me, there is nothing Christian about turning away from someone whom I've called a friend for a long time, simply because they longer conform to the image I had of them*
– ***institutions that might discriminate against homosexual people:*** *I'm not sure but I think church institutions would probably not want me looking after young children during summer camp if they knew I was gay; however, I think there would also be many parents who would not want me to look after their children in the summer holidays, either; I wonder whether you would get a job working in a kindergarten if you told them in your application that you were gay*

D5 **Seite 99**

Lösungsvorschlag/Erwartungshorizont:
Good morning – and let me begin by saying how proud I am to be a student at this school.
I feel very strongly that our school should implement an anti-discriminatory sexual identity policy. Let me tell you why.
In our English class the other day we listened to a podcast about a woman who decided to come out at the age of 18 and who was subsequently dropped by all the people who were dear to her and who had known her for years. This left the woman feeling humiliated and hurt but also scared and guilty. And I don't think anyone should be made to feel that way. Your sexual orientation does not harm anyone so we should not discriminate against anyone because of their sexual identity.
Lesbian or gay people should have our support. Ideally, their coming out should not be treated as a big deal. Let's acknowledge it – and then get on with in. The day people's sexual orientation is as irrelevant as the colour of their hair is the day we can phase out the policy again.
But for now I believe that we need such a policy. Our school spirit is based on basic human values: on respect, fairness and equality. Everyone at our school should feel that this is a safe place, a place where they can be themselves, a place that will help them understand who they really are.
Thank you very much.

Getting started

A1 Seite 100

Lösungsvorschlag/Erwartungshorizont:

a)

```
        F R E E D O M
    S T U D Y
        T E C H N O L O G Y
      S U R P R I S E S
    W O R K
  I N D E P E N D E N T
```

c) *Some people's poems focus on people's private lives, i.e. travelling, studying and family. There are other poems that focus on the future of our society or our world as a whole.*

A2 Seite 100

Placemat: → Seite 27 hier in den *Teacher's notes.*

Lösungsvorschlag/Erwartungshorizont:

a) – *if a third of all websites are pornographic, chances are that there will be even more in future*
- *Americans will continue to have better access to information than people in Africa → the US will change even faster in future, more and more things will be done online; the US will continue to influence what happens elsewhere in the world*
- *there has always been economic inequality; this will continue to be the case for as long as no-one in a position of power cares enough about it to change it*
- *there is enough money in the world; enough money to feed and treat everyone but the people who have the money want to hold on to their money, they don't want to share*
- *the gap between different parts of the world (western countries vs. countries in Africa, rich vs. poor, access to facilities vs. being left behind) will widen*

b) – *human rights are respected (freedom of speech, freedom of religion)*
- *people concentrate on what they have in common, rather than on what divides them*
- *peace for all, no risk of war, no torture, no physical or psychological violence*
- *people everywhere with access to clean water and essential medicines*
- *no-one must go hungry, cold or live in fear*
- *no-one is discriminated against (be it for race, gender, sexual orientation or whatever)*

A3 Seite 101

Lösungsvorschlag/Erwartungshorizont:

a) ***The Handmaid's Tale:*** *a negative, scary, haunting depiction of the future; a "tyrannical Christian fundamentalist society"; personal freedom is restricted; pessimistic view of the future*
Never Let Me Go: *a haunting and scary depiction of the future; personal freedom is restricted; an elite ruling over the lives and fates of everybody else; pessimistic view of the future*
Gone: *a disturbing and scary depiction of the future; adults disappearing, teenagers left to their own devices; with a sinister presence at work behind everything; pessimistic view of the future*
The Circle: *a scary depiction of the future; end of anonymity; a company controlling all aspects of human existence; pessimistic view of the future*

b)

settings	*social groups/society*	*environmental factors*	*consequences for mankind*
tyrannical Christian fundamentalist society	*the ruling elite*	*nuclear radiation*	*unimaginable, dangerous, deadly powers*
a patriarchal, oppressive future America	*dissenters*	*pollution*	*be hanged or die slowly of radiation sickness*
the Republic of Gilead	*donors (of organs)*	*hunger*	*be cloned in order to provide organs*
contemporary England	*teenagers*	*mutations*	*declining birth rate*
not-too-distant future	*a company*		*end of anonymity*
			all aspects of human existence are revealed

c) *The fictional visions are a lot more pessimistic than any of the visions I/we came up with. In fact, there are very few common features between our own ideas and the fictional visions. However, technology seems to be a common feature. Many of us agree with the fictional visions that technology will change our lives in the years to come.*
Another common feature is the widening gap between the ruling class and the rest of the people. Some of us had the same ideas that you can find in the fictional visions: that we will be spied on more and more by our governements.

A4 **Seite 101**

Lösungsvorschlag/Erwartungshorizont:

a) *All four novels fit the definition of a dystopia. All four of them show "a very unpleasant, undesirable or frightening imaginary world".*

b) – *it makes for more interesting reading: a dystopian vision of the future is more complex and will give the reader more to think about than a utopian vision*
– *more potential for character development if there is a central conflict/challenge*
– *we are more likely to develop character strengths in the face of adversity than in the face of everything being hunky-dory*

Practice section

B1 **Seite 102**

Lösungsvorschlag/Erwartungshorizont:

a) *Yes, I know the novel. I've not seen the film, though.*
I think the novel/film is so popular because
– *it shows everyday life in stories that aren't every day: from the way teenagers hang out together, to the frustration with adults*
– *it presents a moral observation about society, even offering solutions to current problems*
– *of the way the characters are oppressed and have to fight to get their voices heard – that's how many young people feel, silenced and unable to really express themselves*
– *it reflects today's uncertain times: young people having to clean up the mess the generation before them has left them / young people's struggle to live up to a new, sometimes unmeetable set of standards / social inequality leading to civil unrest / pollution and over-consumption driving our planet to ruin*
– *the main characters refuse to play the roles written for them → this resonates with today's teenagers: refusing to let anyone else define you*
– *it speaks to the anxieties of young people today: they are facing a future in which very little is a given*
– *the young adult characters in the novel hold the values that the adults have forgotten*
– *it is written in a style that is easy to read*
– *things move on quickly; exciting; chapters often end with a cliffhanger*
No, I know neither the novel nor the film. Of course, I've heard of it but I've never actually bothered reading the novel or watching the film. I'm not into science fiction or fantasy.

B2 **Seite 102**

Lösungsvorschlag/Erwartungshorizont:

– *the event is called the reaping*
– *not entirely clear from the extract what the reaping is about but it's definitely nothing very pleasant; it seems to have something to do with young people between 12 and 18; two of them will be chosen for something (ll. 25–26: "two kids whose names will be drawn")*
– *it is compulsory for everyone to come and watch*
– *it seems as though the lives of the young people are at risk*
– *members of the public can place bets on who will be chosen*

B3 **Seite 103**

Lösungsvorschlag/Erwartungshorizont:

a) *exciting, foreboding, emotional, electrifying, menacing, sinister, thrilling, ominous, captivating*

b) ***exciting***
- *"Family members [...] holding tightly to one another's hands." (ll. 20–22) → the characters are worried/excited about something; as a reader you can tell your pulse quickening*

foreboding
- *"It's too bad, really, but they hold reaping in the square – one of the few places in District 12 that can be pleasant." (ll. 6–9) → something unpleasant will happen*
- *"the two kids whose names will be drawn." (ll. 25–26) → not clear what will happen to the two children but obvious from context that it will not be pleasant, something that will affect their families as well*
- *"Latecomers [...] can watch the event on screens as it's televised by the state" (ll. 41–43) → the fact that the event is not properly explained but referred to only as the "event" makes you realise that this must be something very important*

emotional
- *"Family members [...] holding tightly to one another's hands. But there are others, too, who have no one they love at stake, or who no longer care" (ll. 20–24) → holding tightly because their loved ones are in danger; loving and (not) caring are emotions*
- *"if they will break down and weep." (ll. 28–29) → break down because overcome by emotions*

menacing/sinister/ominous
- *"People file in silently" (l. 15) → very unusual for many people in one place to be quiet*
- *"there's an air of grimness" (l. 12) → grim and sinister are very similar*
- *"but carefully, carefully. These same people tend to be informers" (ll. 30–31) → repetition of "carefully" adds to the sinister atmosphere, it almost makes you hold your breath as a reader*
- *"The space gets tighter, more claustrophobic, as people arrive." (ll. 38–39) → takes your breath away, makes breathing uncomfortable, your chest starts to feel tight*
- *"camera crews, perched like buzzards on the rooftops" (ll. 13–14) → fact that people are being watched/controlled creates a menacing atmosphere; people being compared to animals/birds of prey*
- *"Twelve to eighteen-year-olds are herded into roped areas" (ll. 17–18) → again, people being compared to animals: cattle; people not being treated as human beings but like animals*

electrifying/thrilling/captivating
- *"good opportunity for the Capitol to keep tabs on the population" (ll. 16–17) → population is kept under observation, you can feel your pulse quickening*
- *"Twelve to eighteen-year-olds are herded into roped areas" (ll. 17–18) → it makes you sit up and hold your breath when you read about teenagers being treated like cattle*

B4 **Seite 103**

Lösungsvorschlag/Erwartungshorizont:

a)
- *ll. 39–42: a large square, capable of holding several thousand people; despite the size of the square there is not enough room for everyone*
- *ll. 38–39: people crowded into the tight space of the square → implies an oppressive atmosphere; "claustrophobic" (l. 38)*
- *ll. 7–8: one of the few places in District 12 that can be pleasant → implies that the atmosphere today is anything but pleasant*
- *ll. 8–11: the square is surrounded by shops; on most days there is a nice atmosphere → implies that the atmosphere today is anything but pleasant*
- *ll. 13–14: "camera crews [...] on the rooftops" → people are being watched and controlled by cameras; adds to the oppressive, sinister and impersonal atmosphere*
- *ll. 18–19: "herded into roped areas, marked off by ages" → the square is divided into different sections/areas, according to age (12–18)*

b) ***allusions or connotations***
- *ll. 15–17: "The reaping is a good opportunity for the Capitol to keep tabs on the population as well." → suggests that people are being checked on and controlled at every possible moment; enhances the tense and dangerous atmosphere*
- *ll. 35–36: "Gal and I agree that if we have to choose between dying of hunger and a bullet in the head, the bullet would be much quicker." → narrator comes across as matter-of-fact about death and about dying; also comes across as a strong character who can deal with pressure*
- *ll. 23–24: "others, [...] who no longer care → implies that the event has taken place before → people have been hurt so often and so deeply that they've stopped feeling the pain; act of self-preservation → atmosphere of cruelty and pain*

images
– ll. 17–18: "Twelve to eighteen-year-olds are herded into roped areas" → teenagers treated like cattle; people not treated as human beings but like animals → cruel, heartless atmosphere
sentence structure
– l. 6: "It's too bad, really" → irony; the narrator hides his/her pain behind a facade of irony

B5 **Seite 104**

Lösungsvorschlag/Erwartungshorizont:
I wouldn't change any of the adjectives I chose in B3. To me, the adjectives that describe the atmosphere in extract 1 best of all are foreboding and menacing/sinister/ominous.

B6 **Seite 105**

Lösungsvorschlag/Erwartungshorizont:
a) *the Hunger Games*
- *take place every year*
- *each of the 12 districts in the country (name of country: Panem) nominates/randomly picks one girl and one boy to take part in the Games → 24 in all*
- *over a period of several weeks the 24 participants, called tributes, fight against each other in a big outdoor arena; killing each other one by one; the one surviving tribute wins*
- *the prize: an easy life with all kinds of comforts; the winner's district is given food for a whole year (while the other eleven districts must go hungry)*

b)
- *country is called Panem; used to be called North America*
- *North America was destroyed by natural disasters and by wars*
- *to begin with, all was well in Panem: a capitol plus 13 districts, peace and prosperity for all*
- *followed by the Dark Days, the uprising of the Districts against the Capitol*
- *12 districts were defeated, the thirteenth district was wiped out*
- *once a year, the Hunger Games are organised → punish the people of Panem and show them that they must never rebel/speak out against the Capitol again (ll. 52–53: "If you lift a finger, we will destroy every last one of you.")*
- ***vision of the future:*** *people will be oppressed, humiliated, tortured and tyrannised by their governments, all in the name of peace (ll. 31–32: "new laws to guarantee peace"); won't be allowed to speak out against their governments/the ruling classes; governments will humiliate, torture and tyrannise their people, pretending that it's only for their people's own good → a very bleak vision of the future*

B7 **Seite 106**

Lösungsvorschlag/Erwartungshorizont:
setting
- *ll. 3–4: "temporary stage that is set up before the Justice Building" → the situation depicted, i.e. the reaping that is about to take place, is at odds with the idea of justice → creates an atmosphere of injustice and surreality*
- *ll. 5–6: "three chairs, a podium and two large glass balls, one for boys and one for girls" → podium is elevated → hierarchy; adds to the atmosphere of inequality, atmosphere of superiority of ruling class over people*
- *ll. 17–18: "Just as the town clock strikes two, the mayor steps up to the podium" → everything is organised following a detailed timetable → no room for individuality, eventuality or spontaneity, no freedom, no flexibility → a sterile, cold atmosphere devoid of feelings and emotions*

connotations
- *ll. 2–3: "terse nods" → the boys and girls don't talk; they are under pressure; full of fear*
- *l. 6: "I stare at" → the narrator, Katniss Everdeen, is under pressure; the verb "stare" implies that she is far from relaxed; instead, she is under pressure, paralysed by fear*
- *l. 9: "careful handwriting" → at odds with the situation; a situation of life and death, atmosphere of fear; "careful" implies that the person writing the paper slips was not shaking when s/he wrote the slips; instead, s/he was calm and composed as though s/he was writing invitation cards → the government/ruling class does not feel for its people; no qualms about sending people to their deaths → atmosphere of ruthlessness*
- *l. 30: "obliterated" → an elaborate word (euphemism) in order to avoid the simple but clear word "killed"; means of obfuscation; no atmosphere of openness*

imagery
- *ll. 1–2: "clump of sixteen-year-olds" → immovable mass; numb; not feeling → nothing personal/ individual about a "clump"; atmosphere of anonymity; having to shut down your feelings in order to protect yourself against the pain and the fear*
- *ll. 13–14: "white grin, pinkish hair and spring green suit" → colours in stark contrast to situation; the situation depicted is dark and sinister; Effie Trinket, however, is very colourful; detached from the situation; heartless, no sympathy for how the young people at the reaping must be feeling*
- *l. 13: "white grin" → a grin is artificial; Effie Trinket is putting on a show; hiding her cruelty behind a grin; pretending to have feelings and human emotions when she is in fact ruthless*
- *l. 59: "will be showered with prizes" → atmosphere of plenty; in stark contrast to poverty and starvation in other districts*
- *ll. 62–63: "while the rest of us battle starvation" → emphasises the people's hardships; atmosphere of war although the government pretends that they live in times of peace*
- *ll. 69–70: "The crowd draws in a collective breath" → emphasises that individuality has no place in Panem; also shows that people in the districts all feel the same*
- *l. 20: "the country that rose up out of the ashes" → rise like a phoenix from the ashes, emerge renewed after disaster or destruction → the speaker wants to emphasise Panem's strength*

sentence structure
- *ll. 71–72: "desperately hoping that it's not me, that it's not me, that it's not me" → emphasises the atmosphere of fear and despair*
- *ll. 18–19: "It's the same story every year." → short sentence accentuating the fact that Katniss, the narrator, has heard the story many times before and is sick and tired of hearing it*
- *ll. 31–34: "The Treaty of Treason gave us the new laws to guarantee peace and […] it gave us the Hunger Games." → parallelism to emphasise the contrast between the official party line and the reality for the people; there is nothing peaceful to the concept of the Hunger Games at all*
- *l. 35: "The rules of the Hunger Games are simple." → short sentence; the narrator is so used to the Hunger Games by now that she can talk about them in a very matter-of-fact way; the rules are simple, and the sentence structure is simple, too*
- *ll. 46–48: "how totally we are at their mercy. How little chance we would stand of surviving" → parallelism for emphasis; atmosphere of helplessness*
- *ll. 49–50: "Whatever words they use, the real message is clear." → clear sentence structure = clear message; for the narrator the situation is clear; no matter what the Capitol wants to make them think, the truth is that the Hunger Games are a form of punishment (for the uprising)*

B8 **Seite 106**

Lösungsvorschlag/Erwartungshorizont:

Yes, I think the quotation can be applied to "The Hunger Games". I believe there are tendencies in today's societies that, if they go unchecked, might eventually lead to a society as depicted in the novel.

***Distinctive features and trends in today's world** that we find reflected in "The Hunger Games":*
- *We live in a world where the promise/prospect of peace is used as an excuse to introduce laws violating individual freedom and civil liberties: governments monitoring e-mail and smartphone exchanges; after 9/11 the US government as well as other governments around the world introduced laws in the name of peace and security that infringed on people's freedom of movement, civil liberties and civil rights, without actually making the world a safer or a more peaceful world*
- *governments' attempts to control people's communications and movements (cf. CCTV cameras in public places) → "camera crews, perched like buzzards on the rooftops" (extract 1, ll. 13–14)*
- *dangers of extremist power*
- *huge disparity between the lives of the rich and the lives of the poor*
- *suffering as entertainment: many of today's reality TV game shows focus on making people feel uncomfortable, e.g. "I'm a Celebrity … Get Me Out of Here!" (twelve celebrities spending a few weeks together in a jungle environment)*
- *violence as entertainment: violence in today's television, video games, and movies*
- *social inequality, unjust social hierarchy*
- *hunger and starvation are still prevalent in many parts of the world*
- *disconnect between governments and their people*
- *big, powerful governments have a tendency to become corrupt and intrusive*
- *importance of appearances/lack of authenticity/people putting on a show for effect: Effie Trinket with her "white grin, pinkish hair and spring green suit" (l. 13)*

Getting to the point

C1 **Seite 107**

Lösungsvorschlag/Erwartungshorizont:

a) – *the Second World War ended in 1945*
- *life during the war: people spying on each other, governments spying on their people, governments killing their people (concentration camps killing Jews; soldiers being used as cannon fodder, especially towards the end of the war); extensive use of propaganda to appease and indoctrinate people; atmosphere of random terror*
- *dictators like Hitler and Stalin; Nazi Germany → rise of totalitarian, non-democratic societies in the 1920s and 1930s (e.g. Germany, Soviet Union, Italy, Spain, Portugal)*
- *post-war society → poverty, economically difficult times*
- *beginning of the Cold War: state of political tension and military rivalry between the United States and the Soviet Union*

b) – *a totalitarian society: poverty for the masses while the ruling classes enjoy a comfortable life*
- *use of propaganda to appease and indoctrinate people*

C2 **Seite 107**

Lösungsvorschlag/Erwartungshorizont:
- *a totalitarian society ruled by "the Party" (l. 120)*
- *total control of its people, posters of Big Brother everywhere (ll. 52–54: The blackmoustachio'd face gazed down from every commanding corner"): Big Brother is watching you!*
- *regular power cuts: "the electric current was cut off during daylight hours" (ll. 17–18)*
- *poor infrastructure (cf. ll. 15–16: lifts not working)*
- *telescreens (l. 37) everywhere: people being indoctrinated and controlled at the same time (ll. 71–72: "The telescreen received and transmitted simultaneously."), all the time*
- *citizens have no chance of escaping the watchful eye, i.e. the influence, of Big Brother*
- *the Thought Police monitoring its citizens at all times*
- *people living "in the assumption that every sound you made was overheard, [...] every movement scrutinized" (ll. 85–87)*
- *people seem to have been stripped of their memories (ll. 110–112)*
- *positive values have turned negative and vice versa (ll. 121–123)*

C3 **Seite 107**

Lösungsvorschlag/Erwartungshorizont:

setting
- *ll. 1–6: "a bright cold day in April, and the clocks were striking thirteen. [...] the vile wind [...] a swirl of gritty dust" → not inviting at all; atmosphere of desolation*
- *ll. 93–95: "this was London, chief city of Airstrip One, itself the third most populous of the provinces of Oceania" → chief city: capital city; London is still called London but there is no mention of Europe; instead, London is the capital of a province called Airstrip One; Airstrip One is one of many/various provinces that make up Oceania*
- *ll. 99–103: "rotting nineteenth-century houses, their sides shored up with baulks of timber, their windows patched with cardboard and their roofs with corrugated iron, their crazy garden walls sagging in all directions" → grimness, decay and neglect; London as a dilapidated, rundown city*
- *ll. 8–10: "The hallway smelt of boiled cabbage and old rag mats." → desolate, decaying and not at all inviting or hospitable*
- *ll. 125–126: four Ministries, each of them containing "three thousand rooms above ground level, and corresponding ramifications below" → by far the largest buildings in London → intimidating*
- *no mention of people out and about on the streets → atmosphere of desertedness and neglect*

connotations
- *ll. 41–42: "blue overalls which were the uniform of the party" → making everyone look the same as though individuality were something negative or dangerous → atmosphere of anonymity*
- *l. 44: "blunt razor blades" → the razor blades have lost their effectiveness → atmosphere of helplessness and powerlessness*
- *ll. 45–47: "the winter that had just ended. Outside, [...] the world looked cold." → the winter has ended but it is still cold → emphasis; the cold is down to more than the weather*
- *ll. 55–56: "BIG BROTHER IS WATCHING YOU"; also ll. 121–123 → capital letters for emphasis; overpowering*

- *ll. 57–58: "the dark eyes looked deep into Winston's own" → might the dark eyes actually be able to look into Winston's soul? → mind control, psychological manipulation*
- *ll. 128–130: "So completely did they dwarf the surrounding architecture" → atmosphere of oppression; not just the architecture is dwarfed but also the people living in the buildings → atmosphere of insignificance as far as people/citizens are concerned*
- *ll. 135–141: description of the four Ministries → human values are turned into their opposites → makes you feel as though you might lose your mind if you had to live in a society like that: what to believe in if everything you once knew has changed its meaning, which is of course the whole idea behind the society depicted → psychological manipulation, language as mind control; also, citizens are discouraged from believing in human values*
- *ll. 68–69: "the voice from the telescreen was still babbling away" → the choice of the word "babbling" implies that Winston has learned to ignore the telescreen; to him, it is nothing but background noise; however, he chooses to turn it down (cf. ll. 34–35) so it probably still affects him*
- *ll. 72–74: "Any sound that Winston made, above the level of a very low whisper, would be picked up by it" → foreboding? it makes you wonder whether whispering will, at some point in the novel, serve as a means to undermine the authorities and start a revolution or uprising*
- *ll. 87: "except in darkness, every movement scrutinized" → foreboding? will Winston makes use of the fact that there is freedom of movement when it is dark/at night?*
- *ll. 12–14: "a man of about forty-five, with a heavy black moustache and ruggedly handsome features" → description seems to resemble Josef Stalin, dictator and leader of the Soviet Union*

imagery

- *weather: winter, cold, harshness → cold atmosphere, devoid of warmth, i.e. of feelings/emotions*
- *l. 47: "the world looked cold" → cold atmosphere, lacking in warmth*
- *ll. 50–51: "there seemed to be no colour in anything" → grim and grey → unhappy, atmosphere of depression*
- *l. 96: "He tried to squeeze out some childhood memory" → it takes a lot of effort of Winston's part to remember anything about the past/about his childhood → psychological manipulation*
- *ll. 128–130: "So completely did they dwarf the surrounding architecture" → overpowering; emphasises the Party's power, the Ministries' powers; the citizens are 'dwarfed', i.e. they are insignificant and oppressed*
- *ll. 60–62: "a helicopter [...] hovered for an instant like a bluebottle" → being controlled and watched by insects, no contact with human eyes, i.e. an atmosphere of anonymity*
- *ll. 108–109: "like chicken-houses" → people being treated/housed like animals*
- *l. 152: "gorilla-faced guards" → guards being compared to animals; devoid of human emotions*
- *l. 152: "guards in black uniforms" → colour black a symbol of evil, sinister, menacing*

sentence structure

- *ll. 98–99: "Were there always these [...] nineteenth-century houses [?]" → rhetorical question that emphasises the contrast as readers will know that London has not always been like this*
- *ll. 143–144: "The Ministry of Love was the really frightening one." → short sentence; a sentence that most readers will read a second and third time; a sentence full of contrast, a sentence that turns human values on its head and gives the reader an idea of what it must feel like to live in such a society → psychological manipulation, language as mind control*

C4 **Seite 107**

Lösungsvorschlag/Erwartungshorizont:

- *tendency of today's governments to want to control and monitor their citizens (cf. CCTV cameras in public places)*
- *NSA spying on Americans and citizens all over the world*
- *after 9/11 many governments were quick to curtail civil liberties*
- *Big Brother: bank cards, shoppers' loyalty cards, membership cards etc. help companies obtain a lot of personal information about us*
- *many of us leave a lot of traces being online all the time → useful information that is exploited by companies and websites*
- *manipulation of media stories by governments, political parties, countries, people in power*
- *social inequality, unjust social hierarchy*
- *citizens rarely have access to government buildings, you do not really know what goes on inside; government buildings are inaccessible*
- *Newspeak (euphemisms): let people go = make redundant; enhanced interrogation methods = torture; collateral damage = deaths of civilians; depopulate = kill; economical with the truth = lie*
- *TV show 'Big Brother': viewers watching people go about their daily lives*

Getting started

A1 **Seite 110**

Lösungsvorschlag/Erwartungshorizont:

a) *How often do you shop for clothes?* ***every season***
Do you follow the latest trends? ***sometimes***
How much do you spend every month? ***less than €40***
Where do you shop? ***chains and Internet***
Are fashion labels important for you? ***not really***
How important are the clothes on a person you meet for the first time? ***not really important***

b) *It seems that fashion is more important for the girls in our class than for the boys.*
However, very few of us spend a lot of money on fashion. Some of us spend between 40 and 80 euros every month but none of us spend more than 80 euros.
Fashion labels are important for some of us. Ten people in our class say that fashion labels are absolutely important for them.
The majority of people in our class shop at chain stores. But about a quarter of us also shop on the Internet. Only about five of us shop in department stores.
Two people in our class think it is essential what a person they meet for the first time is wearing. However, the majority of people, i.e. more than twelve of us, think it is irrelevant.

A2 **Seite 110**

Lösungsvorschlag/Erwartungshorizont:

a) *Turkey, Portugal, Bangladesh, China, India, USA, Mexico, Germany*

b) *I think it was predictable that many of our clothes were produced in Bangladesh. Most of us use our pocket money to buy our clothes. So we don't have that much money to spend on fashion, and clothes produced in Bangladesh, India or China are a lot cheaper than clothes produced in Europe or the USA.*
I'm surprised that one of my pullovers was produced in Germany. I thought clothes produced in Germany would be too expensive for me to buy. I don't remember how much I paid but it can't have been all that much as I'm not prepared to spend that much on clothes.
The only thing produced in Europe is a cardigan that belongs to my mum. My mum is very careful about what she buys. She's prepared to pay extra if she knows it was produced in Europe and people were paid a fair wage.

A3 **Seite 110**

Dauer: 4:35 min

Lösungsvorschlag/Erwartungshorizont:

a) *– a documentary about the effects of the global clothing industry on people and the planet*
– fast fashion is unsustainable and unethical
– if we want cheap clothes, we have to accept that someone somewhere is suffering for it, e.g. garment workers dying in factory fires
– working conditions have become secondary to making money/making a profit
– fast fashion production industry = a slave trade
– consumers prefer to stay ignorant about the conditions in which their clothes were produced
– outsourcing of production seems to inevitably lead to outsourcing of responsibility
– outsourcing of production → historically low prices → radically increased consumption
– fast fashion is produced with little regard for the workers who make it and little regard for the environment, both in terms of natural resources and the chemicals used during production
– fast fashion leads to unprecedented amounts of waste

b) *– pictures of people crying in agony and grief, either because they have been injured in a factory fire or because they have lost colleagues, friends or loved ones in a factory fire*
– statistics stating that since 1960 the US has outsourced more than 98% of its clothing production to developing countries
– statistics saying that the average American generates 84 pounds of textile waste a year (→ the figures for us in Germany are probably not that much more favourable)

c) **A** *sweatshop*
B *garment, apparel*
C *unsustainable*

D *unethical*
E *unprecedented*
F *labour*
G *developing countries*
H *working conditions*

A4 **Seite 110**

Lösungsvorschlag/Erwartungshorizont:
advantages *of fast food*
– *saves time because you don't have to spend much time preparing it*
– *often cheaper than food prepared from scratch at home; most certainly cheaper than food prepared from scratch in restaurants*
disadvantages *of fast food*
– *not very healthy: high in salt, sugar and fat; also high in additives and preservatives*
– *you feel hungry again before long*
– *often comes with a lot of packaging → generates a lot of waste → pollution*
– *people working in fast food restaurants earn very little money → minimum wage or even less*

advantages *of fast fashion*
– *cheaper than 'slow fashion'*
– *gives you a chance to 'play' with fashion, i.e. to change your outfit regularly*
– *can react to trends very quickly due to short production times*
disadvantages *of fast fashion*
– *poor quality: does not wash well, falls to pieces after just a few washes*
– *unsustainable: short product life cycle*
– *generates a lot of waste*
– *chemicals used during production can be harmful to both the people making the garments and the people wearing the garments*
– *someone somewhere is suffering for the cheap clothes: factory workers living below the poverty line because they do not earn enough, being paid the minimum wage or even less; companies compromising on worker safety (→ factory fires, health hazards due to chemicals)*

Similarities *fast food and fast fashion*
– *both can leave a bad taste in your mouth*
– *both satisfy an appetite (appetite for food vs an appetite for something new to wear)*
– *both generate a lot of waste/more waste than slow food/slow fashion*
– *aim at making you want more and more (fast food, in fact any processed food, is known to contain artificial additives and preservatives that trick your body into wanting more food than it actually needs)*
– *consumers often don't know the origins → confusing ingredients*

A5 **Seite 111**

Lösungsvorschlag/Erwartungshorizont:
a) *Diagram* **1**
– *impact of a pair of jeans on the environment: carbon dioxide, water and energy*
– *comparing what it takes to produce a pair of jeans with every-day situations → putting the cost/impact of producing a pair of jeans into context*
– *most surprising piece of information for me: producing a pair of jeans requires same amount of energy as powering a computer for 556 hours*

Diagram **2**
– *total cost of a denim shirt manufactured in Bangladesh compared with one manufactured in the US: just under four dollars versus over 13 dollars → about four times cheaper to manufacture a shirt in Bangladesh*
– *biggest difference/discrepancy when you compare labour costs: a denim shirt made in Bangladesh costs just 22 cents in labour compared with almost eight dollars for a shirt made in USA*
– *it is a lot cheaper for brands to manufacture in Bangladesh than in the US*

Diagram **3**
– *countries a pair of jeans travels through in production: Korea, China, Bangladesh, the Philippines, Cambodia → no two steps in the process seem to be carried out in the same place*

b) – *fashion's impact on the environment*
– *disconnected consumerism: consumers are disconnected from production, manufacturers and supply chains. We have no idea where our clothes come from, how they are made, what happens to the people who make them.*
– *if we want our clothes to be manufactured closer to where they are sold and worn, we as consumers will have to be prepared to pay more for our clothes*

A6 **Seite 112**

Four corners: → Seite 28 hier in den *Teacher's notes.*

Lösungsvorschlag/Erwartungshorizont:

b) ***"we are looking at a slave trade"***
– *absolutely true: workers have no rights; terrible working conditions; no chance of improving their lot; their lives are worth less than the lives of their employers or the consumers who end up wearing the clothes they make; if 1,000 people died in a factory fire in the US or in Germany or the UK, new laws and regulations would be introduced immediately to make sure something like that would not happen again*
– *I think that's too harsh: as bad as sweatshops are, the alternatives are worse (prostitution, extreme poverty); sweatshops offer workers a way to improve their lives and impoverished countries a way to transform themselves into industrial economies*

"people have a preference to remain ignorant … they will make an effort not to know"
– *I agree with the first part of the sentence but not with the second: I agree that consumers prefer to remain ignorant of fast fashion's working conditions but I think once they/we know, there is no turning back*
– *I don't think people go out of their way to make sure they don't know how bad things are in the fast fashion industry; if you ask me, it's convenience more than anything else*
– *yes, I know people who don't really want to know too much about how their clothes are produced as it would take the joy out of shopping for them*
– *I have friends who will tell me how terrible they find sweatshops, only to then ask me if I would like to go shopping at the mall with them at the weekend*
– *the disconnect between the consumer and the people producing the clothes is so big that it does not cross people's minds to enquire about working conditions in the factories*

"The big brands have been able to outsource their production … They think they have outsourced responsibility"
– *yes, I agree; brands like to blame their suppliers/the manufacturers when something goes wrong; they are more interested in profits and in making money than in social responsibility*
– *this again comes down to a disconnect; there is a disconnect because the brands do not know the people who work for them; if companies knew the people working for them, if there was some sort of personal relationship, working conditions would improve in no time, I think; it is a lot easier to treat people unfairly and cruelly if you don't know them personally*

"as we consume more we're using more resources and generating unprecedented amounts of waste"
– *there is no arguing against this, I don't think anyone could argue that this is not true*
– *that's true but at the same time consuming keeps our economies going and growing; every country needs a healthy, growing economy; saving resources and cutting back on waste does not feed anyone; instead, it will cost jobs; the world economy is more important than issues like resources and waste*

Practice section

B1 Seite 113

Dauer: 3:55 min

Lösungsvorschlag/Erwartungshorizont:

a) ***subject:*** *sustainable fashion; H&M's sustainability efforts*
main idea(s): *sustainability and fashion don't need to contradict each other, you can have both*
purpose: *educate their customers about their company's sustainability policy; attract consumers for whom sustainable fashion is important; attract customers who want to enjoy fashion without feeling guilty*
addressee(s): *consumers for whom sustainability is important; customers who want to enjoy fashion without feeling guilty*

b) **3)** *H&M's efforts to make fashion that is attractive as well as produced sustainably.*

B2 Seite 114

Lösungsvorschlag/Erwartungshorizont:

a)

materials	***fashion/clothes***	***production cycle***	***addressing challenges***
recycled polyester *(organic) hemp* *(organic) cotton* *fabric*	*fashion brands* *dresses* *party wear* *embroidery* *affordable* *rich detailing*	*– suppliers* *– to increase one's profit* *– biggest user of organic cotton in the world* *– recycle PET bottles into fabric* *– produce, transport and sell*	*– sustainability report* *– code of conduct* *– visit factories* *– audits* *– have a dialogue with your suppliers* *– be active in the Better Cotton Initiative* *– work with brands, farmers, WWF and Unicef* *– educate farmers (to use less water and fewer chemicals in the cotton production)* *– increase the farmers' profits* *– improve the lives of children in the cotton-cultivating area in Tamil Nadu, India* *– improve people's access to health and nutritional care (in Tamil Nadu)* *– customers becoming more aware of sustainability issues* *– produce, transport and sell garments in a sustainable way* *– CSR: corporate social responsibility*

B3 Seite 114

Lösungsvorschlag/Erwartungshorizont:

a) ***H&M's main goals when making their products***
– sustainable
– fashionable
– affordable
– accessible to more and more people around the world

How they want to ensure that the conditions in their suppliers' factories are acceptable
– have been working with a code of conduct since 1997
– auditors visit the factories daily
– a very close dialogue with their suppliers in order to implement improvements

What role does the environment play in their business?
– H&M is the biggest user of organic cotton in the world
– H&M is very active in the Better Cotton Initiative
– they educate farmers to use less water and fewer chemicals in the cotton production

What is special about their new collection?
– party wear: made from organic cotton and organic hemp and recycled polyester
– beautiful party dresses with lots of detailing
– dresses from the collection have been worn by celebrities on the red carpet

How H&M tries to improve the lives of the people living where the cotton …
– educate farmers to increase the farmers' profits
– five-year project with UNICEF to make sure children go to school instead of work
– improve access to health and nutritional care
How they describe their customers
*– more and more **aware** and **conscious** of the environment, social issues and sustainability*

b) *The presentation by Helena Helmersson, Head of Corporate Responsibility, and Ann-Sofie Johansson, Head of Design at H&M, deals with H&M's efforts to make fashion that is attractive as well as produced sustainably.*
One of the things that H&M have done is introduce their Conscious Collection, which is partywear made from organic hemp, organic cotton and recycled polyester.
In addition, H&M want to ensure that the conditions in their suppliers' factories are acceptable, which is why they are constantly in contact with their suppliers, and company auditors, of which there are approximately 70, visit the factories daily.
H&M are the biggest user of organic cotton in the world. They are a member of the Better Cotton Initiative and work together with other brands, farmers, WWF and Unicef.
Furthermore, it is one of H&M's aims to educate farmers to use less water and fewer chemicals in the cotton production. They also hope to educate farmers to be able to increase their profits. H&M try to improve the lives of the people living where the cotton for their products is grown and harvested by making sure the children can go to school instead of having to work. This is part of a five-year project with UNICEF. Another company goal is to improve access to health and nutritional care for the people living in the cotton areas.

B4 **Seite 115**

Lösungsvorschlag/Erwartungshorizont:

a) *– even if H&M use organic cotton, they are still producing fast fashion*
– fast fashion will never be sustainable, no matter what you do; ethical fast fashion is a contradiction in itself; fast fashion is the root of the problem, so it can't ever be part of the solution
– if H&M were serious about sustainability, they would improve the quality of their garments to make sure they last longer; they would ask their customers to buy fewer clothes
– H&M's business model is nothing but a PR attempt to attract new customers

b) *– H&M's prices are too low to be sustainable; low prices will always tempt consumers to part with their money; so if H&M were serious about sustainability, they would increase their prices*
– H&M don't have any factories of their own but instead work with suppliers they have no control over → lack of transparency in supply chains

c) ***Newman's message:** Fast fashion is bad. Don't give in to the temptation of low prices.*
aim of Maddie Newman's blog:
– discourage readers/consumers from buying fast fashion/giving in to fast fashion's seductively low prices/shopping at the new H&M store in Melbourne/shopping at H&M in general
– comes across as wanting to offend; she would probably argue that you need to provoke and offend people if you want to change people's behaviour

B5 **Seite 117**

Lösungsvorschlag/Erwartungshorizont:

b)

example/quotation	*effect*	*function*
"wallet-friendly clothes" (ll. 16–17)	***euphemism for "cheap", which has negative connotations (e.g. poor quality); "wallet-friendly" is more sophisticated and less negative/aggressive than "cheap"***	***Newman wants to come across as considered and conciliatory***
"fast fashion empires" (l. 22)	***"empires" implies a form of hierarchy; someone superior ruling over normal people***	*describes both the size of the companies and their business style*
"Stefan Persson is making mad bank (est. $32.8 billion)" (ll. 24–25)	***show readers that at the end of the day it is all about money***	***make readers jealous of H&M's profit and start criticizing H&M for it***

"rapid-fire supply chain" (l. 34)	*"supply chain" is put into an almost militaristic context and gets a negative connotation*	***demonise fast fashion and fast fashion companies***
"squeeze[s] margin" (l. 34)	***"squeezes" has negative connotations, it implies that things are very tight and uncomfortable for somebody***	***describe H&M's business model and its implications for H&M garment workers***

c)+d)

example/quotation	*effect*	*function*
"mindless consumerism" (ll. 14–15)	*many people/consumers will object to being called "mindless"; consumerism with no concern for the consequences*	*criticize consumers for their behaviour*
"a lovely little euphemism" (l. 18)	*lovely little: alliteration; irony*	*show how two-faced the fast fashion industry is*
"were chomping at the bit" (ll. 3–4)	*evokes the picture of a wild, excited animal (like a horse desperate to start moving)*	*criticize consumers (and media people)*
"H&M is not all evil." (l. 60)	*"not all" pretends to soften the blow/criticism*	*criticise H&M; appeal to readers on an emotional level; protect Newman against criticism that she is demonising H&M*
"evil" (l. 60)	*"evil" is a very negative word*	*appeal to readers on an emotional level; make this about more than just money; making it into something immoral*
"achievements are dwarfed" (ll. 67–68)	*metaphor; evokes mental image of opposites (dwarf vs. giant)*	*criticise/ridicule H&M's whitewashing of facts*
"please take a moment to think about" (l. 95)	*"please" is very polite, asking for a favour*	*end blog entry on a conciliatory note (after some of what came before was provocative and harsh)*

e) – *harsh, emotional, emotive, provocative, manipulative*
- *I think the text will only appeal to readers who are already critical of the fast fashion industry*
- *as far as I am concerned, Newman does nothing to win over unbiased readers: her criticism is too harsh ("not all evil") and emotional ("chomping at the bit") to win over considered people*
- *many people/consumers will object to being called "mindless" (l. 14)*
- *many people shop at H&M because they can't afford to shop anywhere else, and they do not buy lots but a normal, sensible amount of clothes*
- *people will argue that, of course, they care about the environmental and human costs but that there is so little information available that it is difficult to tell the good guys from the bad guys*

B6 **Seite 118**

Lösungsvorschlag/Erwartungshorizont:
- *I am sure that you mean well but I do not see how your blog entry is doing your cause any favour*
- *I feel put off by the tone of your blog entry. I do not like it when people try and demonise others in order to get their point across; so I am finding myself defending H&M although I do in fact share your fast fashion criticism*
- *you seem to ignore the fact that there are plenty of people out there who shop at H&M out of necessity, that is because they cannot afford anything more expensive; so they might go there to "buy cheap" (ll. 15–16) but not necessarily to "buy lots" (l. 16)*
- *I agree with you that fast fashion is worrying but I do not see how you will change people's minds by demonising H&M; you will always encounter resistance if you criticise others too harshly*

Getting to the point

C1 Seite 119

Lösungsvorschlag/Erwartungshorizont:
The responsible consumer
*... **is aware of** where his or her clothes are produced.*
*... **does not** buy from chains like H&M, Zara, Primark and Topshop.*
*... **is considerate of** the environmental and human costs of fashion.*
*... **buys** quality clothes from independent shops and small brands.*
*... **wears** clothes that are sourced or produced as locally as possible.*
*... **tries to** reduce/limit his or her carbon footprint.*

C2 Seite 119

Lösung:
A–10 *resources*
B–2 *chain*
C–4 *turnover*
D–5 *shipment*
E–7 *mark-up*
F–6 *merchandise*
G–8 *high-end designers*
H–3 *bargain shopping*
I–1 *thrift store*
J–9 *low-wage countries*
K–11 *manufacturing centres*

C3 Seite 119

Dauer: 5:54 min

Lösungsvorschlag/Erwartungshorizont:
– ***how Elizabeth Cline used to shop:*** *used to shop at thrift stores*
– ***how that has changed:*** *started shopping at fast fashion chains like Forever 21 and H&M*
– ***consequences for her as well as for others:*** *virtually impossible to walk out empty-handed from places like Forever 21 and H&M because the products are "very, very cheap" and the design is "pretty attractive" / shopping "casually and continually" / amassing items of clothing, some of which you never wear / chains constantly turning over merchandise, introducing ever-trendier clothing and feeding their customers' desire for novelty / relentless focus on speed: end of the two-season fashion calendar, even for high-end designers / creativity has become "a constant challenge" for fashion brands / customers expecting a constant stream of new fashions / manufacturing in low-wage countries / fast fashion has brought a level of style to the masses but at a price: poor quality, cheap, synthetic materials / poor quality has turned the term 'fast fashion' into a pejorative, so much so that chains like H&M now reject the term / growing public consensus that mass production of so much cheap clothing is an enormous waste of resources like fuel and water / days when fashion gets faster and cheaper every year are probably coming to an end*

C4 Seite 119

Lösungsvorschlag/Erwartungshorizont:
– *easygoing, laid-back and relaxed, conversational style, as though he was having a chat with you (l. 21: "when we're, say); not strict, in no way condescending or provocative*
– *ll. 18–22: "Let's face it, while most of us [...], the majority of us don't consider the problem when [...]" → not arguing from a position of criticizing but from a position of understanding; includes himself; accepts that we're only human and we all make mistakes → not expecting his readers to be super-human and disciplined at all times → much more likely to make someone rethink their behaviour if you accept and acknowledge that none of us are perfect; not lecturing his readers but suggesting baby steps of change*
– *ll. 35–39: "Even if you're not recycling or upcycling every item or even one in several items that come through your house, taking a moment to consider what could be done with an object before tossing it out can make a difference." → does not expect much from his readers, no unrealistic expectations, thereby probably appealing to a fair number of readers to give it a try; most readers don't take well to know-alls who come across as perfect and demanding major changes → most people don't take well to the idea of change*
– *"we", "our" → message: we're in this together, I'm as guilty of consumerism as we all are*
– *ll. 23–33: statistics to support his argument that upcycling is worth a try*
– *ll. 59–62: "we need to do what we can to encourage the process and drive others [...]. [...] the best way to get there is to lead by example." → appeals to the good in people; united together*

C5 Seite 120

Lösungsvorschlag/Erwartungshorizont:

- **No,** *I don't see "upcycling" as a real alternative to so-called "fast fashion". In order to use clothes for "upcycling", they have to be good quality. However, most fast fashion garments will have fallen apart at the seams before you have had time to upcycle them.*
- *In addition, if we decided to do away with fast fashion, there would be no need for upcycling.*
- *On the one hand, I see upcycling as a nice idea but it does not really address what is at the root of the problem: that we consume more than we really need. If each and every one of us managed to restrict ourselves to what we really need, we would not feel attracted to fast fashion and there would be no need for upcycling. We would use everything up and would only then throw it away and replace it, without having to feel bad about generating more and more waste all the time.*
- *I might go as far as to say that upcycling helps to soften the devastating effect that fast fashion has had and continues to have on the environment but that is it. It does not achieve more than a softening of the effect.*
- *In my opinion, upcycling will appeal to responsible consumers but they are not really the ones who buy fast fashion in large quantities anyway. I am not saying that they never buy fast fashion but not on a regular basis.*

Mediation

D1 Seite 121

Lösungsvorschlag/Erwartungshorizont:

a) *opening of Primark store in Cologne in May 2014*

b) *a report for my employers*

c) – ***the new shop itself:*** *four levels, more than 8,000 square metres, 5,000 items of fashion for women, men and children; staff of 800, 100 of them full-time; twelfth Primark store in Germany; changing rooms include 80 cabins, plus one big room with full-size mirrors to enable customers to discuss and go over each other's outfits*
- ***its importance for the Primark strategy in Germany:*** *very important; one of the leading Primark stores in Germany; total of twelve Primark stores in Germany*
- ***motivation of consumers:*** *low prices*
- ***reaction of consumers:*** *mainly young and female; started queueing at six o'clock in the morning; their pocket money pays for a number of items*

d) *Primark's 8,000-square metre, four-level store in Cologne opened in May 2014.*
The Cologne store is one of the leading Primark stores in Germany. There are a total of twelve.
The store houses 5,000 items of fashion at low prices for women, men and children.
The number of staff at the store is 800, 100 of them full-time.
Not only are there changing rooms with a total of 80 cabins, there is also a big room with full-size mirrors, which allows friends to discuss and comment on each other's outfits.
The store attracts consumers who are on the lookout for low prices. At Primark you can easily put together a whole outfit for under 30 euros.
The opening of the Cologne store was very popular. The predominantly young and female customers started queueing hours before the store opened and there was a long queue outside by the time the store opened at ten o'clock.

Theme 1 Reading and writing (→ Kopiervorlage Seite 109)

1. Comprehension

- *in the current economic climate it is difficult for university graduates to find a job; taking a gap year will increase your chances of finding a good job*
- *however, the emphasis is on "constructive" (l. 11) gap years; the author is not talking about gap years that are mostly about travelling and volunteering*
- *"constructive" gap year: an activity/employment that shows your focus and your dedication; a possible synonym for the author's understanding of "constructive gap year" would be "work experience"*
- *a gap year can help you find out what it is you want to do with your life, i.e. it makes you more focused, which will pay off later in life*
- *a gap year can help you show what it is you are interested in, i.e. show future employers your character, your personality and your goals → a gap year can help you find a good job*
- *a gap year can help you get into university; good grades will always be more important than any gap year experience but with university candidates with similar grades, your gap year experience might well make the difference*
- *a gap year looks good on your CV because it will make you stand out from others; again, this is not about any gap year but about a "constructive" one*
- *a gap year gives you the opportunity to try out various activities/jobs, so might save you time in the long run*

Der Schüler/Die Schülerin ...
fasst in einer Einleitung die Hauptaussage des Zeitungsartikels zusammen
nennt die Argumente, die der Autor für ein *gap year* anführt: – gerade in wirtschaftlich schlechten Zeiten ist ein *gap year* eine attraktive Option (Zeile 8–9) – erhöht die Chancen, an der Wunschuniversität angenommen zu werden: gute Noten sind nach wie vor wichtiger als Lebens- und/oder Berufserfahrung, aber bei gleich guten Noten können einschlägige Vorerfahrungen den Ausschlag geben (Zeile 18–22) – erhöht die Chancen auf dem Arbeitsmarkt: vermittelt potentiellen Arbeitgebern, dass man weiß, was man will; hebt einen von durchschnittlichen Standard-mitbewerbern ab (Zeile 38–39) – bietet die Möglichkeit, sich besser kennenzulernen, festzustellen oder bestätigt zu finden, was die eigenen Ziele sind, neue Fähigkeiten zu entwickeln und Arbeiten auszuprobieren → all das macht einen sowohl für Universitäten als auch für spätere Arbeitgeber interessant und attraktiv
erkennt, dass es dem Autor nicht um klassische *gap years* geht, bei denen es vorwiegend um Reisen und Freiwilligendienst geht, sondern um *gap years* mehr in Richtung Berufspraktikum *(constructive gap years)* (Zeile 10–15)
schließt mit einer Zusammenfassung

2. Analysis

- *characteristics of both an **argumentative article** and an **evaluative article***
- ***strong adjectives:** "nasty" (l. 1); "bland" (l. 39); "robotic" (l. 44) → emphasis; adjectives are directed in particular at people not taking a gap year*
- ***humour/irony/ridicule:** "Bank of Mum and Dad" (l. 4); "the yellow brick road to university" (l. 5) → to lighten up the article; make it more readable*
- ***informal/colloquial language:** short forms (ll. 10, 11, 23, 48); "Bank of Mum and Dad" (l. 4); "the yellow brick road to university" (l. 5); "jump out from" (l. 38)*
- ***ellipsis:** "And quite rightly so." (l. 7); "Far from it." (ll. 10–11) → ties in with the general tone of the article, i.e. informal*
- ***parallelism:** "demonstrate focus, showcase their abilities, and discover a life path" (ll. 12–14) → emphasis*
- ***awakening human interest:** "Sitting in a bath of cat food to raise money for a six-month placement shadowing a vet on a lion project in Kenya, or a 10,000-mile adventure in a pink tuk-tuk raising funds for charity" (ll. 33–37)*
- ***metaphor:** "robotic exam-factory clones" (ll. 44–45); "life path" (ll. 14, 44, 47–48) → creates an image in the reader's mind and makes the description more powerful*

- ***rhetorical question:*** *"What marine biology course wouldn't choose a candidate fresh from a year on a Malaysian reef project over an identical student unable to show even a basic interest?" (ll. 22–26)*
- ***quoting experts:*** *"two of the thousands I see each year" (ll. 37–38) → emphasis, as the author of the article is the founder of gapyear.com; to prove his point*
- ***alliteration:*** *"facts are facing the class" (l. 1)*
- ***facts vs. opinions:*** *article is more strongly geared towards being argumentative or even manipulative, i.e. pushing the author's viewpoint/agenda that young people will find it harder to be successful if they don't take a constructive gap year*
  important to note who the writer is: Tom Griffiths, the founder of gapyear.com; his agenda is to get people to sign up for gap years by writing about the advantages, so it is no surprise that the article is heavily biased

Der Schüler/Die Schülerin ...
führt mit einer Einleitung zur Textanalyse hin
erkennt einige der im Artikel verwendeten Stilmittel, belegt sie am Text und benennt, zumindest teilweise, die beabsichtigte Wirkung auf den Leser, z. B.: – Sprachregister: informell *(short forms, humour/irony, informal/colloquial language)* – *strong adjectives,* um diejenigen zu kritisieren/beschreiben, die sich gegen ein *gap year* entscheiden: *"bland"* (Zeile 39) und *"robotic"* (Zeile 44) – *humour/irony/ridicule: "Bank of Mum and Dad"* (Zeile 4), *"the yellow brick road to university"* (Zeile 5) – *informal/colloquial language: "Bank of Mum and Dad"* (Zeile 4), *"the yellow brick road to university"* (Zeile 5), *"jump out from"* (Zeile 38) – *ellipsis: "And quite rightly so."* (Zeile 7), *"Far from it."* (Zeile 10–11) – *parallelism: "demonstrate focus, showcase their abilities, and discover a life path"* (Zeile 12–14) – *awakening human interest: "Sitting in a bath of cat food to raise money for a six-month placement shadowing a vet on a lion project in Kenya, or a 10,000-mile adventure in a pink tuk-tuk raising funds for charity"* (Zeile 33–37) – *metaphor: "robotic exam-factory clones"* (Zeile 44–45), *"life path"* (Zeile 14, 44, 47–48) – *rhetorical question: "What marine biology course wouldn't choose a candidate fresh from a year on a Malaysian reef project over an identical student unable to show even a basic interest?"* (Zeile 22–26) – *quoting experts: "two of the thousands I see each year"* (Zeile 37–38) → führt seine persönliche Erfahrung als Beweis an; stark persönlich gefärbter Artikel, subjektiv; entspricht weitestgehend der Textsorte *comment*
schließt mit einer Zusammenfassung der wichtigsten Erkenntnisse

3. Comment

Sir or Madam,

I am writing to you in response to your article "Constructive gap years help students stand out to employers and universities" from 17 August.

I absolutely agree with Tom Griffiths's view that a gap year is a fabulous opportunity to increase your chances of both landing a good job after university but also landing a place at the university of your choice.

It has now been more than eight years since I took my gap year, and I am currently working as an admissions tutor at a university in the north of England. I am convinced that my gap-year experience was valuable work and life experience. During my gap year I had to deal with many different people, with different and sometimes difficult personalities, and I had to get used to having to quickly adjust to new people and situations.

In my present position it is a bonus if you are flexible and have a feel for different personalities and are able to possibly recognize people's hidden agendas, e.g. whether they have applied for a place at our university because they are truly committed to the given course or whether they are, in fact, still trying to figure out what it is they want to do with their lives.

I will admit that because of my own gap year experience I am biased when it comes to applications by young people who have previously taken a gap year. I just find that there is a certain seriousness to those applicants as compared to applicants who have applied coming straight from school.

To everyone in their last year at school reading this: do it! Think about what it is you want to do with your life and then find a gap year experience that fits in with that. Not only will you have the time of your life but also you will benefit from it in years to come, both emotionally and financially.
Deirdre Vincent
Salford, England

Sir or Madam,
I am writing to you in response to your article "Constructive gap years help students stand out to employers and universities" from 17 August.
I agree that gap years are a great opportunity for young people nowadays but I totally disagree that they are the only way for young people to find their place in the world, both emotionally and financially.
I presume you would not really expect Tom Griffiths, the founder of gapyear.com, to write an article discouraging young people from taking a gap year. But I was surprised that he was focusing so much on career, ambition and achievement.
In my opinion, young people should not worry so much about what some potential employer thinks or does not think. Maybe not everyone at the age of 18 knows exactly how their career is going to pan out. And there is nothing wrong with that. Some of the happiest, and also most interesting and most successful, people I know did not know what they wanted to do with their lives when they were 18. There are too many "robotic clones" who just take decisions based on career moves out there already. We do not need any more of them.
I would encourage any young person to take a gap year if they so wish. But their decision should be based on their present, not on their potential professional future.
Patrick Charman
Brighton, England

Der Schüler/Die Schülerin ...
macht mit einem einleitenden Satz die eigene Meinung deutlich: – die Hauptaussagen des Zeitungsartikels unterstützend – oder ihnen widersprechend
führt mindestens zwei Argumente an und aus, um die eigene Meinung zu untermauern
strukturiert die Argumente
nimmt Bezug auf mindestens einen in dem Zeitungsartikel genannten Aspekt, allerdings nicht nur den Aspekt wiedergebend, sondern darüber hinausgehend
schließt mit einer pointierten Zusammenfassung oder Aufforderung
beachtet die Merkmale der Textsorte *letter to the editor:* Anrede *Sir or Madam,* eindeutiger Bezug (Überschrift, Erscheinungsdatum und ggf. Autor des Artikels), keine Textzitate sowie Abschluss mit Name und Wohnort

Theme 1 Listening – version A (→ Kopiervorlage Seite 110)

DVD

1. a. *how to make the most of your gap year in Australia.*
   b. *much easier if you use the Internet and join forces with other gappers.*
   c. *allows you to travel and look for a job all over Australia.*
2. *Working in telesales is a common job for gappers.*
   If you are afraid you might not find a job, you can contact companies in the UK that help you ...
   If you are willing to meet and talk to people, you will have no problems making friends ...
   In order to prepare for your gap year, it's a good idea to read gappers' blogs.
   There are a number of companies specializing in assisting gap-year travellers with anything ...

Theme 1 Listening – version B (→ Kopiervorlage Seite 111)

DVD

1. a. *what you can do to have the best possible gap year in Australia.*
   b. *is less difficult for gappers who use the Internet and join forces with gappers they have ...*
   c. *gives you the right to go anywhere in Australia and look for a job.*
2. a. *true* b. *true* c. *false* d. *false* e. *true* f. *false* g. *true* h. *true* i. *false*

Theme 2 Speaking (monologue) (→ Kopiervorlage Seite 112)

A. 1. – *volunteering in wildlife rescue station in Australian outback for a year*
- *no salary, but board and lodging and pocket money*
- *costs for flight and travelling extra*

2. – *find out more about type of work (working with animals, volunteering)*
- *location (Australia, the outback)*
- *financial arrangements*
- *consider overall career plan (e.g. no gap year planned after* Abitur*)*

B. 1. – *internship at UK branch/partner company of a company you already know*
- *minimum of five weeks next summer*
- *flight and accommodation must be covered by pupil's family*

2. – *previous work experience in class 9 or 10 → was it attractive enough to consider doing a similar internship abroad?*
- *general career plan and whether the internship would tie in with that (e.g. matching the intended university course, changes in career goals since work experience at home)*
- *timing (five weeks of internship would leave just one week of summer holidays for leisure) and cost (relatively expensive, money maybe better spent on a holiday)*
- *fears and hopes connected with such a project (e.g. good for CV, afraid of language barrier)*

C. 1. – *idea of doing* duales Studium *with local company following a friend's suggestion*
- *you would be expected to spend eight months abroad (UK plus either France or Spain) and be fluent in the relevant languages; if not, you would need to attend language courses*

2. – *pupil's career perspectives (for/against* duales Studium, *subject of the degree course)*
- *possible wish to stay in one's home town and not spend time abroad*
- *fact that two foreign languages must be mastered (interest and talent for languages?)*

D. 1. – *friend's suggestion to go to Canada after* Abitur: *nine months of work and travel*
- *approximately €3,000 needed to cover expenses*
- *make list of possible jobs to do while in Canada*

2. – *idea of a work and travel programme together with a friend*
- *attractivity of Canada as a destination*
- *personal plans for the future, e.g. interest/lack of interest in gap year after* Abitur
- *cost*
- *nature of jobs he/she might have to/be willing to do*

E. 1. – *family in Manchester, friends of friends of your parents, are looking for an au-pair; two children: 3 and 4 years old*
- *you would have to look after the children*
- *you would earn only a little pocket money, but would join the family whenever they go on holiday to exotic locations, all expenses paid*

2. – *does the prospect of working as an au-pair appeal?*
- *connection via your parents' friends: advantage or disadvantage?*
- *attractivity of place (Manchester)*
- *financial arrangements (little pay, but chance of travelling to faraway places)*
- *general plans for the time after* Abitur

F. 1. – *home for orphans and disabled children in the Gambia: playing with children, helping them get dressed, putting them to bed etc.*
- *risk of malaria; however, so far very few got sick and those who did made a full recovery*

2. – *does the prospect of looking after orphans and disabled children appeal?*
- *thought of moving to Africa for several months: potential health risks like malaria*
- *general plans for the time after* Abitur

Anforderungen sprachlicher Art
1. Schüler/in stellt die Situation sprachlich treffend dar. Je eigenständiger und sprachlich unabhängiger von der Vorlage dies erfolgt, desto höher ist die Leistung einzustufen. (Allgemein dient der Aufgabenteil dazu, dass die S in die Prüfung „hineinfinden".)
2. Die persönliche Stellungnahme erfolgt strukturiert, mit Wortschatz zur Gliederung und Strukturierung (z. B. Gebrauch von *connectives*) sowie zur Meinungsäußerung. Für eine höhere Punktzahl sind sprachlich komplexere Strukturen und eine größere Bandbreite in den Äußerungen nötig (z. B. nicht beständig *I think …, In my opinion …,* sondern abwägende Äußerungen, Verwendung von Nebensätzen, Überleitungen (z. B. *Although …, I'm not convinced that …, What I don't understand is …*)).

Anforderungen inhaltlicher Art
1. Schüler/in stellt die auf der Karte umrissene Situation unter Berücksichtigung der wesentlichen Informationen treffend dar.
2. In der persönlichen Stellungnahme erfolgt eine strukturierte Auseinandersetzung mit der Situation, die die Bestandteile der Situationsbeschreibung kommentierend aufgreift und mit verschiedenen persönlichen Argumenten verknüpft und das Für und Wider der eigenen Reaktionsmöglichkeiten abwägt, ehe ein reflektiertes Fazit gezogen wird.

Theme 2 Speaking (dialogue) – job advertisements

(→ Kopiervorlagen Seite 113–117)

Interviewer
I'm glad you were able to come and see us here in person.
I hope you've had no problem finding your way here.
Please tell me a little bit more about what …
I hope coming to see us here didn't mean too much hassle for you.
You sent in a very interesting application, so …
It would be great if you could …
Coming back to …
What is your greatest weakness?
What is your greatest strength?
How would you describe yourself?
How do you handle stress and pressure?
What are your hobbies?
What motivates you?
Describe a difficult work situation and how you overcame it.
What do people most often criticize about you?

Applicant
Thank you for inviting me.
As I already pointed out in my application, …
There are basically two reasons why … First of all, … Secondly, …
It would be a great opportunity to …
I know that you are a firm that …
I don't know if it is possible, but …
I would really like to …
As I have already written in my CV, …
I hope I could be of help in that respect.
Maybe there are other skills that might be useful to you.

Anforderungen sprachlicher Art
Schüler/in übernimmt nacheinander die vorgegebenen Rollen und verhält sich sprachlich angemessen durch Gebrauch eines formalen und höflichen Registers und eines passenden thematischen Wortschatzes zum Wortfeld *jobs/job interview.*
Anforderungen inhaltlicher Art
Schüler/in berücksichtigt die Informationen zur ausgeschriebenen Stelle sowohl als Bewerber/in als auch als Vertreter/in der Personalabteilung zutreffend und ergänzt nur dort, wo die Informationen lückenhaft sind, sinnvollerweise die Vorgaben (z. B. fehlende Informationen zum Verdienst).
Als Bewerber/in achtet der Schüler/die Schülerin darauf, sich gut zu präsentieren und möglichst präzise eigene Vorzüge und Qualifikationen darzulegen und sich dabei auf die Ausschreibung zu beziehen. Außerdem lässt er/sie Interesse an der Stelle und der Firma erkennen und stellt daher selbst zielgerichtet Fragen. Je präziser der Bezug auf die Ausschreibung und die Darlegung der eigenen Voraussetzungen erfolgen, desto höher ist die Leistung zu bewerten.
Als Vertreter/in der Personalabteilung berücksichtigt der Schüler/die Schülerin die Kernaussagen der Stellenanzeige und befragt den Bewerber zielgerichtet und zeigt Interesse am Bewerber.

Theme 2 Mediation (→ Kopiervorlage Seite 118)

- *Erasmus is a European exchange program for university students.*
- *It was started in 1987.*
- *Students are given a scholarship.*
- *By 2012, when Erasmus was in its 25th year, almost three million young Europeans had taken part and had been abroad as part of the program.*
- *Erasmus is not only about studying abroad but also about meeting young people from other European countries.*
- *For German Erasmus students, Spain is the most popular country. In 2011, 30,000 students from Germany took part in the EU program, either to study abroad or to do an internship abroad. 20 per cent of them chose to go to Spain.*
- *The program is particularly popular with students of economics. (They seem to be more mobile than students of natural sciences or of engineering and technology.)*
- *If students are lucky, the courses they take while abroad will be accepted by their home universities upon their return. However, it does not always work that way. But universities all over Europe are working on a solution to this problem.*

Der Schüler/Die Schülerin ...
beachtet die Aspekte der Aufgabenstellung
gibt die im Sinne der Aufgabenstellung wichtigen Informationen präzise und situations- bzw. adressatenorientiert wieder
gliedert die Inhalte klar und logisch und löst sich, der Aufgabenstellung entsprechend, ggf. von Struktur und Reihenfolge des Ausgangstextes
beachtet die sprachlichen Erfordernisse der Aufgabenstellung
verwendet den nötigen thematischen und funktionalen Wortschatz treffend
erläutert relevante kulturspezifische Begriffe, wie z. B. „Technikwissenschaftler“
verzichtet auf wortwörtliche Übersetzungen und das Äußern der eigenen Meinung
ergänzt keine Informationen, die im Ausgangstext nicht enthalten sind

Theme 3 Reading and writing (→ Kopiervorlage Seite 119)

1. Comprehension

- *Manjit and his friend Ady are walking through a busy area/a busy part of town/Leicester that is about 90% Asian, i.e. white people are the exception*
- *Manjit feels very much at home in Leicester: he likes that it is very multicultural, i.e. some areas are predominantly white, some black, some Asian, with the city centre being a complete mix of cultures and ethnicities*
- *feels at home in England, was born there, knows how things work, would not feel at home in India*
- *neighbourhoods around Evington Road are full of contrast, which Manjit enjoys:*
  the Highfields side: rough; drugs, prostitution and gangs,
  the London Road side: well-off and posh
- *Manjit enjoys moving back and forth between rough and posh parts of town, moving back and forth between different lifestyles ("messing about in the narrow back streets" (ll. 65–66) vs. playing football or cricket on the hockey pitch or shoplifting at a supermarket)*

Der Schüler/Die Schülerin ...
umreißt in einer Einleitung den Inhalt des Romanauszugs
stellt die Situation dar: – Manjit ist mit seinem Freund Ady unterwegs – sie befinden sich in einem Stadtteil von Leicester, in dem es kaum Weiße gibt
beschreibt die Umgebung und was Manjit daran mag: – einige Stadtteile Leicesters sind überwiegend weiß, andere schwarz, wieder andere *Asian;* im Zentrum selbst gibt es keine Trennung, stattdessen schmelzen alle Kulturen zu einem großen Ganzen zusammen – Gegensätze der Stadtteile, nur durch eine Straße getrennt: auf der einen Seite Drogen, Prostitution, Banden, auf der anderen Seite vornehme Wohngegenden – Manjit wechselt gerne zwischen den verschiedenen Stadtteilen, zwischen den Gegensätzen hin und her und passt sein Verhalten entsprechend an
beschreibt Manjits Einstellung zu *multiculturalism:* – er mag den Mix aus Kulturen: so sollte die Welt aussehen, wenn es nach ihm ginge
stellt heraus, dass England Manjits Zuhause ist: – in England kennt er sich aus; weiß, wie die Dinge laufen – in Indien wäre er verloren

2. Analysis

- *first person narration: emphasizes Manjit's view of Leicester because he lets us in on how he feels about Leicester and multiculturalism in general; provides a personal, subjective view*
- ***direct, explicit** love and appreciation for his hometown Leicester*
  ll. 9–10: "It was one of the things that I loved about Leicester." → implies that there are many other things he loves about Leicester
  ll. 11–13: "everyone kind of melted into the city centre so that it was all multicultural. I liked that – it was the way it should be"
  ll. 17–23: "I was born in England. I liked being born in England. It was my home. […] In England I knew how things worked. Man, England was my country"
  ll. 33–35: "As I crossed over […], I realized why I loved this part of Leicester so much"
  ll. 60–64: "That was what I loved about living where I did. Evington Road was like a fence that I could sit on. Each day I could make a choice about whether I wanted to jump over to the Highfields side or the London Road side."
- ***metaphor:** ll. 11–13: "everyone kind of melted into the city centre so that it was all multicultural" → "melted" implies that you can no longer tell different cultures apart; they turn into something new together; dividing lines are blurred, until, finally, they disappear altogether; no hierarchy; instead, "melted" implies harmony and ease*
- *Manjit's view on multiculturalism vs. cartoon: the cartoon goes against what Manjit believes; Manjit does not expect different cultures to behave like the 'original', dominant culture; cartoon expects new, immigrant cultures to do as told by dominant culture; Manjit wants harmony, ease, melting into sth new together, blurring and disappearance of differences; cartoon advocates hierarchy (we were here first, so we can tell you what to do, we're the boss)*

Der Schüler/Die Schülerin ...
führt mit einer Einleitung zur Textanalyse hin
erkennt und benennt die Erzählperspektive: *first person narration;* Erzähler: Manjit
benennt die Vorteile der Erzählperspektive im Hinblick auf die Aufgabenstellung: Manjits direkte, explizite „Liebeserklärung" an Leicester, inkl. Textstellen/Zitate: z. B. Zeilen 9–10, 11–13, 17–23, 33–35, 60–64
erkennt und untersucht die Metapher *melted,* Manjits Wunschbild für *multiculturalism: "everyone kind of melted into the city centre so that it was all multicultural"* (Zeile 11–13) → Grenzen verwischen und verschwinden und bilden ein neues Etwas; Harmonie; Leichtigkeit; ohne Hierarchie; gleichberechtigt
umreißt die Kernaussage des Cartoons: sich tolerant nennen, ohne es tatsächlich zu sein
vergleicht Manjits Vorstellung von *multiculturalism* mit der Vorstellung im Cartoon: – für Manjit gibt es keine Hierarchie zwischen den verschiedenen Kulturen: Wunsch, dass kulturelle Grenzen verwischen und sich auflösen – im Cartoon zeigt sich eine Hierarchie: die Ursprungskultur fühlt sich überlegen, entsprechend stellt sie die Ansprüche an die zuwandernden Kulturen und erwartet, dass sie sich unterordnen (sich dabei versteckend hinter *"We're a very tolerant society, but"*)

3a. Comment

- *Yes, I think Manjit's view of multiculturalism is "the way it should be". His view sounds peaceful, quiet and happy. His view implies that there is no hierarchy between people and cultures, that we are all one, that we are all in this together. Why should the place where somebody's family originates from determine their place in the society they choose to live in?*
- *I am not sure I really agree with Manjit's view of multiculturalism: I would find it a shame if all the different cultures melted into one → I much prefer the idea of different cultures living together peacefully, accepting and respecting each other, without doing away with their unique cultural customs and traditions. I find it enlightening to get to know different cultures. It is not as though all immigrants really wanted to leave their home countries, quite a few of them were/are forced to leave their homes, because of wars, discrimination for political or other reasons (e.g. sexual orientation). So why ask them to give up their cultural background and melt into something new with other cultures? I don't see that melting is the only way for us to live together peacefully on this planet. What is wrong with living peacefully side by side, with respect for the other, but a deep love and attachment to your own cultures and traditions? I think it would be a shame if our backgrounds melted away and became unrecognisable.*
- *Manjit's view of multiculturalism strikes me as wishful thinking; there are still too many people who, however openly, would much rather agree with the cartoon than with Manjit*
- *As far as the cartoon is concerned, I hate people starting their sentences with "I'm very tolerant but ...". Personally, I find it easier to deal with people who will openly say what they think, without safeguarding themselves against criticism. I would prefer people to openly say that they think the 'original' culture should be able to determine the rules for integration and immigration, rather than for them to hide behind sentences like "We're a very tolerant society, but". Introducing your ideas with a sentence like that reveals you to be a hypocrite and bigot.*
- *Fact is that deep down we all know that telling someone to "go back to where you bloody came from" goes against everything that we as humankind stand for. I strongly believe that humans are basically good and kind. We all want to be perceived as good and kind, which is why so many people like to hide behind introductory sentences like "I'm very tolerant but ...".*

Der Schüler/Die Schülerin ...
formuliert eine auf das Thema hinführende Einleitung
formuliert deutlich die eigene Sicht der Dinge
führt mindestens zwei Argumente an und aus, um die eigene Meinung zu untermauern
strukturiert die Argumente
bezieht sich auf Manjits im Text angelegte Vorstellung von *multiculturalism* sowie auf die Aussage des Cartoons
rundet seinen/ihren *comment* mit einem Schluss ab

3b. Re-creation of text

I walked on up the road. The whole area was about ninety per cent Asian. I knew that Manjit often came here with his friend. Ady, this English friend of his. Not a good influence. I knew it the minute I lay eyes on him. Wanted to turn Manjit into some English boy. Made him forget his roots. Made him read English books. Made him think he was something better than us, his family: his brothers, his father. Just because of his clever books and his grades at school. If he could change the colour of his skin, he would do that, too. Ashamed of his roots and his culture.
Manjit called England home. He was born in England, so that's his home, he would say. How dare he. Show some respect for your forefathers, son. If it wasn't for them, you wouldn't be here. This was not home for me. Who was Manjit fooling? The English certainly never made me feel at home here. Most of them would like to send us back to where we'd come from. I would never feel at home in a place where people accused me of taking their jobs away.
I passed by a pizza takeaway that included tandoori chicken, keema, and mutter paneer in its list of toppings – a clever thing to do in a mainly Asian neighbourhood, even though most of the shop's customers were white students. We Asians didn't eat pizza. And we certainly weren't going to eat tandoori chicken cooked up by some white Englishmen.
My home was India. And it would always stay that way. There was nothing wrong with that. Why mix? I don't want to mix with white English people. They don't know anything about me and my people. They don't want to mix with us, either. Keep us in our ghettos. Well, fine with us. Just you stay where you are.
I wasn't happy with the way things were changing around here. Years ago, all the shops were owned by Asians. But now there were white shopowners everywhere: a fish restaurant, a couple of hairdressers and a florist. Give it a few more years, and there wouldn't be anything but white shopowners around here. Driving us away. Because we weren't good enough for them.
I knew that Manjit saw it differently. Of course he did. All this talk of us as one, cultures melting into one. Respect your roots, is what I say. Respect your elders. You come home tonight, and I'll beat some sense into you.

Der Schüler/Die Schülerin ...
schreibt als *first-person narrator* als Manjits Vater
vermittelt einen Einblick in das kulturelle Denken von Manjits Vater: Abgrenzung von England und *the whole Western culture thing* (TB, *line 35f.*)
berücksichtigt die im Romanauszug im Schülerheft (TB Seite 50f.) angelegte Charakterisierung von Manjits Vater: – unversöhnlich, aggressiv, unnachgiebig – *got angry all the time* (TB, *line 4*) – *working-class Punjabi* (TB, *line 85*) – Abgrenzung von England und *the whole Western culture thing* (TB, *line 35f.*) sowie das schlechte Verhältnis zwischen Manjit und seinem Vater: – [*Manjit's father*] *definitely didn't like the fact that Manjit's best friend wasn't Asian* (TB, *line 37f.*) – *thought that school was a waste of time* (TB, *line 84*) – Manjits Vater schlägt Manjit regelmäßig (TB, *lines 15–21, 25–26, 38, 80–81*)
knüpft mindestens zweimal an Textstellen aus der Vorlage (Romanauszug) an, um einen Zusammenhang zwischen Ausgangstext und Aufgabenstellung herzustellen
beachtet die durch die Textsorte vorgegebene Sprachebene mit informellem Charakter, Kurzformen und ggf. umgangssprachlichen Wendungen

Theme 4 Reading and writing (→ Kopiervorlage Seite 120)

1. Comprehension

- *author Bill Thompson argues that children should not be allowed to use Internet chat rooms/ should not be allowed access to Internet chat rooms*
- *there have been too many worrying cases of children meeting up with people they met online, with negative consequences*
- *many people argue that cases like these are not the Internet's fault but the parents' fault who do not pay close enough attention to what their children get up to online*
- *these same people argue that there are more advantages to the Internet than disadvantages*
- *the author is not arguing that children should be banned from using the Internet altogether; he is aware that in today's world being online is part of growing up, and he agrees that there are many advantages for children to be online*
- *however, according to the author, it is not e-mails that are the problem but chat rooms: there are too many adult men in chat rooms whose intention it is to meet and potentially (sexually) abuse children*
- *Internet chat rooms are OK for children if both they and their parents know the people they are chatting with, i.e. if they have been approved by the child's contact list and by the parents*
- *public chat rooms, i.e. chatting with strangers, should be strictly forbidden for children*
- *society's responsibility to protect children from the risks and potential dangers of the Internet*

Der Schüler/Die Schülerin ...
fasst in einer knappen Einleitung die Hauptaussage des Artikels zusammen: – Kindern sollte der Zugang zu Internet-Chatrooms verweigert werden
benennt die zentralen Aspekte des Artikels ganz oder zum überwiegenden Teil: – zu viele Fälle mit unschönem Ausgang, in denen Kinder im realen Leben Leute trafen, die sie im Internet kennengelernt hatten – Befürworter des Internets führen als Gegenargument immer wieder an, dass nicht das Internet schuld ist, sondern die Nutzer bzw. die Eltern der Kinder – es ist für Eltern unmöglich, jede Aktion ihrer Kinder im Internet zu kontrollieren – Internetnutzung ist eine unumstößliche Tatsache im Leben heutiger Kinder und Jugendlicher und hat auch viele Vorteile – das größte Problem stellen Chats und Chatrooms im Internet dar – Eltern/Gesellschaft sind verpflichtet, Kinder vor den Risiken des Internets zu schützen
erkennt, dass der Autor nicht grundsätzlich gegen die Internetnutzung durch Kinder ist: – Problem sind nicht E-Mails und geschützte Chatrooms, sondern öffentliche Chatrooms – Chatrooms, in denen die Kinder mit Freunden/Leuten chatten, die sie und ihre Eltern kennen, sind völlig in Ordnung – in öffentlichen Chatrooms, in denen keine Alters- und Personenkontrolle erfolgt, sollte Kindern der Zutritt verweigert werden, denn es ist unumstritten, dass sich in solchen Chatrooms viele Pädophile aufhalten, auf der Suche nach dem nächsten Opfer
schließt mit einer Zusammenfassung und/oder Schlussfolgerung

2. Analysis

a. – ***the author's point of view:*** *children should be kept out of chat rooms*
- ***facts vs. opinions:*** *opinion presented in a matter-of-fact way*
- ***point of view is presented openly and directly:*** *"Ban teens from chat rooms" (headline), "I don't propose to do this." (l. 16), "Shevaun's disappearance was the net's fault and we have to accept this." (ll. 17–18), "The only answer is to keep kids out of these spaces" (ll. 63–64)*
- ***tone is predominantly matter-of-fact:*** *"I don't propose to do this." (l. 16), "we have to accept this" (l. 18), "Certainly, parents need to be aware [...]" (l. 20), "a new understanding is required" (ll. 33–34)*
- ***tone is ironic in parts:*** *"It was, it seems, the Internet's fault." (l. 1), "Young and foolish, 12-year-old Shevaun Pennington" (ll. 1–2)*
- ***formal language:*** *"leap to the net's defence" (l. 11), "parental ignorance" (l. 12), "benefits which far outweigh any risks it may pose" (ll. 13–14), "I don't propose to do this." (l. 16), "We can restrict their access" (l. 23), "strike up conversation" (l. 60)*
- ***informal language:*** *short forms (ll. 16, 55)*

- ***listing possible counter-arguments:*** *"It is traditional for those of us who have been online for many years to leap to the net's defence [...], arguing that [...]" (ll. 10–12), "Certainly, parents need to be aware of what their children are doing online, but [...]" (ll. 20–21), "We can restrict their access, or install safety software, but [...]" (ll. 23–24), "Monitoring every e-mail, sitting in on every chat and checking web access logs is not the way" (ll. 27–28) → makes the article more convincing; you are more likely to win someone over if you don't just present your arguments, but also address possible counter-arguments*
- ***balancing arguments:*** *"While there are significant benefits [...], the balance between these benefits and the dangers needs to be [...]." (ll. 30–33) → ditto*
- ***quoting experts, i.e. technology analyst Bill Thompson*** *→ author of the article is described as a "technology analyst", which is supposed to give extra weight to his opinion / "as far back as February I argued that [...] " (ll. 38–39)*
- ***triad/parallelism:*** *"Monitoring every e-mail, sitting in on every chat and checking web access logs" (ll. 27–28)*
- ***facts to back up the arguments:*** *case of 12-year-old Shevaun Pennington (ll. 2–4, 44) / "my 12-year-old daughter has started chatting to her friends online" (ll. 47–48, ll. 50–55) → mentioning his 12-year-old daughter helps to make him a credible expert on the topic of children*
- ***alliteration:*** *"always alert" (l. 22), "benefits to being online" (ll. 30–31), "balance between these benefits [...]" (l. 32), "change the way we let children [...]" (ll. 36–37), "prevalence of predatory adult males" (ll. 39–40), "keep kids out" (l. 63), "persuade us to expose" (l. 68) → helps to make the text flow and read well*

Der Schüler/Die Schülerin ...
führt mit einer Einleitung zur Textanalyse hin
formuliert die Meinung des Autors: kein Zugang zu Internet-Chatrooms für Kinder
erkennt einige der im Artikel verwendeten Stilmittel, belegt sie am Text und benennt, zumindest teilweise, die beabsichtigte Wirkung auf den Leser, z. B.: – *facts vs. opinions: opinions* überwiegen; aber sachlich formuliert – *point of view is presented openly and directly:* Überschrift, Zeile 16, 17–18, 63–64 – *tone* vorwiegend *matter-of-fact* (Zeile 16, 18, 20, 33–34), zum Teil *ironic* (Zeile 1–2) – vorwiegend *formal* (Zeile 11–16, 23, 60), zum Teil *informal* (*short forms,* Zeile 16, 55) – berücksichtigt mögliche Gegenargumente: Zeile 10–12, 20–21, 23–24, 27–28 – wägt Argumente ab: Zeile 30–33 – Expertenmeinung: der Autor ist, wie es im Untertitel heißt, *technology analyst* – *triad/parallelism: "Monitoring every e-mail, sitting in on every chat and checking web access logs"* (Zeile 27–28) – Fakten, um die eigene Meinung zu stützen und zu untermauern: Zeile 2–4, 44 / *"my 12-year-old daughter has started chatting to her friends online"* (Zeile 47–48, 50–55) → erwähnt seine Tochter, um seine Glaubwürdigkeit zu erhöhen – *alliteration,* dient der Lesbarkeit und dem Lesefluss: *"always alert"* (Zeile 22), *"benefits to being online"* (Zeile 30–31), *"balance between these benefits [...]"* (Zeile 32), *"change the way we let children [...]"* (Zeile 36–37), *"prevalence of predatory adult males"* (Zeile 39–40), *"keep kids out"* (Zeile 63), *"persuade us to expose"* (Zeile 68)
schließt mit einer Zusammenfassung der wichtigsten Erkenntnisse

b. – ***visual elements:*** *cartoon is in black and white / the father is depicted as stupid, infantile and naive: bulging eyes, playing with his fingers / girl with her arms folded → not impressed; not taking her father seriously; hearing him out; quietly amused / parent-child roles reversed*
- ***text elements:*** *caption/punch line presented as direct speech by the father / "Daddy's" → talking about himself in third person: baby talk, i.e. the way you talk to really young children; he treats his daughter as though she were a baby who doesn't know anything about the real world, i.e. about staying safe on the Internet / "switchy thingy" → doesn't really know what he is talking about*
- ***what makes the cartoon humorous:*** *father is talking to daughter as though he knew what he was talking about; does not want to admit that he doesn't have a clue / in fact, chances are that the daughter could teach her father a thing or two about the Internet/computers*

- ***cartoonist's message:*** *children know a lot more about computers than their parents think they do and than the parents themselves do / it's naive for parents to think they can or need to teach their children about the Internet / it's time for parents to catch up with their children, i.e. to accept the Internet and computers as a part of their lives*

Der Schüler/Die Schülerin ...
umreißt in einer Einleitung die Kernaussage des Cartoons
beschreibt den Cartoon: – visuelle Elemente: Körpersprache von Vater und Tochter – sprachliche Elemente, insbesondere *"Daddy"* und *"switchy thingy"*
analysiert, wie die Intention des Cartoons mithilfe der visuellen und sprachlichen Elemente transportiert wird, etwa: – visuelle Elemente: vertauschte Rollen (Kind steht, Vater sitzt; Kind mit verschränkten Armen, abwartend, weiß Bescheid; Vater unsicher/infantil) – sprachliche Elemente: unterstützt die visuelle Aussage des Cartoons; Vater ist unsicher, hält seine Tochter für ein kleines Kind, das keine Ahnung hat; in Wirklichkeit ist es genau andersherum
erkennt und beschreibt, was den Cartoon lustig macht: – vertauschte Rollen, allerdings ohne dass sich der Vater dessen bewusst ist
schließt mit einer Zusammenfassung der Erkenntnisse

3. **Comment**
   - *both the article and the cartoon are biased*
   - *the article argues that it is parents' or society's responsibility to protect their children from the risks and potential dangers of the Internet; according to the article, it is asking too much that children themselves should know and understand about the dangers and risks of the Internet*
   - *the cartoon suggests quite the opposite: that parents don't know enough about the Internet/ about staying safe on the Internet to teach their children; parents are naive to think that just because they are adults, they know more than their children do; in fact, most parents don't even know how to start a computer*
   - *whereas the article argues that parents know more and know better than their children, the cartoon argues the exact opposite, i.e. that most parents have no idea about what is happening online, that their children know a lot more about modern technology than they do*
   - *in my opinion, the father in the cartoon represents a typical parent; I agree with the cartoonist that in most families it is the children who know more about computers than their parents; it's certainly true for our family*
   - *I would think that technology analyst Bill Thompson's family is the exception to the rule: it is his job to know more about computers and online safety than most other people, so the Thompson family will be one of the few cases where the children can learn from their parents, as far as being online is concerned*

Der Schüler/Die Schülerin ...
formuliert eine in das Thema einführende Einleitung
fasst zunächst knapp und getrennt voneinander die Kernaussagen des Artikels und des Cartoons zusammen
vergleicht die Kernaussagen von Artikel und Cartoon miteinander
erkennt, dass die beiden Textsorten gegensätzliche Meinungen desselben Themas darstellen: – Artikel: Eltern wissen besser Bescheid über das Internet als ihre Kinder und sind daher verpflichtet, die entsprechenden Vorsichtsmaßnahmen zu ergreifen – Cartoon: Eltern hinken den technologischen Entwicklungen hinterher; ihre Kinder sind ihnen weit überlegen, daher ist es als Eltern naiv zu meinen, man kann die Kinder belehren
rundet seinen/ihren *comment* mit einem Schluss ab

Theme 5 Viewing, reading and writing (→ Kopiervorlage Seite 121)

DVD

1. Comprehension

(Es empfiehlt sich, den S das Wort für „Seilbahn" vorzugeben: *zip-line*)

The scene starts with Mark and his team enjoying life in their house in California. They're in their garden, having fun in the pool, using a zip-line to dive into the water. Mark is filming the others when the chimney they have fastened the zip-line to suddenly collapses. No-one is hurt.

The door bell rings and when Mark goes to open, he's surprised to see Sean Parker and his girlfriend outside. Sean Parker is just as surprised to see Mark. It turns out (that he was helping his girlfriend move out from the place opposite,) they heard the sound of the chimney collapsing and have come to check everyone is OK.

Sean Parker is impressed that Mark has moved out to California and tells him he's made the right choice.

Mark asks them in and shows them around. Sean is visibly impressed with both the place and the team and tells Mark as much.

The scene concludes with Sean asking about Eduardo. Mark replies that Eduardo has stayed in New York to do an internship. It is obvious from both Mark's and Sean's facial expressions and reactions that this is a sore topic: Mark seems embarrassed, and Sean seems very pleased with himself.

Der Schüler/Die Schülerin …
umreißt in einer Einleitung den Inhalt des Filmausschnitts
stellt dar, wie Zuckerberg und sein Team das Leben in Palo Alto, Kalifornien, genießen: – vergnügen sich am Pool, springen von selbstgebauter Seilbahn in den Pool; Zuckerberg filmt, bis der Schornstein, der die Seilbahn trägt, einstürzt – gewisse Bestürzung, aber niemand ist verletzt
erkennt, dass selbst intensive Arbeit verschiedener Mitglieder des Facebook-Teams offensichtlich mit Spaß verbunden ist
beschreibt die überraschende Begegnung mit Sean Parker: – Klingeln an der Tür – Zuckerberg öffnet und sieht sich Sean Parker und dessen Freundin gegenüber, die den Unfall von gegenüber beobachtet haben → Überraschung auf beiden Seiten – Sean Parker ist beeindruckt, dass Mark mit seinem Team nach Kalifornien gezogen ist – Sean gratuliert Mark Zuckerberg zu Haus und Team
stellt Sean Parkers Frage nach Eduardo und Marks Antwort, dass Eduardo in New York geblieben ist, als wichtig und ggf. zukunftsweisend heraus

2. Analysis

in the film extract:

- *relaxed and laid back (loud music playing; healthy work-life balance: some members of the team are fooling around in the pool, others are working ("wired in") and mustn't be disturbed)*
- *drinking beer; not worried about broken beer bottles and beer spilled in the living room → oblivious to cost of clean-up? because Facebook is generating enough money already?*
- *but at the same time it's clear that Mark is the one calling the shots: he is the one filming the others; he is the one who goes and opens the door when the door bell rings*
- *he films the others fooling around but doesn't actually join in; the others are in their swim shorts, Mark isn't → outsider; socially awkward; too cerebral to fool around*
- *proud and pleased that Sean Parker approves of his coming out to California*
- *embarrassed at having to tell Sean Parker that Eduardo decided not to come out → feels as though he is betraying Eduardo; considers Eduardo his friend and can tell that Sean is pleased*

in the extract from the novel:

- *exceptionally bright: "whiz kid" (l. 30)*
- *hard-working: "working round the clock" (l. 45)*
- *becoming famous: "thefacebook […] was slowly becoming the talk of the town" (ll. 28–29)*
- *unpredictable; you could never be sure what Mark was up to next: because of his intelligence but also because of his habit of never consulting with anyone (ll. 2–5, ll. 36–41)*
- *socially awkward, socially inept, doesn't interact with people the usual way: "hard enough to read in person, but on the phone he was a complete mystery. Sometimes it was like talking to a computer." (ll. 36–39)*

– *lacking emotional intelligence: doesn't call his friend Eduardo in New York to bring him up to date (cf. ll. 5–6)*
– *seems to be under the influence of/dependent on Sean Parker: Sean introduces Mark to the people that matter (ll. 16–23, 26–27)*
– *runs and expands the company, on the one hand, by "adding features to the site, and signing up more and more schools" (ll. 46–47) and, on the other hand, by networking with investors and people that matter in California (ll. 19–21, 27–30, 33–35)*
– *work is fun/healthy work-life balance: "have a blast, get some work done" (ll. 13–14)*

similarities in the way Mark's character is presented in film extract vs. extract from novel:
– *not very talkative; not great at communicating with other people but can do it if necessary (is OK communicating with Sean Parker in film extract; and according to the extract from the novel he spends a lot of time at parties, dinners and whatever it takes to get investors interested in thefacebook)*
– *socially awkward, lacking emotional intelligence (film: doesn't show much reaction when he throws beer bottles past Sean Parker's girlfriend; novel: doesn't call Eduardo)*
– *health work-life balance (partying and developing thefacebook website at the same time)*

Der Schüler/Die Schülerin ...
geht einleitend auf die unterschiedlichen Darstellungsformen Roman und Film ein
analysiert, wie Mark Zuckerberg in dem Filmausschnitt dargestellt wird, ggf. unter Berücksichtigung der eingesetzten filmischen Mittel, etwa: – gesellig, mitten im Geschehen (*establishing shot* am Pool, zunächst von hinten als einer der Akteure, Poolszene filmend, dann zur Kamera drehend; *panning shot* und *tilting shot,* bei dem ihm die Kamera die Poolstufen hinauf folgt) – dominante Rolle im Zentrum der Ereignisse, selbst bei dem Unfall (*low angle shot,* der seine Bedeutung unterstreicht) – entschlossen, bestimmt, für Organisation zuständig (*panning shot,* der Zuckerberg auf dem Weg zur Haustür zeigt, den Teammitgliedern Anweisungen gebend, ohne aufzuschauen) – in überraschender Begegnung mit Sean Parker zeigen *reverse angle shots* und *eye-level shots,* dass er mit Sean Parker auf Augenhöhe spricht – *medium shots* und *close-ups* zeigen Stolz über seine Entscheidung, nach Kalifornien gekommen zu sein, aber auch Unsicherheit, Verlegenheit, Bedauern bzw. Erleichterung und Verschwörergeist angesichts Eduardos Abwesenheit (knappes Kopfschütteln, ausweichender Blick zur Seite, beide nehmen einen Schluck aus ihrer Bierflasche)
analysiert, wie Mark Zuckerberg in dem Romanauszug dargestellt wird, etwa: – Genie: *"whiz kid"* (Zeile 30) – hart arbeitend: *"working round the clock"* (Zeile 30) – erfolgreich: *"slowly becoming the talk of the town"* (Zeile 29) – unzuverlässig, unaufrichtig und unfair, vielleicht sogar rücksichtslos, aber zumindest unberechenbar in seinem Streben nach Erfolg, was sich aus Eduardos Befürchtungen ableiten lässt, dass Entwicklung von *thefacebook* an ihm vorbeigeht: *"anxious"* (Zeile 1), *"concerns"* (Zeile 10), *"more and more concerned"* (Zeile 32–33) – eigentümlich und eigenbrödlerisch: *"Mark was Mark"* (Zeile 36) – unzugänglich und schwer zu durchschauen: *"hard to read* [...], *a complete mystery"* (Zeile 36–38) – unkommunikativ und gleichzeitig manipulativ, wenig an klaren Verhältnissen interessiert: *"like talking to a computer* [...] *only if he felt a response was necessary. Sometimes didn't respond at all."* (Zeile 38–41)
untersucht, wie Zuckerbergs Arbeitsweise dargestellt wird, etwa mit Hinweisen auf: – euphorische, alles vereinnahmende Arbeitsweise: *"have a blast, get some work done, and everything would be copacetic. And it would all start with a bang."* (Zeile 13–15) – Arbeit an der Website: *"adding features to the site"* (Zeile 46) – *networking* mit Investoren/Multiplikatoren: *"meet with more investor types,* [...] *some major Silicon Valley players, even a few Internet celebs"* (Zeile 19–21) – schnelle Entwicklung, die sich an ständig neuen, besseren Partnern orientiert: *"each time he spoke to Mark, and heard about another milestone, party, or dinner that he had missed"* (Zeile 33–35)

vergleicht die Darstellung Mark Zuckerbergs in Filmausschnitt und Romanauszug: – Parallelen in der Charakterisierung: knappe, reduzierte Redeweise, die Mark als wenig kommunikativ zeigt / unzuverlässig hinsichtlich der Wahl seiner Partner (billigt Eduardos Abwesenheit und nutzt sie zugleich als Chance, um Facebook hinter Eduardos Rücken weiterzuentwickeln) / fehlende Empathie (Unfall; kaputte Bierflaschen) – Parallelen in der Arbeitsweise: Team arbeitet intensiv und konzentriert *("wired in")*, dennoch ausgelassene, unkomplizierte, lockere Atmosphäre im Haus / Hinweis auf Wichtigkeit des *networking* / Hinweis auf Entfremdung bisheriger Freunde/Partner, z. B. *Eduardo didn't come out*

3a. Comment

- *Yes, I would think that Eduardo's concerns are justified.*
- *As you can see from the film extract, Mark is pleased to see Sean Parker again. He appreciates Parker telling him that it was the right decision to move Facebook to California.*
- *Sean Parker's opinion seems to be important to Mark, he seems pleased, proud and flattered that Sean Parker approves of his coming out to California. And Sean Parker's reaction when he hears that Eduardo did not join Mark and the others in California makes you wonder what his agenda is. His facial expression suggests that he is pleased that Eduardo seems to be out of the picture.*
- *Also, you can tell by Mark's reaction in the film extract that he does not feel entirely comfortable when Parker asks him about Eduardo. The scene seems to refer to an earlier scene, possibly a scene where Mark, Eduardo and Sean Parker were discussing Parker's suggestion that they should move Facebook to Palo Alto, California. Both Mark's and Sean Parker's reactions and facial expressions seem to indicate that Eduardo was against the idea, but that Mark decided to move the company to Calfornia all the same. Again, this suggests that Mark is willing to listen to Sean Parker more than to Eduardo.*
- *I believe that Eduardo is justified in feeling that Mark should keep him up to date about what is happening in California. After all, Eduardo played an important part in the creation of Facebook. It was Eduardo's algorithm that helped launch the website Facemash, which got Mark into big trouble but which eventually led to the development of Facebook.*
- *In additon to providing the algorithm for the Facemash website, Eduardo financed Facebook's early stages, so it is fair to say that without Eduardo's help, support and assistance there would be no Facebook and Mark and his team would not have moved to Palo Alto.*
- *Eduardo must be aware that Mark is fairly oblivious to other people's feelings; he witnessed the nasty blog entry that Mark posted about his ex-girlfriend Erica shortly after she had dumped him; so Eduardo will be painfully aware that Mark would not think twice about dropping him if a new friend or business partner came along.*
- *We also know about Mark's ambition to make it into society's exclusive circles; so again, he might well decide against Eduardo's friendship/business partnership if a more useful/profitable business partner came along.*

Der Schüler/Die Schülerin ...
formuliert eine Einleitung, die sich z. B. auf den Erfolg von Facebook oder die Schnelllebigkeit der neuen Medien bezieht oder an den Film anknüpft
berücksichtigt Eduardos Rolle, auf der Basis von Film und Arbeitsanweisung, etwa: – lieferte den Algorithmus für die *Facemash*-Website, – stellte das Startkapital für Facebook bereit – war anderer Meinung, was den Umzug nach Kalifornien betrifft – favorisiert eine andere Strategie der Vermarktung und ging deshalb nach New York und leitet daraus seinen Anspruch auf Beteiligung am Facebook-Unternehmen ab
setzt sich mit den Charaktereigenschaften Zuckerbergs auseinander, im Hinblick auf seinen Umgang mit Menschen und die mögliche Ausbootung von Eduardo, etwa: – Rücksichtslosigkeit gegenüber Ex-Freundin Erica, die er in seinem Blog diskreditierte – fehlendes moralisches Bewusstsein bei der Eröffnung der *Facemash*-Website – unerschrocken manipulativer Umgang mit den Winklevoss-Brüdern, auf deren Angebot er nur eingeht, um Zugang zu Harvards Elite zu erhalten – Gereiztheit und Ungeduld gegenüber weniger intelligenten Leuten – die Neigung, sich Partnern zuzuwenden, die seinem Erfolg dienlich sein können
kommt zu einer abschließenden Einschätzung

3b. Creative writing

Mark: *Welcome to California!*
Eduardo: *Good to see you. How's life?*
Mark: *Great. Wait until you've seen the features we've added to the site.*
Eduardo: *Great. How's everyone?*
Mark: *Fine. Sean is amazing. He knows everyone, and everyone knows him.*
Eduardo: *Ah, Sean. Don't you think you're coming to depend on him a little too much?*
Mark: *Don't start, Eduardo. thefacebook is becoming the talk of the town. And that's all because of Sean. We've been meeting with some huge Silicon Valley players. Sean was right, Eduardo: Palo Alto is where it's at. You'll see.*
Eduardo: *But thefacebook is our project, it's our company, Mark. You and I started it. Remember how I helped you with the algorithm for Facemash? Remember how you said we needed some money to get this idea of yours started? I'm a part of Facebook, it's not just you. I want to be involved in the business decisions you take. Or at least let me know what you're doing. The fact that I'm in New York working my ass off doesn't mean you can't still call and tell me what's happening.*
Mark: *But things are happening so fast. You wouldn't believe it. We've been signing up more and more schools.*
Eduardo: *That's great.*
Mark: *Remember that party I was telling you about? The one Sean has gotten us invited to? That's tonight. It'll be fun but there'll also be the opportunity to meet with more investor types, some more major Silicon Valley players, even a few Internet celebs. You'll see for yourself. They just all want to meet us.*
Eduardo: *(sighs) Sure, I'll come.*
Mark: *And take that look of your face. We're in this together. You and I, we're Facebook.*
Eduardo: *Did I tell you I've made some real progress with advertisers back in New York?*
Mark: *Yeah? Great. Listen, have you eaten?*
Eduardo: *What?!*
Mark: *How about we stop for breakfast before heading back to the house? I've not had breakfast, and the fridge is empty, the guys were at it last night. Well, apart from beer, that is.*
Eduardo: *OK, right. Let's have breakfast. It's good to see you, Mark.*
Mark: *Good to see you, too, Eduardo. Welcome to California!*

Der Schüler/Die Schülerin ...
findet einen Einstieg in die Unterhaltung, der das unterschiedliche Lebensumfeld (New York / Kalifornien) thematisiert
bezieht die unterschiedlichen Auffassungen in Bezug auf Vorgehensweise und Bewertung neuer Partner wie Sean Parker in die Unterhaltung ein
vermittelt einen Eindruck von Eduardos möglichen Sorgen und seinem Anspruch bezüglich seiner Position im Unternehmen und als Freund und bezieht dabei Fakten über Eduardos Rolle als Wegbegleiter ein, z. B.: – Freund und Partner, der den Algorithmus für die *Facemash*-Website lieferte, – der das nötige Startkapital bereitstellte – der das Unternehmen von New York aus unterstützt, indem er dort um Investoren und Werbepartner wirbt
nimmt in dem Gespräch Bezug auf Entwicklungen in Kalifornien und spiegelt Marks Zurückhaltung, Verlegenheit, Ausweichen, klare Ablehnung oder scheinbar versöhnliche Haltung
beachtet die durch die Textsorte vorgegebene Sprachebene mit informellem Charakter, typischen Merkmalen gesprochener Sprache und umgangssprachlichen Wendungen
imitiert die Sprechweise von Zuckerberg mit kurzen, knappen Beiträgen

Theme 5 Speaking (monologue) (→ Kopiervorlage Seite 122f.)

A. 1. – *two teenage girls talking to each other in a garden*
– *girl on the left is holding an exercise book, indicating that both girls are students/pupils*
– *posture/body language of girl on the left indicates that she is agitated/angry/upset*
– *girl on the left is complaining to her friend that her mum wants to be her Facebook friend → girl feels checked up on, compares it to surveillance cameras in school*

2. – *growing up has changed a lot over the years: surveillance cameras in schools, Facebook*
– *teens misinterpreting/suspicious of adults' good intentions: surveillance cameras are there to protect pupils against harm/shootings; her mum might just want to be nice/have fun*
– *technology can be used against you: protection turns to control and surveillance*

B. 1. – *a boy and a girl talking to each other outside a house*
– *schoolbags/backpacks and books indicate that they are pupils*
– *boy talking: telling the girl that continuously posting on Twitter about his homework keeps him from getting his homework done*

2. – *social media = waste of time*
– *most of what happens on Twitter is telling others what you are doing → not very interesting; time could be spent doing something useful/worthwhile/getting your work done*

C. 1. – *two men meeting for the first time, man on the left is older than the man on the right*
– *both men are wearing ties → indicates that it is a work/business situation*
– *younger man on the right tells the other one that he knows quite a bit about him already, all through Facebook*

2. – *you can find out a lot about other people through social media without ever meeting them*
– *play on words; you often say "It's a pleasure to meet you. So-and-so has told me so much about you" → Facebook is personified*
– *makes fun of the fact that many people use social media to check up on people before they meet them for the first time*
– *gone are the days when you would need a network of friends and contacts to find out information about other people → Facebook has replaced people*

D. 1. – *school situation: male English teacher is sitting at his desk, talking to female student*
– *he explains to her what an essay is, by using social media/Twitter language, explaining that an essay is many tweets put together*

2. – *addresses the fact that many young people are more familiar with social media and social media kind of texts than with 'classic' kinds of texts, e.g. essays*
– *teachers need to know what goes on in their students' lives if they want to reach them and teach them important, 'classic' information; today's teachers need to dumb down*

Der Schüler/Die Schülerin
1. beschreibt den Cartoon unter Berücksichtigung der visuellen und sprachlichen Elemente. Je eigenständiger und sprachlich unabhängiger von der Bildunterschrift dies erfolgt, desto höher ist die Leistung einzustufen.
2. erläutert die Intention des Zeichners und wie diese Intention mithilfe der visuellen und sprachlichen Elemente transportiert wird. Es erfolgt eine strukturierte Auseinandersetzung mit der Vorlage. Je eigenständiger und sprachlich unabhängiger von der Bildunterschrift dies erfolgt, desto höher ist die Leistung einzustufen.

Theme 5 Reading and speaking (dialogue) (→ Kopiervorlage Seite 124–129)

A. **Discussion card 1:** *arguments from article (**yes**, it's a parent's duty to respect …)*
– *your children will not have had a chance to "decide whether they want to participate or even whether the narrative is true to their own vision of self" (ll. 58–60)*
– *"We've created a sense of normality about a world where what's private is public. The sense of being entitled to privacy has been devalued" (ll. 73–76)*
– *"no delete key for the Internet. Once it's out there, it's probably out there forever." (ll. 104–106)*
– *"never before have parents had the ability to publish the details of their children's lives in such a widespread manner" (ll. 113–115)*
– *"We have a right to control how much we want the world to know about us. […] Our children deserve the same protections." (ll. 136–140)*

Discussion card 2
- *equal rights for all, i.e. parents and children*
- *each family member has the right to veto photos/personal information going online*
- *no photos of family members are posted without approval by said family members*
- *possibly two separate sets of rules, depending on whether photos/information are posted on a private account or public account, i.e. visible to all*

Discussion card 3: *arguments from article (**yes**, there is no need to be concerned about this)*
- *"new research findings indicate that openness and information sharing are a way of life for many adults, and personal privacy is readily compromised" (ll. 7–10)*
- *"40% reported a low level of concern" (ll. 23–24) about online privacy*
- *"Nearly 70% […] have shared their own photos online and post about nine personal pictures each year" (ll. 25–27)*
- *"a sense of normality about a world where what's private is public" (ll. 73–75)*

B. **Discussion card 1**
- *most of what people post on social media is about what they are doing this minute, the banalities of life: food they are eating, sitting on public transport, watching TV → not very interesting; time could be spent doing something useful/worthwhile/getting work done*
- *people post information on social media that they wouldn't dream of telling people face to face because they know it is too boring to waste other people's time with*
- *any information condensed to a set number of letters or words is bound to be superficial*

Discussion card 2: *arguments from article (**no**, it's not about more than that)*
- *"the relationship between social shares and actual reading is complex. People do sometimes share stories because they are under discussion on Facebook or Twitter" (ll. 99–102)*
- *"it is quite possible to suggest that someone should read something even though they personally have not done so" (ll. 113–116)*
- *"relationship between an opinion expressed and an opinion held is fundamentally unknowable" (ll. 119–120)*

Discussion card 3: *arguments from article (**yes**, they use social media to exchange ideas …)*
- *Twitter, in particular, is all about exchanging ideas and opinions in no more than 140 letters; however, if you ask me, it is more about stating your own opinion than about wanting to hear and possibly discuss other people's opinions*
- *"The number of users who changed their opinion was very small" (ll. 36–37)*
- *"relationship between an opinion expressed and an opinion held is fundamentally unknowable" (ll. 119–120)*

C. **Discussion card 1:** *arguments from article (**yes**, they give teenagers the "controllability" …)*
- *"These technologies give their users a sense of increased controllability" (ll. 57–58)*
- *"having the power to reflect on and change what you write before you send it" (ll. 66–68)*
- *"'Controllability' […] is about three things" (ll. 62–71)*

Discussion card 2: *arguments from article (**yes**, the advantages outweigh the risks)*
- *"'I'd rather […] give up […] a kidney than my phone." (ll. 1–2)*
- *"It's actually very practical if you forget what that day's homework is" (ll. 8–9)*
- *texting has become "the preferred channel of basic communication between teens and their friends" (ll. 24–26)*

Discussion card 3: *arguments from article (**no**, people's personalities are not affected …)*
- *"Our research gives no reason at present for concern about the social consequences of online communication" (ll. 146–148)*
- *"Our research shows face-to-face time between teenagers hasn't changed over the past five years. Technology has simply added another layer on top" (ll. 152–155)*
- *"These technologies change lives, absolutely" (l. 165) but not necessarily personalities*

Der Schüler/Die Schülerin …
verhält sich sprachlich angemessen durch Gebrauch eines formalen und höflichen Registers und eines passenden thematischen Wortschatzes
berücksichtigt Informationen und Argumente aus dem Ausgangstext
liefert sachgerechte und aufgabengemäße Argumente und beweist ein angemessenes Maß an Sachwissen
geht auf den Partner/die Partnerin ein und erhält das Gespräch durchgehend aufrecht

Theme 6 Reading and writing (→ Kopiervorlage Seite 130)

1. Comprehension

Nigel:
- *"great" idea (l. 22); gets all excited at the thought of girls wearing them (cf. l. 22)*
- *wristbands save time because you know right away how far a girl will go (ll. 24–25: "Means you won't be wasting your time")*
- *it's great for girls to wear the wristbands but he wouldn't want to wear them himself (cf. l. 28) → clearly differentiates between boys and girls*
- *is a lot more critical of girls being sexually experienced than of boys → it's OK for boys to have sex with many girls but the other way round "that's just not attractive" (ll. 37–38)*

Darren:
- *not convinced that the wristbands are a good idea (cf. l. 23)*
- *more thoughtful than Nigel (cf. l. 39); not as excited about the whole wristband thing as Nigel*
- *questions Nigel's enthusiasm for the wristbands (cf. ll. 27, 29–31, 34)*
- *seems aware of the issue of gender equality: why should different rules apply for girls?*

Karen:
- *stage directions reveal that Karen lies to Sarah about her wristbands (cf. ll. 62–64): in line 64 she claims not to have any but in fact she is wearing all four possible colours (yellow, red, blue and green), as is revealed by stage directions in lines 62–63*
- *although Karen is wearing them herself, she starts bitching/being negative about them and about Jane, who is openly wearing them*

Sarah:
- *says she probably won't "bother with it" (l. 74); but on closer inspection: she just pretends not to be bothered; in fact, her short replies indicate that she wants to avoid the topic*
- *in fact, she is quite bothered, as is revealed in line 77: "Yeah well … fuck Jane." / This strong reaction implies that Karen/Jane is right when she says "anyone who doesn't wear it hasn't done anything at all." (ll. 75–76) → Sarah is sexually inexperienced but doesn't want to admit it, so she pretends not to be bothered*

Jane: *we only hear of her (ll. 65 and 75–76): according to Karen, Jane is wearing the wristbands (all four colours) quite openly*

boys: *more open about the wristbands; they might not agree about them, but they don't tell lies about what they think of them, which puts them in contrast to the girls, or to Karen at least, who quite obviously does not want to admit that she likes the idea of the wristbands and is already wearing them; which proves Nigel's point (cf. ll. 37–38), i.e. that peer pressure labels sexually experienced girls as not "attractive", they are considered sluts by most people*

girls: *not open about either the wristbands or their sexual experiences; both girls pretend to be/probably consider themselves good friends but don't trust each other well enough for Karen to admit to Sarah that she is already wearing the wristbands and for Sarah to admit to Karen that she is sexually inexperienced / at the same time they both bitch about Jane*

→ the girls suffer from peer pressure: they judge each other, whereas the boys don't seem particularly bothered by what the other one says / what other people think of them is a much bigger deal for (the) girls than for (the) boys / instead of sticking together, girls lie to each other, judge each other and bitch about each other, e.g. about Jane, who isn't there

Der Schüler/Die Schülerin …
führt mit einer Einleitung in die Aufgabenstellung ein
beschreibt die unterschiedlichen Reaktionen der Jugendlichen auf die Armbänder: – Nigel: tolle, aufregende Vorstellung; möchte aber selbst keins; misst mit zweierlei Maß – Darren: differenzierter als Nigel; sieht nicht, warum für Mädchen und Jungen unterschiedliche Maßstäbe gelten sollen – Karen: trägt die Armbänder, traut sich aber nicht, es zuzugeben; stattdessen zieht sie sogar über Jane her, die die Armbänder offen trägt – Sarah: gibt sich unbeeindruckt; lässt vermuten, dass sie sexuell unerfahren ist, was sie aber nicht zugibt, sondern worauf sie stattdessen heftig reagiert
verallgemeinert die Reaktionen der Mädchen vs. Jungen: – Jungen: sind unterschiedlicher Meinung; aber spielen einander nichts vor – Mädchen: weder Karen noch Sarah ist der Freundin gegenüber offen und ehrlich
fasst die wichtigsten Erkenntnisse abschließend zusammen

2. Analysis

ellipsis: *"And the red one?" (l. 5), "Red one means" (l. 6), "How much further?" (l. 7), "Where?" (l. 9), "Upstairs." (l. 10), "Seriously?" (l. 11), "What about the blue?" (l. 13), "And the green?" (l. 17), "All the way." (l. 18), "Is it?" (l. 34), "You get some yet?" (l. 60), "Green?" (l. 67) → atmosphere of awkwardness/embarrassment; uncomfortable talking about sex*
hesitation: *"Red one means ... that she'll go further." (l. 6), "Well ... like, she'll let the guy ... have a feel ..." (l. 8), "Fucking hell ... and they can't [...]?" (l. 19), "Fucking hell ... that's just ... that's great, isn't it?" (l. 22), "one who won't ... you know ... do anything." (ll. 25–26), "It is ... but if it wasn't ... would you [...]? Let everyone know exactly how ... exactly what you've been doing?" (ll. 29–31), "Yeah, I mean ... I can do what I like [...] but if a girl ... you know ... puts it out a bit ... well, a lot ... then that's just not attractive, is it?" (ll. 35–38), "Couldn't be greener ... it's weird, letting everyone know how far you've ... what you've done ... isn't it? I mean, letting people you don't even know ... know ... letting them judge you" (ll. 68–72), "Yeah well ... fuck Jane." (l. 77) → atmosphere of hesitation, i.e. embarrassment, awkwardness and insecurity; again shows how uncomfortable they are talking about sex*
alluding to sexual acts/euphemism: *"have a feel" (l. 8), "Upstairs." (l. 10), "Downstairs" (l. 15), "who won't ... you know ... do anything." (ll. 25–26), "exactly how ... exactly what you've been doing?" (ll. 30–31), "if a girl ... you know ... puts it out a bit" (ll. 36–37), "how far you've ... what you've done ..." (ll. 69–70) → embarrassment, awkwardness and insecurity; avoiding any mention of the word "sex"*
discrepancy dialogue/stage directions: *stage directions reveal that Karen is lying to Sarah about her wristbands (cf. ll. 62–64): she claims not to have any but in fact she is wearing all four of them (which means she is prepared to have sex), as is revealed by stage directions in lines 62–63 → atmosphere of lying, dishonesty and distrust; peer pressure*
swearing by Sarah: *"Yeah well ... fuck Jane." (l. 77) → strong reaction, overreacting, strong emotions; suggests that Sarah is hiding something, that what Jane says about girls who don't wear a wristband is true, i.e. that they have no sexual experience; Sarah is embarrassed/ashamed that she is sexually inexperienced; the fact that she doesn't trust Karen well enough to tell her adds to the atmosphere of lying, dishonesty and distrust*
short replies by Sarah: *"Yeah." (l. 59), "No." (l. 61), "Green?" (l. 67), "Yeah well ... fuck Jane." (l. 77) → wants to give as little away as possible; would like to avoid the topic of wristbands because she is worried that Karen will ask her how sexually experienced she is*
body language/silence: *"Darren nods." (ll. 12, 16), "Darren says nothing." (l. 39) → atmosphere of embarrassment; feeling uncomfortable*
swearing/exclamation by Nigel: *"Fucking hell" (ll. 19, 22) → atmosphere of excitement/fun*
short answers by Nigel: *"isn't it?" (l. 22), "isn't it?" (l. 33), "is it?" (l. 38) → insecure, looking for confirmation*

Der Schüler/Die Schülerin ...
umreißt einleitend die Aufgabenstellung
erkennt einige der sprachlichen und stilistischen Besonderheiten der Textauszüge, belegt sie am Text und benennt die Stimmung/Atmosphäre, die so geschaffen wird, z. B.: – *ellipsis, hesitation* und *euphemism:* → Verlegenheit und Unsicherheit – Fluchen: → starke Emotionen (Nigel: Aufregung, Sarah: Stress/Angst/Unsicherheit) – Sarahs einsilbige Antworten: → Verlegenheit, will dem Thema aus dem Weg gehen – Diskrepanz zwischen Gesagtem und Regieanweisungen (Zeile 62–64)
fasst die wichtigsten Erkenntnisse abschließend zusammen

3a. Comment

- *I personally cannot imagine wearing wristbands to show my level of sexual experience but I am sure not everyone feels like that; I can imagine people who are looking for a one-night stand enjoying the idea; it provides them with a thrill and, as Nigel puts it, it saves you time*
- *I do not believe in sex just for the sake of having sex; I would not want to have sex with anyone but my girlfriend/boyfriend so I would never wear these wristbands; and I would not care whether that would make other people think that I have never had sex*
- *I would think that many of those people who think wristbands are a cool idea would be embarrassed to wear them themselves; they might like the voyeuristic idea of others labelling themselves according to how far they are prepared to go, but would not be courageous/stupid/self-confident/unashamed enough to wear the wristbands themselves*

Der Schüler/Die Schülerin …
formuliert eine in das Thema einführende Einleitung
macht mit einem einleitenden Satz die eigene Meinung deutlich: – dem Konzept der Armbänder als äußeres Zeichen der eigenen sexuellen Erfahrung und der eigenen sexuellen Bereitschaft zustimmend oder – ihm widersprechend
– berücksichtigt mögliche Motive, warum Menschen die Armbänder tragen würden
kommt zu einer abschließenden Einschätzung

3b. Creative writing

Nigel: *Hey look, there's Jane over there. (shouts) Jane! Jane!*
Jane: *Oh, hi Nigel, hi everyone. What's up?*
Nigel: *Not much. Good to see you. You going to the end-of-year do?*
Jane: *Sure. Are you?*
Nigel: *Sure. I'll be there. Hey, what's that on your wrist?*
Jane: *Come on, Nigel. Don't play dumb. Don't tell me you've not heard of the wristbands?!*
Nigel: *Yeah. I think Darren mentioned them the other day.*
Darren: *You think? You were salivating like one of Pavlov's dogs when I told you about them. Jane is right: don't play dumb, Nigel.*
Nigel: *Thanks, mate. OK then, fess up, Jane: what colours are you wearing?*
Jane: *(grins) All four of them.*
Nigel: *Wow … Does that mean … I mean … you know …*
Jane: *Get a grip on yourself, Nigel. Does it mean am I prepared to go all the way? Yeah.*
Darren: *Why would you want others to know?*
Jane: *Sex is fun. It's nothing to be ashamed of. Hey, Karen, Sarah: what about you? What colours are you wearing?*
Sarah: *I think they're a dumb idea. Won't bother with it.*
Jane: *Ah, so you haven't done anything at all.*
Sarah: *That's not true. And none of your business.*
Jane: *Yeah, right. So what about you, Karen?*
Karen: *(pulls up her sleeve to reveal all four wristbands) All four.*
Nigel: *Fucking hell … Karen, does that mean … I mean … Wow, that's cool!*
Sarah: *Karen, you said you weren't going to get any! You lied to me!*
Karen: *No, I didn't. I only got them yesterday. Calm down. What's the big deal?*
Sarah: *You said you weren't going to get any. What about all this talk about not letting people judge you for who they think you are and not who you actually are?*
Jane: *Grow up, Sarah. Jealous, are you?*
Sarah: *Fuck you. … Fuck all of you. (storms off)*
Nigel: *Fucking hell … what was that all about?*
(Darren says nothing.)
Jane: *You want to come shopping, Karen? Look for something to wear to the end-of-year do?*

Der Schüler/Die Schülerin …
findet einen Einstieg in die Unterhaltung
stellt in den Redeanteilen die in den Textauszügen angelegten Einstellungen der Jugendlichen zu den Armbänden dar, etwa: – Jane: offen – Nigel: tolle Idee; aufgeregt und nachgerade geifernd bei der Vorstellung, dass einem Mädchen am Handgelenk abzulesen ist, wie sexuell erfahren es ist – Darren: differenzierter als Nigel; zurückhaltend; sieht nicht, warum für Mädchen und Jungen unterschiedliche Maßstäbe gelten sollen – Karen: hat die Armbänder, traute sich aber nicht, es Sarah gegenüber zuzugeben; stattdessen zog sie sogar über Jane her, die die Armbänder offen trägt – Sarah: will nicht zugeben, dass sie sexuell unerfahren ist, möchte am liebsten das Thema wechseln
beachtet die durch die Textauszüge vorgegebene Sprachebene mit Ellipsen, Euphemismen, Vermeidungen und Verzögerungen sowie typische Merkmale gesprochener Sprache und umgangssprachliche Wendungen

DVD Theme 6 Listening (→ Kopiervorlage Seite 131)

1. *The podcast is about marriage between same-sex couples.*

2. a. *The couples interviewed had come to the county courthouse to **get married.***
   b. *Many of them had been together for **a long time/for up to 25 years.***
   c. *They had not been through this ceremony before because the law **did not allow same-sex couples to get married.***
   d. *Ed Golembiewski, the county chief deputy clerk, explained that the county clerk had informed him the night before that **he could issue marriage licences to/marry same-sex couples.***
   e. *Reverend Dean Ware came to the county courthouse to show that the church supported all loving couples regardless of **gender identity or sexual orientation.***
   f. *For some of the same-sex couples one of the practical benefits of the ceremony was that they could now **be legal parents** to their children.*
   g. *Not only the couples were present at the event but also **friends, family and supporters.***
   h. *After the ceremony one of the brides, Stephanie Williams, said that she no longer felt like **a second-class citizen.***

Theme 7 Reading and writing (→ Kopiervorlage Seite 132)

1. **Comprehension**
   – *public execution/hanging of three women*
   – *witnessed by an audience of women only (there are also Salvagings for men only)*
   – *the women in the audience must participate in the hangings:*
   first by placing their hands on a rope that is connected to the noose around the woman's head, the woman that is being hanged/that is dying [not clear from extract whether they just have to touch the rope or whether they actually tug at the rope, to counterbalance the woman's body],
   followed by putting one hand on their heart to show their "unity with the Salvagers and [their] consent, and [their] complicity in the death of this woman" (ll. 74–76)
   – *Salvagings do not happen often, it has been two years since the last one (ll. 35–36: "I've only been to one of these before, two years ago. Women's Salvagings are not frequent.")*
   – *Salvagings are organised at very short notice, i.e. announced "the day before" (ll. 13–14)*
   – *takes place outside: the actual hanging takes place on a wooden stage, with the female audience on the lawn in front of the stage*

Der Schüler/Die Schülerin …
umreißt die in dem Romanauszug dargestellte Situation in einem Einleitungssatz
stellt die Situation unter Berücksichtigung der wichtigsten Aspekte dar: – öffentliche Hinrichtung durch Erhängen – drei Frauen werden hingerichtet – Publikum besteht ausschließlich aus Frauen – das Publikum ist an der Hinrichtung beteiligt: die Frauen müssen das Seil, das sie mit der Frau, die erhängt wird, verbindet, mit beiden Händen berühren/festhalten/ziehen?; in einem zweiten Schritt müssen sie eine Hand aufs Herz legen, als Zeichen ihres Einverständnisses, ihrer Verbundenheit mit den *Salvagers* und ihrer Komplizenschaft.
erwähnt ggf. weitere Aspekte des *Salvaging:* – *Salvagings* finden nur selten statt, das letzte vor zwei Jahren – Ankündigung erfolgt kurzfristig: 24 Stunden vorher – Geschlechtertrennung: *Salvagings* erfolgen nach Geschlecht getrennt, d. h. es gibt auch *Salvagings* für Männer – findet draußen statt; das eigentliche Erhängen erfolgt auf einer für den Zweck errichteten Holzbühne, das Publikum befindet sich auf einer Rasenfläche vor der Bühne

2. **Analysis**
   atmosphere: oppressive, gruesome, sinister, ominous, foreboding
   setting
   – *ll. 4–9: "a heavy contingent of guards [...] with riot gear [...] in cordon around the outside of the Wall" → atmosphere of being controlled, atmosphere of fear*
   – *ll. 16–17: "paths once used by students, [...] buildings that were once lecture halls and dor-*

mitories" → contrast between then and now, the good old times/the better past vs. the harsh, gruesome present; repetition of "once" for emphasis
- *ll. 20–21: "the blinds on most of the windows are drawn down" → atmosphere of secrecy*
- *l. 25: "a wooden stage erected on the lawn" → stage is elevated → hierarchy; atmosphere of oppression; atmosphere of superiority vs. inferiority*
- *ll. 25–27: "stage erected on the lawn, something like the one they used every spring, for Commencement, in the time before" → harks back to better times; contrast*
- *l. 34: "the television camera is discreetly off to the side" → irony and pretence; nothing discreet about the hanging of three women / also: atmosphere of control and of being watched*
- *ll. 45–46: "The rope is thick and brown and smells of tar" → unpleasant smell*
- *ll. 54–55: "All of them sit on folding wooden chairs" → discomfort and tension*

connotations
- *"Salvaging" → a word with positive connotations (to salvage = to rescue) is used to describe the exact opposite (euphemism) → psychological manipulation, language as mind control*
- *l. 10: "The hooks on the Wall are empty." → foreboding?; ominous; implies that the hooks will be filled, something will be hung there; the fact that the hooks are mentioned at all implies that it will not be coats or hats that will be hung there …*
- *l. 14: "It's not enough time, to get used to it." → foreboding*
- *ll. 18–19: "From the outside you can't tell that anything's changed" → translates as: a lot has changed, basically nothing is as it was before*
- *ll. 22–23: "in front of what used to be the library" → emphasis, contrast; a library is a peaceful, quiet place dedicated to reading, learning, freedom of speech, education, culture, the arts → the situation described is far from anything resembling culture and education*
- *l. 27: "in the time before." → in the time before what?; everything has changed; too painful for narrator to elaborate on how things used to be*
- *l. 39: "I don't want to be telling this story." → foreboding; you can tell that what is going to follow is not going to be pleasant, almost too painful to bear for Offred, the narrator*
- *ll. 59–60: "so they won't make a fuss. It's better if things go smoothly" → foreboding; something gruesome is going to happen, something you would want to make a fuss about*
- *l. 60: "It's better if things go smoothly" → euphemism: "things"; not calling it what it is (because it is too painful for the narrator to bear), i.e. hanging/execution of dissenters*
- *ll. 68–70: "her hand over the mike, to stifle the other sounds coming from behind her" → "the other sounds" is a euphemism for the sounds of a person dying, suffocating; calling it "the other sounds" gets the reader's imagination going; reader will most likely read sentence twice, think about what "the other sounds" might be and then feel his/her stomach turn*
- *l. 76: " I have seen the kicking feet" → the kicking feet, which means that the woman is dying from being hanged; again, the reader has to put two and two together to understand what is being described here; attention is drawn away from the neck, which is mirrored by the narrator saying "I don't want to see it any more. I look at the grass instead" (ll. 79–80) → too painful to bear; averting attention away from the person dying; atmosphere of powerlessness, having to witness a person dying without doing anything to help/prevent it*
- *ll. 79–80: "I don't want to see it any more. I look at the grass instead." → the narrator looks down/bows her head → atmosphere of defeat and shame; inferiority; facing reality is too painful → shows the ruling class's style of governing: making people look away in order to survive; looking away as an act of self-preservation, a basic instinct in human beings*

→ words 'hang', 'hanging', 'execution' or similar do not come up once; the narrator does not explicity say what is happening but the connotations/implications/asides are clear/strong enough for readers to know/understand, which makes the scene all the more powerful
- *ll. 3–4: "When we reach the main gate we file through it, two by two." / l. 22: "We file onto the wide lawn" → to file: to walk in an orderly manner → cannot/must not behave naturally, they are restrained, oppressed and under control*

imagery
- *l. 5: "a heavy contingent of guards, special-detail Angels, with riot gear" → the guards are anything but angels → meanings of words are distorted, turned into their opposites → psychological manipulation, language as mind control*
- *ll. 6–7: "the bulging dark plexiglass visors that make them look like beetles" → simile; being controlled and watched by insects, no contact with human eyes → atmosphere of anonymity*
- *ll. 41–42: "There's a long piece of rope which winds like a snake" → simile; a snake is dangerous and poisonous; will kill without warning, i.e. giving you no chance to fight or defend yourself; an animal that makes no noise when it kills*

- *ll. 41–45: "There's a long piece of rope [...], bending like a very old, very slow river viewed from the air, down to the back." → simile; contrast; at odds with the situation*
- *ll. 47–48: "It's like a fuse, or the string of a balloon." → contrasting similes; a fuse implies that a bomb is about to explode; however, a balloon makes you think of carefree times, e.g. birthday parties in the sun → atmosphere of contrasts and contradictions, which causes stress*
- *ll. 54–56: "All of them sit on folding wooden chairs, like graduating students who are about to be given prizes." → simile; contrast between being hanged and receiving a prize adds to the cruelty and gruesomeness of the scene; contrast between the old times and the present*
- *ll. 64–65: "the noose adjusted delicately around the neck, like a vestment" → simile; contrast between vestment and noose that will kill adds to cruelty and gruesomeness of the situation*
- *ll. 23–24: "the white steps going up are still the same, the main entrance is unaltered" / ll. 61–62: "the white bag placed over the head" → white = colour of innocence → contrast, as the situation described is far from innocent; the ruling class wants to whitewash its gruesome rituals/behaviour*
- *ll. 66–67: "I've heard the long sigh go up, from around me" → emphasises that individuality has no place in this society; also shows that the women in the audience all feel the same*
- *ll. 67–68: "the sigh like air coming out of an air mattress" → simile; suffocation, air = life; life is being drained from the women in the audience; the women are being drained*

sentence structure

- *l. 10: "The hooks on the Wall are empty." → foreboding?; the sentence is very short, too short to be insignificant; it makes the reader wonder when the hooks are going to be 'filled'; the fact that the empty hooks are mentioned implies that this is going to change very soon ...*
- *ll. 37–38: "There is less need for them. These days we are so well behaved." → These short sentences accentuate the fact that people have no choice but to obey. No long explanations or discussions are necessary. The same goes for ll. 9–10, 13–14.*
- *ll. 79–80: "I don't want to see it any more. I look at the grass instead." → parallelism to emphasise the contrast between what is and how the narrator would like things to be*

Der Schüler/Die Schülerin ...
führt mit einer Einleitung in die Aufgabenstellung ein
analysiert und belegt am Text das *setting* und die dadurch hervorgerufene Atmosphäre, z. B.: *oppressive, gruesome, sinister, ominous, foreboding*
nennt und analysiert die sprachlichen Mittel und die so hervorgerufene Atmosphäre aus Beklemmung, Bedrohung, Scham. Die untersuchten Kategorien sollten mindestens zwei der folgenden umfassen: – *connotations* – *imagery* – *sentence structure*
fasst die wichtigsten Erkenntnisse abschließend zusammen

3. Comment

- *demonstration of power and strength; to show people who is in charge*
- *to intimidate, to indoctrinate, to keep people quiet*
- *streamlining and brainwashing; psychological manipulation*
- *do away with individuality; the individual mind is a totalitarian society's worst enemy*
- *crush people's morale/create a feeling of shame: witnessing a gruesome situation/a person's death but not having the courage to intervene/being able to react/resist/rebell*
- *in the extract: the women in the audience symbolically hang the women themselves → later feel humiliated and ashamed of their "complicity in the death of this woman" (ll. 75–76) → humiliation and shame will keep the women from speaking out against the regime*
- *having to witness a person dying from a position of powerlessness → emotional trauma*
- *make the people complicit in whatever is happening → shame → weakening of spirit*
- *mass events affect people's minds; people have neither time nor space to think, they just go along; might think about what happened later but will find the memory either too painful or too shameful to reflect on their behaviour or will go into denial about what happened*
- *rational thinking takes a back seat in mass events; people will do things they would usually be ashamed of doing if they were by themselves*
- *masses make people feel strong; make people ignore the needs of the individual*
- *create and strengthen the collective experience and memory*
- *feeds into people's desire to belong to a group, to be part of something bigger*

- *addresses emotions, i.e. silences the rational mind*
- *witnessing something in a group reduces the individual's feeling of responsibility; justify your own passive behaviour by arguing that the others did not intervene/object, either*
- *masses make people do and agree to things they would not do or agree to if they were alone*
- *appeals to base instincts: unity of a crowd lifts an individual's self-confidence, bestowes a feeling of power on the individual (possibly followed by a sense of shame → weakening of spirit)*

Der Schüler/Die Schülerin ...
führt mit einer Einleitung in die Aufgabenstellung ein
erkennt mindestens drei Funktionen von Massenveranstaltungen in totalitären Gesellschaften, z. B.: – Machtdemonstration → Einschüchterung und Indoktrination der Massen – Scham, Erleben der eigenen Machtlosigkeit → potentielle Kritik am Regime verstummt – das Individuum tritt seine Kritikfähigkeit und Eigenverantwortung an die Masse ab
strukturiert die Argumente
fasst die wichtigsten Erkenntnisse abschließend zusammen

Theme 8 Listening, reading and writing (→ Kopiervorlage Seite 133)

1. Comprehension

- *upcycling = adding on to something that already exists (as opposed to recycling = using more resources to reproduce)*
- *ideally, not buying anything new at all; all you need is a needle and a piece of thread to begin*
- *all materials used are found locally, e.g. in thrift stores*
- *in fashion terms: upcycling = ethical fashion*
- *benefits: saves water and electricity; reduces carbon pollution, i.e. cuts your carbon footprint*

Der Schüler/Die Schülerin ...
führt mit einer Einleitung in die Aufgabenstellung ein
fasst zusammen, was mit *upcycling* gemeint ist: – Umwandlung von gebrauchten, eigentlich ausgedienten Stoffen zu neuen Produkten – Wiederverwertung von bereits vorhandenem Material
benennt die Vorteile von *upcycling:* – Wasserersparnis – Energieersparnis – verbessert die eigene CO_2-Bilanz
fasst die wichtigsten Erkenntnisse abschließend zusammen

2. Analysis

author's attitude

- *fast fashion and sustainability is a contradiction in itself; exclude one another (ll. 1–2)*
- *companies' efforts are nothing but PR attempts (l. 23: "greenwashing") to attract new customers, critical customers who would otherwise refrain from buying from those companies*
- *if companies were serious about sustainability, they would produce fewer clothes and they would ask their customers to buy fewer clothes*
- *asks readers "to boycott the fast fashion industry and resist the urge to buy new clothes on a weekly or monthly basis" (ll. 34–36)*

the means by which the attitude is conveyed

- *ll. 38–56: use of **imperatives;** provides her readers with a checklist, enabling them to tick off the things they might already do; most people enjoy lists, gives them a feeling of accomplishment and effectiveness*
- *ll. 1–2: "Fast fashion and sustainability are an oxymoron." / ll. 11–12: "They create sustainable and eco-friendly lines" → **clear sentence structure (subject, verb, object),** typical of blog entries: not as complex as the sentence structures you will find in traditional newspapers*
- *predominance/enumeration of **main clauses,** not many subordinate clauses → possibly monotonous but easy to understand; many people read blog entries on their mobile devices, i.e. while on public transport or in public places, with a limited attention span*
- ***point of view is presented openly and directly:** checklist in ll. 38–56*

- ***quoting experts to give weight to arguments:*** *quotes from an article in Al Jazeera (ll. 13–24) and quotes by Livia Firth of Eco Age, a consulting firm in London (ll. 28–31) (Livia Firth also happens to be the wife of actor Colin Firth)*
- ***choice of language/words that trigger(s) associations***
  "churn out" (l. 3) → impersonal choice of words, no mention of the people behind it
  "entice" (l. 12) → acknowledging that shopping is about emotions ('retail therapy')
  "resist the urge" (ll. 34–35) → acknowledging that clothes shopping has a lot to do with emotions; and that saying 'no' can be difficult; just as difficult as losing weight, for example
  "hopping on the eco-friendly bandwagon" (l. 61) → hopping is a carefree way of moving, i.e. fast fashion companies are not really serious about wanting to change their ways

Der Schüler/Die Schülerin ...
führt mit einer Einleitung zur Textanalyse hin
formuliert die Meinung der Autorin: Fast Fashion und Nachhaltigkeit vertragen sich nicht, sind ein Widerspruch in sich
erkennt einige der im Artikel verwendeten sprachlichen und stilistischen Mittel, belegt sie am Text und benennt, zumindest teilweise, die beabsichtigte Wirkung auf den Leser
schließt mit einer Zusammenfassung der wichtigsten Erkenntnisse

3. **Comment**

- ***Yes,*** *I am convinced that the suggestions from both the news report and the blog entry present real alternatives to buying fast fashion. However, I believe that the suggestions from the blog entry are a lot more helpful than the idea of upcycling from the news report.*
  The idea of upcycling will appeal to people who are interested in arts and crafts. But for people like me, who have never held a needle and a piece of thread in their life, it is asking a lot. I cannot see myself taking to upcycling any time soon although I agree that it is a nice idea.
  However, most of the suggestions from the blog entry are easy to put into practice. Thrift stores or charity shops have become very popular in Germany over the past few years, and my mum and I often stop by our local charity shop when we are in town. We have both been able to pick up some nice clothes from there. They are usually not very expensive, and we feel a lot better buying from a charity shop than from a fast fashion chain.
  The thing I like about the suggestions from the blog entry is that you could start with just one or two things from the list. In my opinion, the suggestions acknowledge that small changes to our behaviour make a difference, too, and will hopefully make our world a better place.
- ***No,*** *I do not see how any of the suggestions presented will help. Clothes shopping is about so much more than clothes shopping. Just think of the term 'retail therapy', which suggests that shopping is therapeutic for many people, that there are psychological needs which make people shop casually and continually. And I do not see that those needs would be met by doing "a clothing swap with friends" (l. 55). This approach reminds me of wanting to tell someone how to wean themselves off chocolate, e.g. by doing sports more often, an approach which does not really acknowledge what is going on. In order to change people's behaviour, we need to address the emotional needs governing their actions.*
  In addition, I think there is a major problem with all of this: I do not think that many people are serious about wanting to do something to help the environment. I think that for the majority of people sustainability is not really an issue. They might want to protect the environment on paper, but not when it comes to actually having to change their ways. To be honest, I think there are very few people who are prepared to make even the smallest sacrifice if they cannot immediately see the effect. I am sorry to sound so negative or pessimistic.
  The majority of articles suggesting alternatives to buying fast fashion will be read by "those slightly more discerning or skeptical customers" (ll. 12–13 of blog entry), who in most cases are not the ones buying fast fashion in large quantities.

Der Schüler/Die Schülerin ...
formuliert eine in das Thema einführende Einleitung
macht die eigene Meinung deutlich: ob die in *news report* und Blogeintrag vorgestellten Ideen sinnvolle, realistische Alternativen zum Kaufen von Fast Fashion darstellen
strukturiert die Argumente und greift dabei mindestens zwei Aspekte aus *news report* oder Blogeintrag auf, um daran anknüpfend den eigenen Standpunkt zu erläutern
schließt mit einer Zusammenfassung

Theme 8 Mediation (→ Kopiervorlage Seite 134)

1. *claims/criticism by German government official/politician/minister in charge of developing countries that the official Adidas shirt celebrating Germany winning the football World Cup was manufactured in sweatshops in Bangladesh; shirt is sold for 85 euros, of which the garment worker will have received a mere 15 cents; Adidas is the official sponsor of Germany's national football team*
2. *press release stating that the shirts were produced in China, not in Bangladesh; accusing the politician of not knowing his facts and not having contacted Adidas directly to find out more*
3. *Adidas's football shirts are selling well; sales figures January to September 2014: > two million*
4. *garments sell really well; sports brands not prepared to accept responsibility for working conditions in the countries where their garments are manufactured; not prepared to pay garment workers in countries with cheap labour fair wages*

Der Schüler/Die Schülerin ...
gibt die im Sinne der Aufgabenstellung wichtigen Informationen präzise und situations- bzw. adressatenorientiert wieder
gliedert die Inhalte klar und logisch und löst sich, der Aufgabenstellung entsprechend, ggf. von Struktur und Reihenfolge des Ausgangstextes
beachtet die sprachlichen Erfordernisse der Aufgabenstellung
verwendet den nötigen thematischen und funktionalen Wortschatz treffend
erläutert relevante kulturspezifische Begriffe, hier z. B. Entwicklungsminister, DFB
verzichtet auf wortwörtliche Übersetzungen und das Äußern der eigenen Meinung

Theme 8 Reading and writing (→ Kopiervorlage Seite 135)

1. Comprehension
   - *clothing companies are trying to make their customers believe that the workers producing their garments are well looked after; that their working conditions meet the standards set by the International Labor Organization, including a guarantee that no child labour is involved*
   - *actual situation: child labour, very low wages, workers being fired and/or beaten if they speak up for their rights, workers not being paid their agreed wages, people speaking up for workers' rights receiving death threats*

Der Schüler/Die Schülerin ...
führt mit einer Einleitung in die Aufgabenstellung ein
benennt den Eindruck, den die Bekleidungsindustrie ihren Kundinnen und Kunden gegenüber vermitteln möchte: – dass die Bedingungen für Arbeitnehmer in den Herstellerländern gut sind – dass die Industrie sich internationalen Bestimmungen zum Schutz von Arbeitnehmern verpflichtet fühlt, u. a. dem Verzicht auf Kinderarbeit
fasst zusammen, wie sich die Situation in Billiglohnländern tatsächlich darstellt, u. a.: – Kinderarbeit – sehr niedrige Löhne – Mitarbeiter, die sich arbeitsrechtlich organisieren, erhalten Morddrohungen, werden entlassen oder verprügelt

2. Analysis
   - ***use of strong or emotive, i.e. negative, adjectives:*** *"defeated" (l. 12), "horrific factories" (l. 13), "gloomy mood" (l. 16), "murderous threats" (l. 41)*
   - *l. 10: "But not that much has changed." → short, clear, simple, to the point*
   - *l. 14: "exposed by", "the Institute secretly met with workers" (ll. 18–19) → implies that some people would have liked to keep the information secret, confidential, out of the public eye*
   - *"expensive sweaters" (l. 21) → emphasis/contrast to highlight the discrepancy between the price of finished product and the wages paid to workers*
   - *ll. 27–28: "Well, that turns out not to exactly be the case." → irony, understatement*
   - *ll. 40–42: "There was every reason to take these murderous threats seriously" → emphasis*
   - *"not even a legally recognized union" (ll. 38–39) → "not even" for emphasis*

– *"Sweatshops still make your clothes" (heading), "most Americans* still *likely know very little" (ll. 28–29) → "still" to emphasise that nothing has changed over the past sixteen years*

Der Schüler/Die Schülerin ...
führt mit einer Einleitung in die Aufgabenstellung ein
untersucht die Wortwahl und erkennt einige der verwendeten sprachlichen Mittel, die – die kritische Haltung *(task a)* bzw. – den negativen Blickwinkel *(task b)* unterstreichen bzw. zum Ausdruck bringen, z. B.: – negativ konnotierte Adjektive: *"defeated"* (Zeile 12), *"horrific"* (Zeile 13), *"gloomy"* (Zeile 16), *"murderous"* (Zeile 41) – Ironie: *"Well, that turns out not to exactly be the case."* (Zeile 27f.) – Betonung/Verstärkung: *"There was every reason to take these murderous threats seriously"* (Zeile 40–42), *"not even a legally recognized union"* (Zeile 38f.) / *"Sweatshops still make your clothes"* (Überschrift), *"most Americans* still *likely know very little"* (Zeile 28f.) – *"exposed by"* (Zeile 14), *"the Institute secretly met with workers"* (Zeile 18f.) → Kritik an denen, die die Informationen lieber unveröffentlicht sehen würden
benennt, zumindest teilweise, die beabsichtigte Wirkung auf den Leser
fasst die wichtigsten Erkenntnisse abschließend zusammen

3. Comment

– ***I agree*** *that our clothing choices might be very limited, possibly even more limited than I think but that does not mean that we should give up and resign ourselves to the situation. I think it is tempting for us to sit back and say that there is so much going on behind the scenes that we do not know about that we might as well not bother about trying to buy ethically. I have often heard it said that people think it does not matter where we buy our clothes as there is no such thing as ethical labour anyway. People are taking the fact that our choices as consumers are limited as an excuse not to get involved in the first place, and that is an attitude I find appalling. In order to change the world for the better, we need to get involved.*

– ***I don't agree*** *with the sentiment put forward in the statement. I think we as consumers are more powerful than we might think. Our clothing choices might be limited but there are still plenty of clothing choices out there for even the most discerning or skeptical customers. And what is wrong with a limited choice? Do your homework, find out about fashion brands that produce their garments locally or domestically and then stick with them. You might be limited to one brand but within this one brand you will have an unlimited choice of ethical fashion.*
It seems to be a sign of our times that limited choice is considered something negative. It seems to be a matter of "The grass is always greener on the other side." If people were more content with what they have, they would not start looking for replacements so soon, which would do our environment a world of good.

Der Schüler/Die Schülerin ...
führt mit einer Einleitung in die Aufgabenstellung ein
macht die eigene Meinung deutlich, bezieht also Position zu den Herausforderungen der Modeindustrie
strukturiert die Argumente und greift dabei mindestens zwei Aspekte auf, die in der Unterrichtseinheit zur Sprache kamen, um daran anknüpfend den eigenen Standpunkt zu erläutern
schließt mit einer Zusammenfassung

Reading and writing

1. **Comprehension:** Read the article and outline the reasons given for taking a gap year.

2. **Analysis:** Analyze the language the author uses to influence the reader's opinion on gap years.

3. **Comment:** Write a letter to the editor commenting on the views expressed in the article.

"Constructive gap years help students stand out to employers and universities"

by Tom Griffiths, founder of gapyear.com

Some nasty facts are facing the class of 2009. Graduate jobs are thin on the ground[1] – and may continue to be so for years to come. The Bank of Mum and Dad is under pressure, and the yellow brick road[2] to university and a career that will pay off student debt[3] is being questioned. And quite rightly so.

Taking a gap year – this year, more than any other – has become a serious option for many. It's not about travel and volunteering. Far from it. It's about a constructive use of time that will enable young people to find and demonstrate focus, showcase their abilities, and discover a life path that works for them, both financially and emotionally.

Constructive gap years help students stand out to employers and universities.

Admissions tutors[4] point out that, while gap-year experiences will never be a substitute for not having the required grades, a constructive year can often add weight to an individual's case, particularly for vocational degrees. What marine biology course wouldn't choose a candidate fresh from a year on a Malaysian reef project over an identical student unable to show even a basic interest?

An ability to demonstrate genuine interest and to talk knowledgeably in an interview around the subject based on real experiences will fast-track[5] you on to the shortlists[6].

Graduate recruiters[7], who now have demand outstripping[8] supply, also place enormous value on gap-year experiences. Sitting in a bath of cat food to raise money for a six-month placement shadowing a vet on a lion project in Kenya, or a 10,000-mile adventure in a pink tuk-tuk raising funds for charity – both real examples, two of the thousands I see each year – jump out from the mass of bland[9], identical, CVs.

Demonstration of character, ambition, achievement, key skills and life experiences trump a generic[10] degree every time. Employers want young people keen to follow a well thought-out life path, not robotic exam-factory clones.

Students need more than just good results to take that important first step on their chosen life path, no matter what they're aiming for. Work experience and proof of an interest in a career are a necessity. The gap year is an ideal time to "test-drive" jobs to get this experience.

The Independent, Monday, 17 August 2009

[1] **thin on the ground** = not available in large numbers [2] **yellow brick road** = golden path to a place of your hopes and dreams [3] **debt** = money that you have to give back [4] **admissions tutor** = so. at a university who reads the incoming applications and decides who should be offered a place [5] **to fast-track** = to make sth. happen more quickly than usual [6] **shortlist** = list of candidates who might be good for a job [7] **graduate recruiter** = so. who helps people who have just finished university to find job [8] **to outstrip** = to become larger than sth. else [9] **bland** = nothing special, boring [10] **generic** = normal, unspecific

name: ____________________

Listening – version A

DVD

1. Listen to a report about gap-year students in Australia and choose the correct/best answers below. You may tick **one** answer only for each question.

   a. The report is mainly about
   - ☐ the experiences of former gap-year students.
   - ☐ tips for gap years worldwide.
   - ☐ the pros and cons of a gap year.
   - ☐ how to make the most of your gap year in Australia.

   b. Finding a flat or house is
   - ☐ something that gappers usually only manage once they have stayed in a hostel for three or four months.
   - ☐ much easier if you use the Internet and join forces with other gappers.
   - ☐ very difficult so you should be grateful if you end up in somewhere like a fire station.
   - ☐ not really necessary in some places as you can camp outside with other backpackers.

   c. The Working Holiday Scheme
   - ☐ is something that exists only in Australia.
   - ☐ provides you with the money you need to get by.
   - ☐ allows you to travel and look for a job all over Australia.
   - ☐ puts you in a particular place where you can earn the money you need.

2. Listen again. Tick the statements that are **true** according to the people interviewed.
   - ☐ Working in telesales is a common job for gappers.
   - ☐ If you are afraid you might not find a job, you can contact companies in the UK that help you with everything (applications, arranging job interviews etc.).
   - ☐ If you want to go to Sydney, you needn't worry because you won't have any problems finding a job that suits you.
   - ☐ If you are willing to meet and talk to people, you will have no problems making friends in Australia.
   - ☐ You should plan your travel route in detail before you arrive in order to not have to worry about travelling around Australia on your own.
   - ☐ In order to prepare for your gap year, it's a good idea to read gappers' blogs.
   - ☐ There are two things you will need if you would like to work in Australia: a work and holiday visa and a bank account in Australia.
   - ☐ There are a number of companies specializing in assisting gap-year travellers with anything they need, even job training.
   - ☐ For anyone working in Australia during their gap year, it is important to bear in mind that they must pay taxes when they leave the country.

name: ______________________________

Listening – version B

1. Listen to a report about gap-year students in Australia and choose the correct/best answers below. DVD

   You may tick **one** answer only for each question.

   a. The report is mainly about
   - ☐ the advantages and disadvantages of gap years.
   - ☐ what previous gap-year students experienced.
   - ☐ what you can do to have the best possible gap year in Australia.
   - ☐ advice for gap years around the world.

   b. Finding somewhere to live
   - ☐ is less difficult for gappers who use the Internet and join forces with gappers they have made friends with.
   - ☐ does not need to be your priority as you can often sleep in tents with other gappers.
   - ☐ is so difficult that you may consider yourself lucky if you can find somewhere as exotic as a fire station.
   - ☐ usually takes three to four months.

   c. The Working Holiday Scheme
   - ☐ provides you with the financial support you need to cover your basic expenses.
   - ☐ gives you the right to go anywhere in Australia and look for a job.
   - ☐ tells you where to look for work and earn the money you need to travel around Australia.
   - ☐ can only be found in Australia.

2. Listen again. Decide if these statements are **true or false** according to the people interviewed.

	true	false
a. Working in telesales is a typical job for gappers.	☐	☐
b. In order to make finding a job abroad less stressful and scary, there are companies in the UK that help you with everything beforehand (looking and applying for a job, arranging interviews etc.).	☐	☐
c. Sydney is such a competitive job market that it's very hard to find a job that suits you.	☐	☐
d. Making friends in Australia is difficult even for open-minded people who like chatting and socializing.	☐	☐
e. Travelling on your own is nothing you need to worry about, so there's no need to plan ahead in any detail.	☐	☐
f. Gappers' blogs are not the best source of information when it comes to preparing a trip.	☐	☐
g. Two things are necessary if you want to work in Australia: a work and holiday visa and an Australian bank account.	☐	☐
h. There are companies in Australia that provide gappers with everything they need, from bank accounts to job training.	☐	☐
i. Gappers must remember to pay taxes when they leave the country.	☐	☐

name: ______________________________

Speaking (monologue)

1. Pick a card and – in your own words – describe the opportunity/challenge that is presented.
2. Comment on what you would do in the situation and why.

Make sure you refer to the information on the card.

A

You have been invited to take part in a volunteering programme in Australia which would allow you to work on a wildlife rescue station in the outback for a year. The programme includes accommodation and food as well as some pocket money, but you would have to pay for your flight as well as for any travelling you decide to do in Australia.

B

The company/institution where you did your work experience in class 9 or 10 has offered you a similar internship at their branch/with a partner company in the UK.
You could do it next summer but you would have to pay for your flight and your accommodation yourself and you would have to stay for at least five weeks.

C

A friend of yours has suggested that you do a *duales Studium* for International Business Studies. The company in question expects their students to spend eight months abroad – four months in the UK and four months in France or Spain. If you do not have the necessary language skills, you will be expected to attend special language courses before and during your time with the company.

D

Your best friend has asked you to join him/her after the *Abitur* when s/he intends to spend nine months in Canada as part of a "work and travel" programme.
You would need about 3,000 euros to cover all the costs of the programme. Also, you should think of jobs you might be good at or willing to do to earn the money needed to cover your living expenses once in Canada.

E

Friends of your parents know a family in Manchester, England, who are looking for an au pair. You would live with the family, look after their two children, aged 3 and 4, take them to kindergarten and pick them up and spend time with them while their parents are at work. You would earn a little pocket money, and you would be expected to join the family, all expenses paid, on their holidays to faraway places like the Maldives and New Zealand.

F

A charity organisation is looking for someone to help at a home for orphans and disabled children in the Gambia, an English-speaking country in West Africa. It would be your job to play with the children, get them up in the morning, put them to bed at night and help with other jobs around the home.
The home is in an area with a significant risk of malaria, but very few previous participants contracted malaria and those who did fully recovered.

name: ______________________________

Speaking (dialogue) – job advertisement A

1. a. One of you is the applicant, the other one is the interviewer.
   b. Study the job advertisement and the support cards.
   c. Do a job interview based on the job advertisement and on what is expected of you in your roles.
2. Follow the steps as in 1., but swap roles.

Note: As the applicant, base what you say on your own qualifications, experience and character.
You may add information if necessary.

Daniels Resorts

Vacancy: Waiting person

When: Summer season

Location: Greece

Our restaurant staff play an important part in making sure our guests receive our special Daniels service in all our hotel restaurants. As well as waiting on tables, our restaurant staff are essential to providing the excellent service and customer relations that our Daniels guests have come to know and love.

You will provide a high level of service at all meal times in buffet and à la carte restaurants providing all service styles, including wine service, tray and table service. As part of a motivated team you will be key in creating a comfortable and welcoming atmosphere in our restaurants. You will be expected to know our wine/cocktails lists as well as snack bar/bistro menus in order to make educated recommendations to our guests during meal times. We will train you in all of these areas, but you need to have the willingness to learn and the character to put it into practice.

You will need to be highly motivated, extremely perceptive in understanding what a customer may want and have the confidence to relate to all types of guests in all situations.
You will have a highly likeable personality, be an excellent team player and a confident salesperson. You will display the highest levels of outward appearance and hygiene and be friendly and approachable at all times.

To join our restaurant team, you will ideally have worked in a similar position before in a hotel, restaurant, café or coffee shop and have proven customer service experience.

name: ______________________________

Speaking (dialogue) – job advertisement B

1. a. One of you is the applicant, the other one is the interviewer.
   b. Study the job advertisement and the support cards.
   c. Do a job interview based on the job advertisement and on what is expected of you in your roles.
2. Follow the steps as in 1., but swap roles.

Note: As the applicant, base what you say on your own qualifications, experience and character.

You may add information if necessary.

Stars & Stripes Summer Camps

Teach Sports in America!

There are hundreds of sports for you to teach and assist in. Any sport you can think of – from tennis to soccer, roller hockey to basketball and everything in between.

So, you're over 18, you're ready to travel and, most of all, you want to have an UNBELIEVABLE summer. Look no further as this placement is for you! Stars & Stripes Summer Camp offers a diverse range of camps all across the US, from California to New York.

Get paid spending your summer having fun, gaining valuable experience as an instructor and doing all the things you really want to do! Seems too good to be true, right? Wrong, it gets even better – it's a known fact that camp friends are friends for life. You'll have the opportunity to meet people from around the world, learn new things and have the option to travel around the States with them.

Preparation

Stars & Stripes Summer Camp will provide the placement which suits you best! We help you through the preparation stage, step by step, right through to your flight departure. We provide all the necessary information, such as choosing the right style of camp. Whether you want to be a "specialist" or a "general" counsellor, there's a place ideally suited to you. Don't worry – we've got it covered.

You must be available for 9 weeks, starting in late May/June and running into August. Following this, you will get about 8 weeks to travel around the US and see as many sights as you wish! It doesn't get much better than that!

Let's Talk Numbers

For an unmissable experience from only £399, you'll get:

- A summer camp placement in the USA
- Return transatlantic flights
- Food and accommodation while at camp
- 90 days comprehensive medical insurance
- Visa documentation
- Up to 8 weeks of travel time in the US
- The summer of a lifetime!

For a further breakdown and more information head to our website now: www.usasummercamp.co.uk
Trust us when we say that there is no better place than camp!
Get on board and prepare for the #bestsummerofyourlife

name: ______________________________

Speaking (dialogue) – job advertisement C

1. a. One of you is the applicant, the other one is the interviewer.
   b. Study the job advertisement and the support cards.
   c. Do a job interview based on the job advertisement and on what is expected of you in your roles.
2. Follow the steps as in 1., but swap roles.

Note: As the applicant, base what you say on your own qualifications, experience and character.

You may add information if necessary.

Helping Hand Au Pair Agency London

Live-in au pair required – Golders Green, North London

About the family

We are a family with two children, aged 6 and 2.
We live in Golders Green (North London) and are looking for a loving and reliable live-in au pair to look after our two girls.

Working hours

Mon: 7.30 am–1.00 pm
Tues: housework only (approx. 3.5 hrs)
Wed–Fri: 7.30 am–6.00 pm

Main duties

- Looking after the younger girl during the day, taking her for walks, going to play groups, doing craft projects, meeting up with other children.
- Looking after the older child when she comes home from school, which will include helping with her homework.
- Other activities include doing the children's laundry, preparing healthy meals for the children, keeping the children's rooms and play areas clean and tidy.
- Three evenings per month of babysitting (arranged in advance).

The ideal person must be

- friendly
- professional
- reliable
- a non-smoker
- prepared to stay for at last a year
- fluent in English

Accommodation

You will have your own room with your own bathroom, Wi-Fi and TV.

Salary

£90–£100 per week, depending on experience

name: ______________________________

Speaking (dialogue) – job advertisement D

1. a. One of you is the applicant, the other one is the interviewer.
   b. Study the job advertisement and the support cards.
   c. Do a job interview based on the job advertisement and on what is expected of you in your roles.
2. Follow the steps as in 1., but swap roles.

Note: As the applicant, base what you say on your own qualifications, experience and character.

You may add information if necessary.

Charity Fundraiser with St John Ambulance

We are a volunteer-led charity providing and teaching about first aid and are currently looking for fundraisers to engage in door-to-door activities, generating fresh support for St John Ambulance.

This exciting role involves joining one of our fundraising teams and communicating with the general public on a daily basis, with the aim of generating an income for charitable activities across the UK.

All our teams are based in fully furnished, family-style homes of a high standard – a real home away from home. A company car is provided for each team.

We are looking for motivated, driven and ethically-minded individuals with the confidence to clearly promote and market our activities and services.

In return for your hard work we provide a unique and rewarding pay structure.

- £1500+ per month
- hourly pay
- high standard of accommodation provided
- funded travel to start working with us

Working hours
36 hours per week

Development
full training provided

With both long-term and short-term jobs available throughout the year, the role of a fundraiser can be a great opportunity for a summer job or an excellent step into the charity sector to build a career.

name: ______________________________

Speaking (dialogue) – job advertisement E

1. a. One of you is the applicant, the other one is the interviewer.
   b. Study the job advertisement and the support cards.
   c. Do a job interview based on the job advertisement and on what is expected of you in your roles.
2. Follow the steps as in 1., but swap roles.

Note: As the applicant, base what you say on your own qualifications, experience and character.

You may add information if necessary.

OWEN'S – The Clothing Company

With over 70 stores around Great Britain, we are always on the lookout for enthusiastic, energetic and fun sales assistants. You will find that our wonderful retail teams have one thing in common – a real passion for our brand!

We are currently looking for **temporary sales assistants** to support us over the summer period in our branch in Falmouth, Cornwall.

We will expect you to create an amazing shopping experience, combining an **expert understanding of Owen's products,** for children, women and men alike, and a friendly, welcoming environment for our customers. A key element of your role will be assisting in maintaining exceptional store standards.

These opportunities offer contracts of 8 hours but candidates must be flexible to take on extra hours if necessary.

In return, we offer lots of on-the-job training and coaching and a fantastic opportunity to develop your career with us – so come and join Owen's now!

Support card: applicant

Explain

- what made you apply for the job
- why your qualifications make you the ideal person for the position
- experiences you have that might be relevant to the job
- what you expect from the job as regards training, social skills, language skills etc.

Make sure you

- refer to the information in the job advertisement
- are polite and use formal language
- react to what the interviewer says
- ask questions about the job/company to show that you prepared the interview well

Support card: interviewer

Ask the candidate

- to say something about himself/herself
- to talk about why he/she applied for the job
- to explain which qualifications make him/her the ideal person for the job
- to describe his/her expectations
- to ask questions about the job/company/ …

Make sure you

- refer to the information in the job advertisement
- are polite and use formal language
- react to what the applicant says

Language support

– *Could you please tell me what/why/…?*
– *What made you apply for the position?*
– *What do you consider your strengths/weaknesses?*
– *What do you expect from the job?*
– *Do you have any questions about the job?*

name: ______________________________

Mediation

Sie besuchen als Austauschschüler/in eine US-amerikanische Highschool und werden von der Sozialkundelehrerin gebeten, das europäische Austauschprogramm Erasmus vorzustellen. Verfassen Sie auf der Grundlage des folgenden Artikels einen Informationstext **auf Englisch,** aus dem hervorgeht, was das Erasmus-Programm ausmacht, wie es funktioniert und was das Besondere daran ist.

„Hey, hier ist Europa, und ich bin mittendrin"

von Amory Burchard

Am Anfang war ein Film, „L'auberge espagnole". Als Marie 16 war, hat sie den Film mit ihren Eltern als Video angeschaut. Ihr Vater hat mitgefiebert, als der französische Austauschstudent Xavier in diese WG in Barcelona kam. Die ganzen Typen aus verschiedenen Ländern, die Kneipen, die Freundinnen, war schon eine tolle Zeit. Von der Uni hat man nicht viel gesehen, aber darauf kam es wohl auch gar nicht an. Immerhin war ihr Vater 1987 einer der ersten gut 600 deutschen Erasmus-Studenten. Ihre Mutter wollte beim Abspann wissen: Und, Marie, wo willst du mal dein Erasmus-Jahr verbringen?

Vier Jahre später, Anfang 2012, hat das Austauschprogramm der EU Geburtstag, es wird 25. Und Marie, die fiktive Musterstudentin, ist inzwischen für Wirtschaftswissenschaften an einer Uni in Ostdeutschland eingeschrieben – und „macht Erasmus" in Madrid.

Nicht gerade originell, hatte der Berater im Auslandsamt gesagt und die Statistik heruntergeleiert. Spanien ist das beliebteste Land bei deutschen Erasmus-Studenten, von den 30 000, die im vergangenen Jahr in dem EU-Programm studiert oder ein Auslandspraktikum gemacht haben, waren gut 20 Prozent dort. Dass sie als Wirtschaftswissenschaftlerin ins Ausland wolle, sei auch typisch, die seien viel mobiler als die Natur- und Technikwissenschaftler. Aber insgesamt wollen doch immer weniger ein Auslandsjahr machen, weil im Bachelor keine Zeit ist?, wollte Marie wissen. Es gab nur einen kleinen Knick, hat der Berater gesagt, 2010/11 war schon wieder ein Rekordjahr. Insgesamt waren schon fast drei Millionen junge Europäer mit dem Programm im Ausland!

Nach ein paar Tagen auf dem Campus, im Café und in den Clubs von Madrid simst Marie an ihre Eltern: Hey, hier ist Europa, und ich bin mittendrin, fühlt sich toll an. Nur das mit der internationalen WG hat nicht geklappt. Die Zimmerpreise sind einfach zu hoch für ihr Auslands-Bafög und die 250 Euro Erasmus-Zuschuss pro Monat. Marie teilt sich im Wohnheim einen Raum mit einer Deutschen. Sie nimmt sich vor, richtig Spanisch zu lernen und zur nächsten Erasmus-Party zu gehen.

Wichtig ist ihr aber auch, dass es mit dem Studieren hinhaut, sie will kein Semester verlieren. Marie hat geklärt, dass die Kurse zu Hause anerkannt werden. Das ist ein echtes Problem im Bachelor, vieles ist so spezialisiert, dass es nicht mal in Deutschland zusammenpasst. Aber die Unis arbeiten daran, hat Marie gehört.

Der Tagesspiegel, 31. Januar 2012

name: ____________________

Reading and writing

1. **Comprehension:** Summarize the following extract from "(Un)Arranged Marriage" by Bali Rai paying particular attention to Manjit and his description of his environment.
2. **Analysis:** Analyze how Manjit presents his hometown and how narrative techniques are used to emphasize his view of Leicester and its multicultural population. Then compare Manjit's view on multiculturalism to the one expressed in the cartoon.

3. Choose task **a.** or **b.**
   a. **Comment:** Comment on the views expressed both in the extract and the cartoon and present **your** view of multiculturalism – do you think it is "the way it should be" (l. 13)?
   b. **Creative writing:** Rewrite the extract from the perspective of Manjit's father as the first-person narrator. Consider what you know about him and his relationship with Manjit. Imagine how he would describe Leicester, its multicultural society and Manjit's role in it.

We walked on up the road as all around us the hustle and bustle[1] of cars, buses, customers and shopowners continued. I was playing a game that I had invented called 'spot the white man'. The whole area was about ninety per cent Asian. All the shops were owned by Asians apart from a fish restaurant, a couple of hairdressers and a florist. Most of the people on the street were Asian too, or black. It was one of the things that I loved about Leicester. Some areas were nearly all white, some black and some Asian. And everyone kind of melted into the city centre so that it was all multicultural. I liked that – it was the way it should be – only it wasn't the way that my family saw it, or even Ady's when it came down to[2] it. We used to say all the time, Ady and me, that it was down to us kids to sort things out. I mean, I was born in England. I liked being born in England. It was my home. If you stuck me on the streets of Delhi or Mumbai I wouldn't have a clue what to do or where to go. In England I knew how things worked. Man, England was my country and Ady's. Ours.

Ady broke my train of thought. 'Bwoi, it's getting to be like little Delhi round here, man.'

I just looked at him and grinned, suggesting that maybe the city council should change the name of the area as we passed by a pizza takeaway that included tandoori chicken, keema, and mutter paneer[3] in its list of toppings – a clever thing to do in a mainly Asian neighbourhood, even though most of the shop's customers were white students.

As I crossed over Beckingham Road, halfway up Evington Road, I realized why I loved this part of Leicester so much. On the one side there was Highfields, an area that loads of people called the ghetto. I suppose a few parts of it were dangerous but mostly it got a bad rep[4] because loads of black and Asian people lived there, and all the racists couldn't handle that. There was this image of it as being full of drugs and prostitutes and gangs. Well, it had all of those things – but then so did lots of other areas of Leicester and if some of the people that slagged[5] the place off ever actually bothered to go see for themselves, they would find big old houses, with huge cellars and attic rooms, named after Greek gods and stuff. [...]

On the other side of Evington Road the streets all ran up towards London Road, which led you into Clarendon Park and, further south, to Stoneygate, two of Leicester's posher areas. In fact, a lot of the houses in the posher areas, especially in Clarendon Park, were dead similar to the ones in Highfields, with the same narrow streets. The only difference was that Clarendon Park was much more middle class and had loads more white families living there which automatically gave it a better reputation in the eyes of some ignorant people.

That was what I loved about living where I did. Evington Road was like a fence that I could sit on. Each day I could make a choice about whether I wanted to jump over to the Highfields side or the London Road side. It was wicked[6] because some days Ady and me would be messing about in the narrow back streets of the ghetto, and the next we'd meet Ben, Penny and Parmy up the London Road to play football or cricket on the hockey pitch they had up there, or cross into Clarendon Park so that we could go shoplifting at the Spar.

[1] **hustle and bustle** = hectic pace (here: of life in the city) [2] **to come down to sth.** = to be the most important aspect of sth.
[3] **tandoori chicken, keema, mutter paneer** = traditional Indian dishes/ingredients [4] **rep** = reputation [5] **to slag sth. off** = to put sth down, talk badly about it [6] **wicked** = here: cool, awesome [7] **bloody** = here: a typical English swear word

name: ______________________________

Reading and writing

"Ban teens from chat rooms"

Children should be kept out of chat rooms, argues technology analyst Bill Thompson.

It was, it seems, the Internet's fault. Young and foolish, 12-year-old Shevaun Pennington[1] found a friend online and decided that what he had to offer was more exciting than the boys in school.

She joins a long line of other children who have met people in chat rooms or over e-mail and been persuaded to turn an online friendship into a real-world one, with consequences that will terrify any parent.

It is traditional for those of us who have been online for many years to leap to the net's defence at times like this, arguing that parental ignorance is to blame and that anyway the net brings benefits which far outweigh any risks it may pose to children.

I don't propose to do this.

Shevaun's disappearance was the net's fault and we have to accept this.

[…]

Certainly, parents need to be aware of what their children are doing online, but none of us is perfect and always alert to danger.

We can restrict their access, or install safety software, but our kids also need space to grow up, privacy from even their parents, and a sense that they are trusted.

Monitoring every e-mail, sitting in on every chat and checking web access logs is not the way, certainly for the over-10s.

While there are significant benefits to being online and to using the resources available on the net, the balance between these benefits and the dangers needs to be better understood, and a new understanding is required.

[…] we should not automatically let problems with chat and e-mail change the way we let children use the web.

The major problem is chat, and as far back as February I argued that the prevalence[2] of predatory[3] adult males in online chat rooms had been demonstrated so clearly that it was time to exclude kids from chat rooms where adults might be present.

The experiences of Shevaun and other children like her have only confirmed my view that kids do not need to use chat rooms to talk to strangers.

In the last couple of months my 12-year-old daughter has started chatting to her friends online, and she enjoys the experience greatly. […]

However we have a deal. She has let me set up her chat service so that only people on her contact list can see she is online or send her messages, and I get to look through her contact list to check that they are all friends I know.

And she doesn't go to public chat rooms.

This is a political, not a technical issue. Whatever age verification schemes we might come up with, a determined adult will find a way around them – or just find a way to steal a child's online identity and strike up conversation in an apparently trustworthy space.

[…]

The only answer is to keep kids out of these spaces – to make them adult-only and require age verification by those hosting them.

[…]

We should not let the net advocates try to persuade us to expose our children to the dangers of public chat rooms.

[1] Shevaun left home and flew to Paris with a man she had met in a chat room; she returned home after five days
[2] **prevalence** = the fact that sth. is very common in a particular place
[3] **predatory** = treat so. badly for your own benefit

"Tonight, Daddy's going to teach you how to stay safe on the Internet – now where's the on off switchy thingy?"

www.CartoonStock.com

1. **Comprehension:** Read the article "Ban teens from chat rooms" by Bill Thompson and summarize the main points.
2. **Analysis:**
   a. Analyze the author's point of view in the article and explain the means used to underline it.
   b. Analyze the cartoon and explain how its message is conveyed.
3. **Comment:** Assess to what extent both the article and the cartoon represent a biased approach towards young people using the Internet.

name: ______________________________

Viewing, reading and writing

A. Extract 4 from the film "The Social Network" (1:15.18–1:17.10) DVD

(Background: Facebook continues to grow, and Mark and most of his team have moved to Palo Alto, California, while Eduardo Saverin, who financed Facebook's early stages, stays in New York for an internship. In the extract, Sean Parker, an Internet entrepreneur who, as a teenager, started Napster, a free file-sharing service for music, visits Mark.)

B. Extract from Ben Mezrich's novel "The Accidental Billionaires. The Founding of Facebook"

(Eduardo Saverin, a friend and fellow student of Mark Zuckerberg's at Harvard, used his money to help Mark start Facebook. When Mark moves the company to California, Eduardo stays behind to do an internship in New York.)

But he couldn't help but be anxious about thefacebook, especially late at night, wondering how things were going in California with Mark and the rest of the team, what they were up to, what progress they had made – and why they weren't calling more often.

He rolled his eyes at himself […] Wasn't that the real reason he had booked the last-minute trip to California, to see for himself that his concerns were unfounded?

By the end of tonight, he was certain things would feel back to normal with thefacebook. He and Mark and the rest would have a blast, get some work done, and everything would be copacetic[1]. And it would all start with a bang.

Mark had said something about a party that Sean Parker had gotten them invited to […]. It would be fun, but there'd also be the opportunity to meet with more investor types, […] some major Silicon Valley players, even a few Internet celebs. According to Mark, Parker had already taken them to a handful of similar parties; over the past month since they'd hit California, Mark had seen all the highs the area had to offer. […]

Sean Parker knew everyone, and everyone knew Sean. Through him, everyone was getting to know Mark, too; thefacebook […] was slowly becoming the talk of the town, and it seemed like everybody wanted to meet the whiz kid behind the much-hyped social network. Eduardo couldn't help but grow more and more concerned each time he spoke to Mark, and heard about another milestone, party, or dinner that he had missed by being in New York. Worse yet, Mark was Mark – hard enough to read in person, but on the phone he was a complete mystery. Sometimes it was like talking to a computer. He heard what you said, digested it, but responded only if he felt a response was necessary. Sometimes he didn't respond at all.

If he was thrilled that Eduardo had finally made some real progress with advertisers […] he certainly wasn't showing it. To be fair, Mark and his team were working round the clock at adding features to the site, and signing up more and more schools.

[1] **copacetic** = in excellent order

1. **Comprehension:** Watch extract 4 (1:15.18–1:17.10) and outline what happens in the scene.
2. **Analysis:** Analyze how Mark Zuckerberg's character is presented in the film extract and in the extract from Ben Mezrich's novel. Give evidence from both the film extract and the text to illustrate Mark's character and the way he runs the company.
3. Choose task **a.** or **b.**
   a. **Comment:** Discuss whether you think Eduardo's concerns about what has been happening in California while he has been in New York are justified.
   b. **Creative writing:** Not having spoken to each other in person for weeks, Mark picks Eduardo up from the airport. On their way to the house, they talk about what they have been up to, how they see Facebook and their relationship as friends and business partners. Use your knowledge from both the film and the extract from the novel to write a dialogue between Mark and Eduardo.

name: ______________________________

Speaking (monologue)

Cartoon A

1. **Describe** the cartoon.
2. **Explain** the cartoonist's view.

"First it's surveillance cameras in schools and now my mom wants to be my friend on Facebook, so she can check up on me."

Speaking (monologue)

Cartoon B

1. **Describe** the cartoon.
2. **Explain** the cartoonist's view.

"The reason I never finish my homework is that I spend too much time tweeting about how I have too much homework."

name: ______________________________

Speaking (monologue)

Cartoon C

1. **Describe** the cartoon.
2. **Explain** the cartoonist's view.

Speaking (monologue)

Cartoon D

1. **Describe** the cartoon.
2. **Explain** the cartoonist's view.

"Think of an essay as a collection of tweets, only joined together."

name: ______________________________

Reading and speaking (dialogue) – text A

1. **Preparation:** Prepare the following article. Look up any words you do not understand and make sure you have a detailed knowledge of the article's contents.
2. **Exam:** With a partner who has prepared the same text, pick one of the three discussion cards for the text and follow the instructions.

'Facebook parenting' is destroying our children's privacy

by Aisha Sultan and Jon Miller

Today's 30-somethings are the first generation whose children are coming of age alongside the social Web.

Technology is making an indelible[1] imprint[2] on modern parenting, and there is a sense that our data, our personal information, are no longer within our control. But new research findings indicate that openness and information sharing are a way of life for many adults, and personal privacy is readily compromised, along with personal information about one's children.

In an attempt to understand how much privacy matters in this digital age, we questioned 4,000 young adults as part of the Longitudinal Study of American Youth, the largest and longest-running nationwide survey of its kind.

The same participants have been surveyed every year since 1987, when they were public middle or high school students across the country. The sample is now 37 to 40 years old.

Nearly a quarter of these Generation X young adults expressed a high level of concern about online privacy, while 40% reported a low level of concern. But the behaviors were more telling: Nearly 70% said they have shared their own photos online and post about nine personal pictures each year.

More than half (55%) said they have shared information or posted pictures from a vacation. Also, nearly two-thirds of parents (66%) reported posting pictures of their children online, and slightly more than half (56%) shared news of a child's accomplishment[3].

Well-intentioned parents with great instincts have a desire to share and connect about their children, which often helps foster[4] and maintain social ties to relatives and friends. Our extended families live in different states, and we enjoy being able to keep up with siblings, nieces and nephews. But there is a cost to connection, and many are unclear about what is lost and what is at stake[5].

By and large, the short-term implications of less-guarded personal privacy may be limited in scope, such as being vulnerable to burglary if vacation plans are publicly announced or victim to possible identity theft[6]. There are also amplified[7] consequences to using poor judgment when posting online, such as getting fired or sustaining damage to one's reputation.

But, there are also the decisions made about us that happen in the shadows, the calculations of who merits credit or constitutes an insurance risk, which are harder to track and weigh.

On the most basic level, we want to be able to tell our story about our lives. But, in the case of our children, a permanent and public story has already been recorded about them before they have a chance to decide whether they want to participate or even whether the narrative is true to their own vision of self.

In our survey, the greatest reported levels of concern about online privacy relate to online credit card use (67% said they were very or somewhat concerned) and online banking services (61%), followed by concerns about social networks (57%). Concerns about social networks were greater than those about online medical records, search engines, instant messaging and texting. How this concern translates into behavior is less clear.

The message from parents, as witnessed from behavior, is clear. Children grow up learning that posting pictures of one's self and sharing personal information is typical. We've created a sense of normality about a world where what's private is public. The sense of being entitled to[8] privacy has been devalued.

And our children will never have known a world without this sort of exposure[9]. What does a worldview lacking an expectation of privacy mean for the rest of society?

The founders of our Constitution could not have imagined a democracy in which our physical movements are tracked by cell phones, our personal correspondence is scanned for key words by corporations and we willingly surrender our reading lists and fleeting private thoughts.

It's an arrangement we've made not just for ourselves but for our children, as well.

When many parents are confronted about what it means to raise children in an era of greatly diminished[10] privacy, the most common responses are: I really have nothing to hide, and who would be interested in my life, anyway?

name: ______________________________

But these rationalizations miss the point, because privacy is one of those nebulous rights that don't matter until it matters. Who worries about Miranda rights[11] until an arrest?

We are living in an era in which every keystroke online, from the information you search for to videos you watch to things you consider buying, is collected, stored, archived, aggregated and potentially shared or sold. And regardless of the false sense of security offered by the key on the upper right corner of your keyboard, there is no delete key for the Internet. Once it's out there, it's probably out there forever.

There is a spectrum, of course, of parental behavior toward their children's private lives, from those who sequester[12] and smother[13] their children in a misguided attempt to protect them to those who exploit and commercialize on the largest stages available.

But never before have parents had the ability to publish the details of their children's lives in such a widespread manner.

A potentially embarrassing anecdote won't faze[14] a toddler[15], but how does the unilateral[16] flow of information affect a tween or teenager?

Recently, a new set of proposed changes to Facebook's privacy policy was revealed. They include giving users more access to the data collected about them and attempts to explain how the company tracks them. But the changes would also allow Facebook to keep certain information longer along with possibly targeting users with ads across the web, not just on the Facebook site. So, the valuable marketing information gleaned[17] from pictures, posts and "likes" is not contained just to Facebook but used throughout the Web.

More than 900 million of us (and counting[18]) willingly participate in this exchange of information for convenience and connection. But we implicate[19] more than ourselves in the transaction.

We have a right for our data to not rise up and destroy us. We have a right to create our own narrative about our lives. We have a right to control how much we want the world to know about us.

These are fundamental to our personal autonomy.

Our children deserve the same protections.

CNN: May 25, 2012

[1] **indelible** = unable to be forgotten or removed [2] **imprint** = effect, impression [3] **accomplishment** = skill or ability [4] **to foster** = to develop [5] **to be at stake** = to be at risk [6] **identity theft** = criminal use of so.'s private identifying information [7] **to amplify** = to increase, to make bigger [8] **to be entitled to** = to have the right to [9] **exposure** = here: publicity [10] **diminished** = reduced [11] **Miranda rights** = the duty of the police to inform a suspect of their right to legal counsel and the right to remain silent under questioning (US) [12] **to sequester** = to isolate or hide away [13] **to smother** = to make so. feel oppressed by being overly protective [14] **to faze** = to upset [15] **toddler** = a young child that is just beginning to walk [16] **unilateral** = affecting only one person or group [17] **to glean** = to collect bit by bit [18] **and counting** = and becoming more and more [19] **to implicate** = to affect, to involve

Discussion card 1 **Text A**

Discuss whether it is a parent's duty to respect their children's privacy by, for example, never posting any photos and personal information about them.

Support your arguments with information from the text and your own experience.

Discussion card 2 **Text A**

Discuss what family rules you would recommend in order to make the use of social media a positive experience for both parents and children.

Support your arguments with information from the text and your own experience.

Discussion card 3 **Text A**

"Today's children are growing up with social media, i.e. they are used to having less privacy, so that there is no need to be concerned about this issue." Discuss.

Support your arguments with information from the text and your own experience.

name: ______________________________

Reading and speaking (dialogue) – text B

1. **Preparation:** Prepare the following article. Look up any words you do not understand and make sure you have a detailed knowledge of the article's contents.
2. **Exam:** With a partner who has prepared the same text, pick one of the three discussion cards for the text and follow the instructions.

Social media: tools or trivial pursuits?

by Andrew Masterson

The cherished[1] idea of the Twitter universe as a gloriously turbulent and fluid place for debate has taken a major hit, thanks to new research from China.

At the same time, findings from the United States have demolished another plank of common wisdom about digital communications. There is, it turns out, no relationship at all between the number of times an online article is shared and the number of times it is actually read.

In a paper published in March, two Chinese social scientists, Fei Xiong and Yun Liu, of Jiaotong University in Beijing, revealed unexpected results from an in-depth study into how opinions form on social media.

The pair analysed 6 million posts from almost 2.5 million Twitter users during a six-month period. In looking at how Twitter users are influenced by the thoughts of other micro-bloggers, the researchers came to what they termed a "non-trivial" conclusion, meaning, pretty much, they aren't.

"Users seldom change their opinions," Fei and Yun wrote in *Chaos,* an academic publication devoted to "non-linear science".

Remarkably, the study was one of the first times actual online data had been used to test a theory in their field, known as opinion dynamics.

The Beijing findings challenge the much-vaunted[2] utility of Twitter as a forum for debate. Fei and Yun found that in tweeted discussions around any given topic, a consensus formed very quickly, with the majority of users adopting one common position, and just a small minority taking an opposing stand.

The number of users who changed their opinion was very small, and that number continued to decrease, along a predicted frequency, as hours elapsed[3].

The interesting thing is that these developments – a big majority with one position, and opinion changing on an ever-decreasing scale – held, regardless of the topic under discussion.

[...]

However, a couple of additional observations made by Fei and Yun moderate[4] this picture, although perhaps not comfortingly.

The largest number of opinion changes, they observed, correlated with topics that didn't get the blood boiling. In other words, Twitter users are more likely to be swayed[5] by argument if they don't give much of a hoot[6] in the first place.

Second, there is no obligation[7] for Twitter posters to admit that they have changed their positions.

"In fact," wrote the researchers, "even if agents can update their internal opinions, they do not always publish posts to share their ideas with the public and may drop out of interaction."

What people really think, therefore, might be hidden. This, it turns out, is certainly the case in the matter of "social sharing", the posting on social networks of links to news articles.

It is often assumed that a huge number of social-media shares indicates lots of people are reading a particular piece. According to findings published by New York data science company Chartbeat, that is pretty much a crock[8].

The company advises media groups on the latest metric[9] for measuring online readership – attention analytics. Previous methods measured only the number of visitors a web page received – the "click-through" – but this method records the amount of time a reader spends actually looking at the thing.

Again, the results are uncomfortable. According to Chartbeat, 55 per cent of people spend less than 15 seconds looking at any page they visit, and the relationship between social sharing and reading, it turns out, is at best minuscule[10], and at worst non-existent.

The company tracked 20 billion visits to 580,000 online articles on 2000 websites and concluded that, on average, pages generated only one tweet and eight Facebook "likes" for every 100 visitors.

Drilling deeper, the relationship between what people like and what they read becomes even stranger.

"Some types of content are barely[11] shared at all, although they're heavily read," Chartbeat strategist Lauryn Bennett says. "How many people tweet links to stock ticker pages? Other types are heavily shared but less read. Any story that Kim Kardashian tweets will instantly have hundreds of other tweets, regardless of whether it's being read," she says.

It is difficult to know which is more depressing here – the idea that lots of people care what Kardashian thinks is a good yarn[12], or that they don't, but still feel compelled[13] to pretend they do.

name: ______________________________

Bennett says the relationship between social shares and actual reading is complex. People do sometimes share stories because they are under discussion on Facebook or Twitter, she says.

Similarly, the appearance of any story on a media outlet's "most popular" or "most emailed" table often results in a rise in shares.

"But it's not to say that those share numbers relate to depth of scrolling or reading the page at all," Bennett says. "In fact, in past research we've done, we've seen no relationship between how much of the page people have engaged with and social sharing."

In other words – and again, Ms Kardashian, perhaps unfairly, comes to mind – it is quite possible to suggest that someone should read something even though they personally have not done so.

There is one point at which Chartbeat and the Beijing researchers find common ground: the relationship between an opinion expressed and an opinion held is fundamentally unknowable.

"So do those social-sharing numbers on the top of the page affect if people will read the full article or share it?" Bennett asks.

"Maybe. Observing reader behaviour on an article helps us understand what people do, but doesn't allow us to understand their intent or what directly influenced them to take those actions."

(If you liked this article, please share it now. Yes, Kim, that means you.)

The Sydney Morning Herald, April 3, 2014

[1] **to cherish** = to like very much, to protect [2] **to vaunt** = to boast about or praise sth. [3] **to elapse** = to pass, to go by [4] **to moderate** = to make less extreme [5] **to sway** = to control or influence [6] **to not give a hoot** = to not care at all [7] **obligation** = rule, must [8] **crock** = complete nonsense [9] **metric** = a system of measurement [10] **minuscule** = very small [11] **barely** = almost not [12] **yarn** = here: story [13] **to compel** = to force, to put under pressure

Discussion card 1 **Text B**

Discuss whether the use of social media is just a superficial sharing of information no one really cares about.

Support your arguments with information from the text and your own experience.

Discussion card 2 **Text B**

Discuss whether using social media is more about wondering about what the others may think about you and your posts than expressing what you really think.

Support your arguments with information from the text and your own experience.

Discussion card 3 **Text B**

Discuss whether young people use social media to exchange ideas and opinions.

Support your arguments with information from the text and your own experience.

name: ______________________________

Reading and speaking (dialogue) – text C

1. **Preparation:** Prepare the following article. Look up any words you do not understand and make sure you have a detailed knowledge of the article's contents.
2. **Exam:** With a partner who has prepared the same text, pick one of the three discussion cards for the text and follow the instructions.

Teenagers and technology: 'I'd rather give up my kidney than my phone'

by Jon Henley

"I'd rather," deadpans[1] Philippa Grogan, 16, "give up, like, a kidney[2] than my phone. How did you manage before? Carrier pigeons? Letters? Going round each others' houses on BIKES?" Cameron Kirk, 14, reckons he spends "an hour, hour-and-a-half on school days" hanging out with his 450-odd Facebook friends; maybe twice that at weekends. "It's actually very practical if you forget what that day's homework is. Unfortunately, one of my best friends doesn't have Facebook. But it's OK; we talk on our PlayStations." [...]

Teens, eh? Not how they were when I was young. Nor the way they talk to each other. Let's frighten ourselves, first: for a decade, the Pew Internet & American Life Project has been the world's largest and most authoritative provider of data on the internet's impact[3] on the lives of 21st-century citizens. [...]

First, 75% of all teenagers (and 58% of 12-year-olds) now have a mobile phone. Almost 90% of phone-owning teens send and receive texts, most of them daily. Half send 50 or more texts a day; one in three send 100. In fact, in barely four years, texting has established itself as comfortably "the preferred channel of basic communication between teens and their friends".

But phones do more than simply text, of course. More than 80% of phone-owning teens also use them to take pictures (and 64% to share those pictures with others). Sixty per cent listen to music on them, 46% play games, 32% swap videos and 23% access social networking sites. The mobile phone, in short, is now "the favoured communication hub for the majority of teens".

[...] 73% use social networking sites, mostly Facebook – 50% more than three years ago. Digital communication is not just prevalent[4] in teenagers' lives. It IS teenagers' lives.

There's a very straightforward reason, says Amanda Lenhart, a Pew senior research specialist. "Simply, these technologies meet teens' developmental needs," she says. "Mobile phones and social networking sites make the things teens have always done – defining their own identity, establishing themselves as independent of their parents, looking cool, impressing members of the opposite sex – a whole lot easier."

[...]

But, as we all recall, adolescence[5] is also a period of excruciating shyness and aching self-consciousness – which can make all that self-presentation and self-disclosure something of a perilous[6], not to say agonising[7], business. So the big plus of texting, instant messaging and social networking is that it allows the crucial identity-establishing behaviour, without the accompanying embarrassment. "These technologies give their users a sense of increased controllability," Valkenburg says. "That, in turn, allows them to feel secure about their communication, and thus freer in their interpersonal relations."

"Controllability", she explains, is about three things: being able to say what you want without fear of the message not getting through because of that humungous[8] spot[9] on your chin or your tendency to blush[10]; having the power to reflect on and change what you write before you send it (in contrast to face-to-face communication); and being able to stay in touch with untold hordes of friends at times, and in places, where your predecessors[11] were essentially incommunicado.

But what do teenagers make of this newfound freedom to communicate? Philippa reckons she sends "probably about 30" text messages every day, and receives as many. "They're about meeting up – where are you, see you in 10, that kind of thing," she says. "There's an awful lot of flirting goes on, of course. Or it's, 'OMG, what's biology homework?'. And, 'I'm babysitting and I'm SOOOO bored.'" (Boredom appears to be the key factor in the initiation of many teen communications.)

Like most of her peers, Philippa wouldn't dream of using her phone to actually phone anyone, except perhaps her parents – to placate[12] them if she's not where she should be, or ask them to come and pick her up if she is. [...]

Philippa also has 639 Facebook friends, and claims to know "the vast majority" (though some, she admits, are "quite far down the food chain"). "I don't want to be big-headed or anything, but I am quite popular," she says. "Only because I don't have a social life outside my bedroom, though." When I call her, 129 of her friends are online.

Facebook rush-hour is straight after school, and around nine or 10 in the evening. "You can have

name: ____________________

about 10 chats open at a time, then it gets a bit slow and you have to start deleting people," Philippa says. The topics? "General banter[13], light-hearted abuse. Lots of talk about parties and about photos of parties." Cred-wise[14], it's important to have a good, active Facebook profile: lots of updates, lots of photos of you tagged.

Sometimes, though, it ends in tears. Everyone has witnessed cyber-bullying, but the worst thing that happened to Philippa was when someone posted "a really dreadful picture of me, with an awful double chin", then refused to take it down. "She kept saying, 'No way, it's upped my profile views 400%,'" says Philippa. It's quite easy, she thinks, for people to feel "belittled, isolated" on Facebook.

There are other downsides. [...] "Privacy's a real issue," says Emily. "I get 'friend' requests from people I don't know and have never heard of; I ignore them. I have a private profile. I'm very careful about that."

A 2009 survey found up to 45% of US companies are now checking job applicants' activity on social networking sites, and 35% reported[15] rejecting people because of what they found. Universities and colleges, similarly, are starting to look online. "You need to be careful," says Cameron Kirk, astute[16] and aware even at 14. "Stuff can very easily get misunderstood." Emily agrees, but adds: "Personally, I love the idea that it's up there for ever. It'll be lovely to go back, later, and see all those emotions and relations." [...]

Emily is fairly confident that social networking and texting aren't changing who she is. "I'm the same online and in person. All this is an extension to real life, not a replacement." Olivia Stamp, 16 and equally self-aware, says she thinks social networking actually helps her to be more herself. "I think of myself as quite a shy person," she says. "So it's actually easier to be myself on Facebook because you can edit what you want to say, take your time; you don't feel awkward. I definitely feel more confident online – more like the self I know I really am, beneath the shyness."

These [...] communications technologies, Olivia says, are "an enhancement, an enrichment actually. They bring people even closer, in fact, without replacing anything. We're not socially abnormal. Look at us!" And the experts *seem* to back that up. Valkenburg says: "Our research gives no reason at present for concern about the social consequences of online communication – but it's early days. What if the constant self-confirmation teens experience online turns into excessive self-esteem, or narcissism? We don't know yet."

Lenhart puts it another way. "Our research shows face-to-face time between teenagers hasn't changed over the past five years. Technology has simply added another layer on top. Yes, you can find studies that suggest online networking can be bad for you. But there are just as many that show the opposite."

We should, she suggests, "Step back. The telephone, the car, the television – they all, in their time, changed the way teens relate to each other, and to other people, quite radically. And how did their parents respond? With the same kind of wailing[17] and gnashing[18] of teeth we're doing now. These technologies change lives, absolutely. But it's a generational thing."

The Guardian, Friday 16 July 2010

[1] **to deadpan** = to say sth. funny while pretending to be serious [2] **kidney** = an organ in your lower body that purifies the blood [3] **impact** = effect or influence [4] **prevalent** = widespread [5] **adolescence** = being a teenager [6] **perilous** = dangerous [7] **agonising** = painful [8] **humungous** = very big [9] **spot** = *Pickel* [10] **to blush** = to go red in the face [11] **predecessor** = so. who has been followed or replaced by another [12] **to placate** = to calm down [13] **banter** = playful and friendly exchange of teasing remarks [14] **cred** = short for 'credibility' [15] **to reject** = to refuse, to turn away [16] **astute** = able to assess situations or people correctly [17] **to wail** = to give a cry of pain, grief or anger [18] **to gnash** = to grind (one's teeth) together

Discussion card 1 **Text C**

Discuss whether the use of social media gives teenagers the "controllability" they seem to wish for. Support your arguments with information from the text and your own experience.

Discussion card 2 **Text C**

Discuss whether the advantages of using social media outweigh the risks for teenagers. Support your arguments with information from the text and your own experience.

Discussion card 3 **Text C**

Discuss whether young people's personalities are affected by using social media. Support your arguments with information from the text and your own experience.

name: ______________________

Reading and writing

1. **Comprehension:** Read the two extracts from Ursula Rani Sarma's play "The Spider Men" and state the different attitudes towards wearing the wristbands[1] as expressed by the boys and girls in the extracts. (Darren, Nigel, Sarah and Karen are all 15 years old and attend the same school.)
2. **Analysis:** Analyze the means the playwright uses to create atmosphere when her characters talk about sexual experiences.
3. Choose task **a.** or **b.**
   a. **Comment:** Comment on the idea of wearing wristbands to show your level of sexual experience. Take into consideration the motives people might have.
   b. **Creative writing:** Add a scene in which Jane meets Darren, Nigel, Karen and Sarah and justifies wearing the wristbands.

Extract I

Darren and Nigel are kicking a football back and forth to each other.

Nigel So what does the yellow one mean, then?
Darren That she'll let the guy snog[2] her.
Nigel And the red one?
Darren Red one means … that she'll go further.
Nigel How much further?
Darren Well … like, she'll let the guy … have a feel …
Nigel Where?
Darren Upstairs.
Nigel Seriously?

Darren nods.
What about the blue?
Darren What do you think?
Nigel Downstairs?

Darren nods.
And the green?
Darren All the way.
Nigel Fucking hell … and they can't wear a colour they haven't done already?
Darren That's what I heard.
Nigel Fucking hell … that's just … that's great, isn't it?
Darren I dunno[3].
Nigel What you mean, you dunno? Means you won't be wasting your time with one who won't … you know … do anything.
Darren Would you wear one?
Nigel Thought you said it was just the girls?
Darren It is … but if it wasn't … would you wear one? Let everyone know exactly how … exactly what you've been doing?
Nigel *(stops and thinks about it)* Yeah, but it's different for a guy, isn't it?
Darren Is it?
Nigel Yeah, I mean … I can do what I like with whoever I like but if a girl … you know … puts it out a bit … well, a lot … then that's just not attractive, is it?
Darren says nothing.

Extract II

Sarah and Karen are in two neutral spaces, on the phone.
[…]
Karen I came home after ten one night, my dad nearly gave himself a stroke shouting.
Sarah My dad doesn't care.
Karen I wish mine didn't.
Sarah *(beat)* No you don't.
Karen *(awkward)* Yeah … I guess … so where do you think they are?
Sarah I don't know.
Karen Maybe they're meeting some girls.
Sarah I doubt it.
Karen Well, whatever it is, I bet it's more exciting than lying in their pyjamas talking on the phone.
Sarah Yeah.
Karen What you wearing to the end-of-year do[4]?
Sarah Dunno.
Karen Everyone's talking about the wristbands.
Sarah Yeah.
Karen You get some yet?
Sarah No.

Karen pulls up her sleeve[5] to reveal[6] four wristbands, yellow, red, blue and green.
Karen Me neither. *(She takes them off one by one.)* Saw Jane in town, wearing hers already – no prizes for guessing what colour.
Sarah Green?
Karen Couldn't be greener … it's weird, letting everyone know how far you've … what you've done … isn't it? I mean, letting people you don't even know … know … letting them judge[7] you for who they think you are and not who you actually are.
Sarah Don't think I'll bother with it.
Karen Jane says anyone who doesn't wear it hasn't done anything at all.
Sarah Yeah well … fuck Jane.

Lights down.

[1] **wristband** = a strip of material worn around the part of your body between your hand and your arm [2] **to snog** = to kiss [3] **dunno** = don't know [4] **do** = party [5] **sleeve** = the part of a piece of clothing that covers your arm [6] **to reveal** = to show [7] **to judge** = to form an opinion about sth.

name: ______________________________

Listening

DVD

1. Listen to the podcast and say in one sentence what it is about.

____

____

2. Listen to the podcast again and complete the following sentences.

a. The couples interviewed had come to the county courthouse to ______________

b. Many of them had been together for ______________

c. They had not been through this ceremony before because the law ______________

____

d. Ed Golembiewski, the county chief deputy clerk, explained that the county clerk had informed him the night before that ______________

____

e. Reverend Dean Ware came to the county courthouse to show that the church supported all loving couples regardless of ______________

f. For some of the same-sex couples one of the practical benefits of the ceremony was that they could now ______________ to their children.

g. Not only the couples were present at the event but also ______________

____

h. After the ceremony one of the brides, Stephanie Williams, said that she no longer felt like

____

name: ______________

Reading and writing

Margaret Atwood's novel *The Handmaid's Tale* is set in the Republic of Gilead, an oppressive Christian fundamentalist society where the ruling elite controls all other social groups. The protagonist and narrator, Offred, is a handmaid with just one function, which is to bear children to members of the ruling class who cannot have children themselves. In this extract the narrator describes the ceremony of Salvaging, during which dissenters (= people who hold or express critical or unpopular opinions) are punished publicly.

1. **Comprehension:** Outline the main features of the Salvaging event as described in the extract.
2. **Analysis:** Analyze the atmosphere created by examining the setting and the use of language.
3. **Comment:** Comment on the function that mass events like Salvagings have in a totalitarian society.

The bell is tolling; we can hear it from a long way off. It's morning, and today we've had no breakfast. When we reach the main gate we file[1] through it, two by two. There's a heavy contingent of guards, special-detail Angels, with riot gear[2] – the helmets with the bulging dark plexiglass visors that make them look like beetles, the long clubs[3], the gas-canister guns – in cordon[4] around the outside of the Wall. That's in case of hysteria. The hooks[5] on the Wall are empty.

This is a district Salvaging, for women only. Salvagings are always segregated. It was announced yesterday. They tell you only the day before. It's not enough time, to get used to it.

To the tolling of the bell we walk along the paths once used by students, past buildings that were once lecture halls and dormitories. It's very strange to be in here again. From the outside you can't tell that anything's changed, except that the blinds[6] on most of the windows are drawn down. These buildings belong to the Eyes[7] now.

We file onto the wide lawn in front of what used to be the library. The white steps going up are still the same, the main entrance is unaltered. There's a wooden stage erected on the lawn, something like the one they used every spring, for Commencement[8], in the time before. I think of hats, pastel hats worn by some of the mothers, and of the black gowns the students would put on, and the red ones. But this stage is not the same after all, because of the three wooden posts that stand on it, with the loops of rope.

At the front of the stage there is a microphone; the television camera is discreetly off to the side.

I've only been to one of these before, two years ago. Women's Salvagings are not frequent. There is less need for them. These days we are so well behaved.

I don't want to be telling this story.

[…]

There's a long piece of rope which winds like a snake in front of the first row of cushions, along the second, and back through the lines of chairs, bending like a very old, very slow river viewed from the air, down to the back. The rope is thick and brown and smells of tar[9]. The front end of the rope runs up onto the stage. It's like a fuse[10], or the string of a balloon.

On stage, to the left, are those who are to be salvaged[11]: two Handmaids, one Wife. Wives are unusual, and despite myself I look at this one with interest. I want to know what she has done.

They have been placed here before the gates were opened. All of them sit on folding wooden chairs, like graduating students who are about to be given prizes. Their hands rest in their laps, looking as if they are folded sedately[12]. They sway[13] a little, they've probably been given injections or pills, so they won't make a fuss. It's better if things go smoothly. […]

I've seen it before, the white bag placed over the head, the woman helped up onto the high stool as if she's being helped up the steps of a bus, steadied there, the noose[14] adjusted delicately around the neck, like a vestment[15], the stool kicked away. I've heard the long sigh go up, from around me, the sigh like air coming out of an air mattress, I've seen Aunt Lydia place her hand over the mike[16], to stifle[17] the other sounds coming from behind her, I've leaned forward to touch the rope in front of me, in time with the others, both hands on it, the rope hairy, sticky with tar in the hot sun, then placed my hand on my heart to show my unity with the Salvagers and my consent[18], and my complicity in the death of this woman. I have seen the kicking feet and the two in black who now seize hold of them and drag downwards with all their weight.

I don't want to see it any more. I look at the grass instead.

[1] **to file** = to walk one behind the other in an orderly manner [2] **riot gear** = protective clothing and equipment worn by police in situations of expected violence [3] **club** = here: a heavy stick, in particular one used as a weapon [4] **cordon** = a line or circle of police, soldiers or guards [5] **hook** = a curved piece of metal for hanging things on [6] **blind** = a screen for a window [7] **the Eyes** = the secret police [8] **Commencement** = a ceremony in which graduating students are given their diplomas [9] **tar** = a dark, thick liquid used in roadmaking [10] **fuse** = a length of material along which a small flame moves to explode a bomb [11] **to salvage** = to rescue [12] **sedate** = calm [13] **to sway** = to move slowly or rhythmically backward and forward or from side to side [14] **noose** = a loop with a running knot, typically used to hang people [15] **vestment** = a ceremonial or official robe [16] **mike** = short for 'microphone' [17] **to stifle** = here: to stop [18] **consent** = agreement

name: ______________________________

Listening, reading and writing

1. **Comprehension:** Listen to the news report on upcycling and summarize the most important facts. Say how, according to the report, upcycling works and what its benefits are.
   www.diesterweg.de/cta/74014/links

2. **Analysis:** Analyze the attitude towards companies' efforts to guarantee more sustainability as shown in the blog entry "Fast fashion will never be sustainable, no matter what companies say" and the means by which this attitude is conveyed.

3. **Comment:** Both the news report and the blog entry suggest solutions to the problems created by fast fashion. Assess to what extent these suggestions present real alternatives to buying fast fashion.

Fast fashion will never be sustainable, no matter what companies say

by Katherine Martinko

Fast fashion and sustainability are an oxymoron[1]. The whole idea behind fast fashion is to churn out[2] cheap new collections and stimulate consumption, and there's nothing sustainable about that. It's impossible to produce ethical, eco-friendly clothing at the quantity and rate that fast fashion demands while maintaining genuinely high and environmentally sustainable standards.

Many clothing companies would have us think otherwise. They create sustainable and eco-friendly lines to entice[3] those slightly more discerning[4] or skeptical customers. An article in Al Jazeera points out that "H&M has its Conscious collection, made of organic cotton and recycled polyester; Puma's biodegradable InCycle Collection; Adidas' Design for Environment gear; Uniqlo's All-Product Recycling Initiative; Zara's eco-efficient stores; and the Gap's P.A.C.E. program, to benefit the lives of female garment workers."

But these efforts are little more than greenwashing[5], as "sustainability and consumerism do not go hand in hand."

Livia Firth of Eco Age, a consulting firm in London, argues that fast fashion brands have to change their business models. As long as they continue to produce "in such volumes and at such ridiculous prices, their sustainability efforts – no matter how genuine – are a form of greenwashing."

[…]

The easiest way to avoid greenwashing is to boycott the fast fashion industry and resist the urge[6] to buy new clothes on a weekly or monthly basis. Contrary to what many people think, you don't have to be rich to do this.

- Support smaller companies, since they are likely to have an easier time tracking the source of their product than companies with high volume.
- Shop at private businesses or buy from a seamstress[7] or tailor[8].
- Seek out[9] pieces that are made locally or domestically.
- If possible, buy high quality items; they're more likely to last, and you're more likely to take care of them.
- Buy clothing and footwear that is repairable.
- Buy second-hand from a thrift store[10], as those items have proven their durability[11].
- Make do with less clothing. Resist the urge for novelty and keep the same clothes as long as possible.
- Do a clothing swap[12] with friends instead of shopping.

When shopping, it's important to discern[13] between companies that truly want to minimize their footprint[14] and improve supply chain transparency, and those that are hopping on the eco-friendly bandwagon only to look better. […]

http://www.treehugger.com, June 19, 2014

[1] **oxymoron** = contradiction [2] **to churn out** = to produce something at regular intervals and in large quantities [3] **to entice** = to attract [4] **discerning** = having or showing good judgment [5] **greenwashing** = disinformation by a company so as to present an environmentally responsible public image [6] **urge** = a strong desire [7] **seamstress** = a woman who sews [8] **tailor** = a person whose job is making fitted clothes [9] **to seek out** = to look for [10] **thrift store** = a secondhand shop [11] **durability** = ability to withstand wear, pressure, or damage [12] **swap** = act of exchanging one thing for another [13] **to discern** = to differentiate [14] **footprint** = carbon footprint, i.e. the amount of carbon dioxide produced through a person's everyday activities

name: ______________________________

Mediation

Imagine you are working for an organization that tries to raise awareness among young customers and help workers in the clothing industry in countries with cheap labour. When a headline from a German newspaper catches your eye, you decide to write a report about it for the website of the organisation. Read the following extracts from the article in the *Frankfurter Allgemeine Zeitung* and give a report on

1. the criticism that was voiced
2. Adidas's reaction to the criticism
3. the sales figures
4. the general problem associated with sports brands and the garments they sell.

Das Trikot und der Lohn – 15 Cent für vier Sterne

von Michael Ashelm

Der Deutsche Fußball-Bund (DFB) hat eine Reaktion zu dem Vorwurf des Entwicklungsministers Gerd Müller (CSU) abgelehnt, das neue Weltmeistertrikot mit den vier WM-Sternen der Nationalmannschaft vom Sponsor Adidas werde in Billiglohnländern wie Bangladesch unter menschenunwürdigen Bedingungen produziert. Der DFB verwies am Mittwoch auf Anfrage auf den Ausrüster Adidas und dessen Stellungnahme. Der Sportartikelhersteller wehrte sich gegen die Äußerungen des Regierungsmitglieds […]: „Wir sind äußerst verwundert über die […] Aussagen von Herrn Minister Müller und weisen seine faktisch falschen Vorwürfe mit Entschiedenheit zurück", teilte Adidas dieser Zeitung mit.

Leider hätte sich der Minister vor seinen Aussagen nicht detailliert genug über die Beschaffungsaktivitäten des Unternehmens informiert und auch keinen der Zulieferbetriebe selbst besucht. „Wir hätten ihm sonst gerne erklärt, dass wir die deutschen Nationaltrikots aus China beziehen, nicht aus Bangladesch. Im Übrigen haben wir die Liste aller WM-Zulieferer bereits 2013 auf unserer Website veröffentlicht, Bangladesch taucht darauf genauso wenig auf wie die von Herrn Minister Müller erwähnten afrikanischen Länder", fügte ein Adidas-Sprecher hinzu.

Müller hatte darauf hingewiesen, dass das neue DFB-Weltmeistertrikot fast 85 Euro koste, wovon eine Näherin in Bangladesch aber nur 15 Cent bekäme. Der CSU-Politiker hatte bei einer Veranstaltung am Dienstag in der Industrie- und Handelskammer Berlin die Ausbeutung von Arbeitern in Asien und Afrika durch Konzerne aus Europa und Nordamerika kritisiert. […]

Die Trikots der DFB-Auswahl setzen sich in diesem Jahr ausgezeichnet ab. Ausrüster Adidas meldete schon mehr als zwei Millionen verkaufte Hemden – und nach dem WM-Triumph in Brasilien wird die neue Linie mit den vier Sternen auf der Brust wohl ebenfalls ein Verkaufsschlager werden. Doch unabhängig von dem aktuellen Streit kritisieren Organisationen, die sich seit Jahren intensiv mit den Bedingungen für Arbeiter in den Billiglohnländern beschäftigen, weiterhin die mangelnde Verantwortungsbereitschaft der dort produzierenden Konzerne. „Die Umsatzzahlen der Unternehmen erreichen immer neue Höhen, während die Reallohnentwicklung der Arbeiter und Arbeiterinnen in den Fabriken nach unten geht. Wir fordern, dass von Firmen wie Adidas oder auch Puma und deren Zulieferern endlich Gehälter gezahlt werden, damit die Arbeiter ein Leben in Würde führen können", sagte Sandra Dusch von der Christlichen Initiative Romero. […]

http://www.faz.net, 11. September 2014

name: ______________________________

Reading and writing

1. **Comprehension:** Describe what some clothing companies are trying to make their customers believe and contrast this with the actual situation as depicted in the article.
2. **Analysis:** Choose task **a.** or **b.**
   a. Analyze how the choice of words underlines the author's critical attitude.
   b. Analyze how the choice of words reveals the author's negative view.
3. **Comment:** Discuss the statement "If you care about ethical labor standards, your clothing choices are more limited than you might think" and give your view on the problems of the fashion industry.

Sweatshops still make your clothes

If you care about ethical labor standards, your clothing choices are more limited than you might think

by Jake Blumgart

It's been 16 years since Charles Kernaghan made Kathie Lee Gifford cry on national television, revealing that her Wal-Mart-sold clothing line was produced by Honduran children working 20-hour shifts. It was an essential moment in bringing labor conditions in the developing world – specifically in the garment[1] industry – to the attention of the American public.

But not that much has changed. Looking back on the movement and its achievements in an interview, Kernaghan sounds defeated[2], even as he reels off[3] the list of horrific factories exposed by his Institute for Global Labour and Human Rights.

Kernaghan's gloomy mood stems[4] from the report he is writing now on a recent trip to Northern Bengal, where the Institute secretly met with workers from the Rosita and Megatex factories [...]. The two factories produce expensive sweaters for an array of European apparel companies, companies which assure their customers that the workers are guaranteed the core[5] rights established by the International Labor Organization (ILO), including freedom of association and the elimination[6] of child labor.

Well, that turns out not to exactly be the case. And it turns out that most Americans *still* likely know very little about the conditions under which the clothes they wear were produced.

"It was ridiculous. In fact it was one of the worst factories we've seen," says Kernaghan. "There was child labor, people were being beaten, cheated[7] of their wages – and wages were very, very low. [...]"

The Institute followed every development: The presidents of the workers' committee (not even a legally recognized union) were both threatened with assassination[8]. There was every reason to take these murderous threats seriously: the Bangladeshi Export Processing Zone Authority, which runs the free trade zone where the factories are located, is run by former military operatives. Police stations are located right outside the factory, and police cars stud[9] the surrounding blocks, but not for the protection of the employees. When workers demonstrated for their rights, hundreds were beaten by the police and then fired.

http://www.salon.com, March 21, 2013

[1] **garment** = clothing [2] **defeated** = demoralized [3] **to reel sth. off** = to say sth. quickly [4] **to stem from** = to originate in or be caused by [5] **core** = central [6] **elimination** = removal [7] **to cheat** = to trick, to act dishonestly or unfairly [8] **assassination** = here: being killed [9] **to stud** = to decorate

name: ____________________

Textquellenverzeichnis

S. 109: "Constructive gap years help students stand out to employers and universities" © Tom Griffiths in *The Independent,* Monday, 17 August 2009.

S. 118: „Hey, hier ist Europa und ich bin mitten drin.", Amory Burchard in *Der Tagesspiegel,* 31. Januar 2012

S. 119: From "(Un)arranged Marriage": S. 33–35 Bali Rai , published by Corgi. Reprinted by permission of The Random House Group Ltd, London, 2001.

S. 120: from "Ban teens from chat rooms" © Bill Thompson, 2003.

S. 121: from "The Accidental Billionaires. The Founding of Facebook" © Ben Mezrich, New York 2009, p. 174f.

S. 124f.: "'Facebook parenting' is destroying our children's privacy" Aisha Sultan and Jon Miller, CNN: May 25, 2012.

S. 126f.: "Social media: tools or trivial pursuits?" Andrew Masterson, The Sydney Morning Herald, April 3, 2014.

S. 128f.: "Teenagers + technology: 'I'd rather give up my kidney than my phone'" by Jon Henley, in *The Guardian,* 16.07.2010 © Guardian News & Media Ltd 2010.

S. 130: from "The Spider Men" by Ursula Rani Sarma in: *Shell Connections 2006. New Plays for Young People,* London (Faber & Faber) 2006, pp. 655f. and 664ff. © Ursula Rani Sarma, 2006.

S. 132: From "The Handmaid's Tale" Margaret Atwood, randomhouse.com.

S. 133: "Fast fashion will never be sustainable, no matter what companies say", Katherine Martinko, http://www.treehugger.com, June 19, 2014.

S. 134: „Das Trikot und der Lohn – 15 cent für vier Sterne", Michael Ashelm http://www.faz.net, 11. September 2014.

S. 135: "Sweatshops still make your clothes" by Jake Blumgart. This article first appeared in Salon.com, at http://www.Salon.com. An online version remains in the Salon archives. Reprinted with permission.

Bildquellenverzeichnis

S. 119: © Ron Tandberg.

S. 120, 122, 123: Cartoon Stock Ltd., Bath.